A Symphony of Possibilities

NCTE Editorial Board

A Symphony of Possibilities

A Handbook for Arts Integration in Secondary English Language Arts

Edited by

Katherine J. Macro
SUNY Buffalo State College

Michelle Zoss
Georgia State University

NCTE

NATIONAL COUNCIL OF TEACHERS OF ENGLISH
1111 W. KENYON ROAD, URBANA, ILLINOIS 61801-1096
WWW.NCTE.ORG

Staff Editor: Bonny Graham

Manuscript Editor: The Charlesworth Group

Interior Design: Jenny Jensen Greenleaf

Cover Design: Pat Mayer

Cover Images: iStock.com/MAXSHOT, iStock.com/PaoloGaetano, iStock.com/Nongkran_ch, iStock.com/BrianAJackson

NCTE Stock Number: 49713; eStock Number: 49720
ISBN 978-0-8141-4971-3; eISBN 978-0-8141-4972-0

Library of Congress Cataloging-in-Publication Data

A catalog record of this book has been requested.

For David, who learned to love to read because of pictures, and Grace, who never stops performing, drawing, imagining, and writing.

—Katherine J. Macro

For Fiona, who is always reading and seeing the world in new ways, and Cordelia, who delights in all the books, drawings, music, and dance.

—Michelle Zoss

Contents

Acknowledgments

We are grateful for our colleagues and fellow members of the NCTE Commission on Arts and Literacies (COAL). This group always supports the arts in their own work and showcases the possibilities of the arts for English each year at the NCTE Annual Convention. This book extends the published work and active involvement of COAL members in both NCTE and classrooms in schools and universities across the United States. COAL is a group under the umbrella of the English Language Arts Teacher Educators (formerly the Conference on English Education), and we extend our thanks to the leaders who sustained our work, especially Mollie Blackburn and Melanie Shoffner.

We owe great thanks to the students in all the classes highlighted in this book who tried out these ideas and brought them to life. Likewise, we thank our teaching colleagues and research participants who also graciously shared their time and wisdom with us as we learned alongside them. One person in particular encouraged this book from the beginning: Roz Linder, who was a strong supporter of writers creating books to change the landscape of education. Though she passed away before this book came out, we are grateful to have shared time, conversation, and laughter with her along the way and hope that this book would have made her proud.

A book like this is possible when a great team gathers toward a common purpose. Many thanks to the editorial team at NCTE, especially Kurt Austin and Bonny Graham, Pat Mayer, our cover designer, and the editing team at the Charlesworth Group. We appreciate too the reviewers of the manuscript who carefully read and gave feedback to us throughout all stages of the publishing process. We also thank Laura Efford and Latricia Oliver, doctoral students at Georgia State University who generously read the manuscript for editing details.

Finally, there are two groups of people without whom this work would not be possible. The first group is our teachers. We thank all the art, drama, English, and music teachers and professors who showed us the way when we were in secondary school, college, and teacher education. In particular, Kathie would like to acknowledge Marlowe Beis, Tim Ward, and Sharon O. Watkinson, and

Michelle would like to acknowledge Carol Morrison, Peter Nazareth, Elliot Eisner, and Peter Smagorinsky. The second is the group closest to home, our families. We thank our loved ones who graciously shared our time and listened to our stories along the way. David Macro and Nick Zoss championed this work and we are most thankful.

Introduction

MICHELLE ZOSS, *Georgia State University*

KATHERINE J. MACRO, *SUNY Buffalo State College*

In an English classroom in New York State, tension dominates the room as students with bowed heads begin to silently write essays. This is not the quiet hush of busy minds and pens excited to commit ideas to paper, though; it is instead the silence that pervades when writing is tested and tied to graduation. They write because they must; the students in this classroom, like many others in New York, write because they have learned to jump through hoops, to write five-paragraph essays, to insert examples of the proper literary elements in a formulaic response to questions posed by people they've never met.

Elsewhere, in an eighth-grade English language arts classroom in Georgia, the situation is eerily similar. As students read through prompts and write responses, they sit in a room empty of instructional materials. All of the bookcases have butcher paper taped over the shelves, while posters the teacher used throughout the year to encourage students to think widely and deeply are now stored out of view until the testing window for the entire school is complete. There are two teachers in the room, required to provide a secure testing environment, who move through the space under strict instructions not to tarry near any given student, and not to look at the exam questions. In this space, both teachers and students are subject to the restrictions set forth by the state, district, and school. These efforts are made to show that the teaching is effective, the learning can be displayed and objectively measured, and the school is accountable for proving its value.

These illustrations of English language arts (ELA) classrooms are just snapshots of the current challenges facing secondary teachers. In contrast to these images, there are stories of hope and delight, creativity and innovation to be told as well. This book is a tribute to those narratives, and a handbook for teachers who seek to renew, revive, or create experiences that are alive with thinking and passion as they strive to push back against the testing and standardization culture depicted above. In this book, we present the strategies and stories of teachers who choose to bring arts in the form of music and drama, creative writing, and visual art into their classes.

Every year at the convention of the National Council of Teachers of English (NCTE), during roundtable presentations, teachers, professors, graduate students, and future teachers gather to talk about and share their expertise for integrating the arts in their schools. The conversations and resources developed in classrooms and shared during the annual convention are key components of the group called the Commission on Arts and Literacies (COAL). As members of COAL, we collectively aim to shed light on the thoughtful and creative work that teachers and students are doing across the country as they bring the full sense of possibilities in arts-based pedagogies into their ELA classes.

Our goal with this book was to create a resource specifically for secondary English teachers to support them as they integrate the arts into their curricula. Teachers need meaningful examples of how to do the work of incorporating creative writing, drama, music, and visual arts into their classrooms so they can challenge students, expand the horizon for student growth, and, we hope, express their own passions for the arts while offering potential learning touchstones for students.

COAL endeavors to generate more conversation about the way the arts intersect with literacies, old and new. As co-chairs of COAL, we feel that the arts provide methods of resisting the testing culture of education today. The arts offer opportunities for students and teachers to be readers, creators, and interpreters of texts (Holbrook, 2010; Macro, 2015; Zoss & White, 2011). We need these opportunities in classrooms across the country today, perhaps now more than ever before. The mission of COAL is to "effect change in English language arts classrooms by advancing teaching, research, and theory in the three areas of the arts, multimodalities, and New Literacies in ways that situate this knowledge as essential components of literacy learning" (NCTE Commission on Arts and Literacies, n.d.). In this book, we bring teaching strategies that use the arts in ELA classrooms, strategies that are multimodal, pedagogically sound, and promote teaching and learning to move beyond the test. Our aim is to show that, in the arts, there is possibility for secondary teachers and their students.

We champion the use of varied art forms in the classroom to facilitate growth and learning. To this end, we explore the arts of drama, music, visual art, and writing to promote discussion and exposure to the diversity of thinking and meaning making that are available to teachers and students alike. Just as there is no one specific art form that works better than others, there is no one voice that can best describe them all. For this reason, we approach this book with the voices of multiple teachers and researchers with the hope that collectively the variety and the expertise shown in our work in secondary classrooms can fill an important void within the field. There are a number of books and resources available to elementary teachers who wish to integrate the arts into their teaching of literacies (e.g., Bogard & Donovan, 2013; Donahue & Stuart, 2010; Goldberg, 2012; McDonald, 2010; McDonald & Fisher, 2006), but the field of resources for secondary English teachers remains relatively small.

As a commission committed to action, COAL seeks to spread ideas widely. We supplement our annual gatherings at NCTE conferences with publications so that we might reach a large audience to share knowledge about arts integration practices. Our work in the present book extends two fairly recent projects. The first is an edited volume of research by members of COAL, *Literacy, the Arts, and Multimodality* (Albers & Sanders, 2010), wherein we present empirical studies conducted across the United States in which teachers have systematically been teaching with the arts for decades. The second project is a special edition of *English Journal*, entitled "Imagination, Creativity, and Innovation: Showcasing the 'A' in English Language Arts" (Emert, Macro, & Schmidt, 2016). The themed issue, coedited by Toby Emert, Katherine Macro, and Pauline Skowron Schmidt (all contributors to this volume), includes eleven articles exploring how teachers bring the arts into secondary English classes. Building on the base of research and practice in these publications, we designed *A Symphony of Possibilities* as a resource volume for secondary English teachers.

We are indebted to the work of Phyllis Whitin (1996a, 1996b, 2005), whose work examining sketch-to-stretch drawings and writing of middle school students opened a number of pathways for teachers, including us, to not only use drawing as a means for responding to, writing about, and talking through literature, but also to provide a strong rationale for administrators that taking the time to imagine, draw, and talk about literature can be a valuable and powerful tool for learning. Other important distant teachers (John-Steiner & Meehan, 2000) showed us how to consider the role of the arts and imagination in schools (Dewey, 1934/1989; Eisner, 2002; Greene, 1995; Wilhelm & Edmiston, 1998), provided keen insights into the development of drama as a way of thinking (Banks, 2014; Heathcote & Bolton, 1994; Schneider, Crumpler, & Rogers, 2006; Wagner, 1976), and encouraged our thinking through vision (Arnheim, 1969) and written expression (Fletcher, 1993; Macrorie, 1976; Morrison, 1997).

In our states of Georgia and New York, the legislative moves of state and local governments have created testing and accountability cultures that may seem antithetical to arts-integration approaches to teaching. For instance, there are school districts in Georgia that mandate a specific number of grades that teachers must generate for student work. Those grades must fit within a prescribed set of categories, and the weight of the categories is set by the district. A teacher may need to have sixty grades per marking period with at least 20 percent in benchmarking tests, 20 percent in homework, and so on, with the testing portions accounting for a quarter of the total grade and the state-mandated standardized test for the grade level accounting for 15 to 25 percent of the grade as well. This is a system that values counting things within the curriculum. A system that measures learning in order to generate results that rank students, teachers, classes, schools, districts, and states. It seems there is no end to the amount of counting a teacher can or must do to show proof of student learning. And yet, there is more to learning and school than can be measured by a standardized test. There is more to teaching than can be measured by a student's performance on a standardized test. Eisner (2002) is adamant in pointing out that not everything that is important can be measured and not everything that is measured is important. In other words, there is more to school than can be captured with standardized tests, quotas for grades, and demands for counting everything in sight.

In New York, the Office of State Assessment writes the standardized tests for ELA, mathematics, and science at every grade level. In grades 6 to 8, students are tested every year in ELA. In high school, at the end of grade 11, students take the Regents Examination in English, which is a graduation requirement. While the assessment scores for grades 6 to 8 do not factor into student records, they have been tied to teacher evaluation. So the exams measure student proficiency but are used to determine teacher effectiveness. The Office of State Assessment advises that it:

> develops and administers tests that are aligned with the New York State Learning Standards and Core Curriculum, are consistent with State and federal mandates, are statistically and psychometrically sound, and yield valuable information that enables the State Education Department to hold schools accountable for the education of all students. (Office of State Assessment, 2014, para. 2)

Statistically and psychometrically sound tests are not helpful when approaching the diversity of students and their needs. Standardized tests do not measure most of the things we value about teaching and learning. Indeed, these tests do not measure the whole of what students can perform, achieve, or even express. Parents in New York State have become increasingly frustrated with testing and have begun a grassroots opt-out movement that has resulted in students boycotting the tests in elementary and middle schools. Scores for these exams in most cases are not available to teachers until the very end of the school year or even the following year, so they cannot inform instruction or remediate weaknesses (Network for Public Education, 2016). Parents now exercise their rights to refuse to have children tested and students are either kept home from school or made to sit and read or do other homework in alternate locations on test days.

In Georgia, tests at the state level are standardized forms given in every year of middle school for grades 6 through 8, then twice in high school for ELA: at the end of grade 9 English and at the end of American Literature courses. These tests are called the Georgia Milestones and, by law, have to account for a specific percentage of the overall grade for the course. Georgia opted out of the Partnership for Assessment of Readiness for College and Careers consortium of states developing tests in relation to the Common Core State Standards, arguing that the state could not afford the technological requirements and wanted more control over the content of the tests (Georgia Department of Education, 2013). The state school superintendent argued that Georgia could not afford the $31 million required to pay for the consortium tests (Capelouto, 2013). Ultimately, Georgia paid CTB/McGraw-Hill, a private company, $107.8 million for a five-year contract to develop tests to be given online across the state. The first round of testing with the Milestones began in spring 2015; the state published the results of the tests in September 2015. Those familiar with the ebb and flow of school calendars will note that this means the results for one year of students was reported in the year following. What can teachers do with results for students they no longer have, since most secondary teachers do not loop with their students? What is really being measured and to what ends? While test scores are no longer used as a metric to determine teacher effectiveness in Georgia, the influence of testing has not diminished. In New York State, even with the efforts of the opt-out movement, there is still no reprieve for any teacher, because everyone has to show that they are contributing to the improvement of student learning as shown on tests.

The Arts as an Act of Defiance

All of the above information on the kinds of increased scrutiny that teachers face begs the question: What is the role of the arts for English teachers? Who would have the audacity to bring in surprise, multiple points of view and endpoints, delight, and innovation in the face of all these accountability measures? English teachers. Creative and innovative ELA teachers enhance the learning environment by offering spaces to think critically and for students to connect their own lives and worlds through the arts. It is these qualities, these enhancements to the educational experience, that, as Eisner (1992) makes clear, the arts offer to both students and teachers alike. This is a time of increasingly loud demands for differentiation to meet the cultural, emotional, and individual needs of students while simultaneously proving that students can perform on a set of shared test performance tasks. It is in this time that teachers need resources to rebuke, to defy, to push against the system that threatens to weaken their reasoned judgments and undermine their professional practices. This moment is the one in which the arts can no longer be on the sidelines or pushed away in favor of more drill and practice in preparation for high-stakes tests in the name of accountability for students, teachers, and administrators. Now is the time for movement with grace, viewing with scrutiny, and action with creativity.

Students need the arts of fiction, poetry, drama, visual art, music, and dance to be welcomed and embraced in schools. The dedicated artists, musicians, performers, and thespians who teach visual art, music, dance, and drama in school are assuredly vital to the future of schools and the nation. ELA teachers are often also avid readers, writers, and creators of ideas and beautiful things. These English teachers can bring the arts with them into discussions of literature, analyses of concepts, and writing about language and culture. We need teachers who can integrate the arts in English classes, and this book is designed to support those teachers and encourage others who can see the promise and the possibility of teaching English as an inclusive and open space for students to express themselves with words and other qualities that words cannot yet contain.

Body and Soul

How then do we enact the arts in defiance? When we think about a teacher's purpose, we think about enabling kids to *learn* while fostering the growth of their lives and bodies. Good teachers strive to inspire, to teach, and to change students' outlook on their subject matter and their lives. Although the current pressures of testing create certain challenges for teachers, there are those who teach beyond the tests and are doing more to educate the whole student than many realize. It is easy to get bogged down in the negativity of a standards-driven educational climate that takes a good deal of personal autonomy out of the teaching practice; however, rather than cater to this negativity and these standards, we prefer to celebrate the creativity and innovation present in many English classrooms today. We prefer to infuse new energy into this climate by exploring the things good teachers do with the arts so that others can also find ways to remain true to what is best for students and still meet the demands of standards and testing.

Now more than ever, teachers need to work with students using curricula and strategies relevant to their lives. We live in a highly interactive society and world. Teachers can find many opportunities for interaction and authentic learning endeavors in the arts. The arts offer creative and interactive possibilities that allow for an individual to be immersed in the subject, to make decisions, to think critically, and to develop their own ideas as they work through a piece of literature, write an essay, or make meaning of a text.

The problem with simply making sure that students can pass a given test is that they are not being given the opportunity to think for themselves. They are not given the room to grow, to learn, and to appropriate knowledge if they are not actively and creatively becoming part of the texts they are reading. Successful teachers encourage students to be part of the construction of knowledge (Applebee, 1996; Freire, 1970; Smagorinsky, 2001). The arts offer many opportunities for students to become part of that meaning making and even to move beyond the texts. In the English classroom, it is possible to get students involved in class discussions, in group presentations, in talking about the things they really believe, desire, feel, love, hate, and so on. Employing the arts in regular instruction can provide a creative outlet to have those conversations and make important moves beyond the text toward new meaning and understanding.

Eisner (2002) talks about the arts as a way to invite children into the learning process; he says that a "major aim of arts education is to promote the child's ability to develop his or her mind through the experience that the creation or perception of expressive form makes possible" (p. 24). Visual arts, drama, music, creative writing, dance, and movement all provide an opportunity in a classroom for students to learn through living, thinking, and interacting with the world around them.

Further, Efland (2002) writes about the cognitive aspect of arts education: the justification, if you will, for arts education to exist and to be placed on par with other subjects. He says the "purpose for teaching the arts is to contribute to the understanding of the social and cultural landscape that each individual inhabits" (p. 171). Students can glean understanding through the arts that ultimately goes beyond textbooks, beyond the banking model of education (Freire, 1970); art allows students to interact with and react to their worlds.

Students can participate in authentic inquiry-based lessons through the arts to explore and learn about things that matter to their own lives and worlds. Art allows students to explore their identities in embodied ways; the arts allow the learning experience to truly become part of the individual in ways that solely reading and writing a text cannot do. When approaching literacy from a multimodal perspective, the arts offer visual, auditory, textual, and kinesthetic ways of making meaning. Finally, the arts facilitate student exploration of spaces between texts in meaningful and useful ways. A learning environment that is transactional, embodied, and multimodal nurtures students and teachers alike.

Our job as teachers goes beyond preparing classes to pass tests. Our job is to feed the bodies and souls of our students; nourishing the things in them that need growth and development is at the heart of any kind of work in the arts. The arts provide ways to explore content, ourselves, and our place in the world. In all art forms, there is higher-order thinking, analysis, synthesis, and reflection. The arts offer authentic inquiry opportunities for students to make meaning of their worlds despite the pressure of tests while making students more readily able to pass tests at the same time (Beach, Campano, Edmiston, & Borgmann, 2010). There will always be standardization in education, but the arts allow us to personalize and humanize our teaching.

A Symphony of Possibilities

Within this volume, we hear from teachers and researchers working with drama, found poetry, music, public art forms, spoken word poetry, and visual arts. The contributors each have a detailed story to tell about classroom practice and the ways in which teachers can navigate using similar methods in secondary classrooms. Each chapter provides a tangible example of real teachers using real methods with real students.

Since music is often so much a part of our students' lives and worlds, Tim Duggan opens our exploration of the arts with his chapter on musical adaptations. He examines how students develop original musical responses to literary and informational texts in the classroom. He provides a theoretical model for using music in the classroom as well as several options for lessons to explore creative adaptations of text and song. Christian Goering and Amy Matthews also write about creating music with high school students. They share their experiences examining and writing protest songs and discuss how the songwriting process connects social justice and activism.

Next, both Wendy Williams and Toby Emert explore the art and performative nature of poetry. Williams shares her experiences with spoken word poetry in high school classrooms and offers accessible approaches to integrating this art into instruction. Emert describes his efforts to broaden the concept of aesthetic response as he offers a brief introduction to the avant-garde Dada movement in order to explore using found poetry as a tool for analysis of, and response to, literary texts.

Dramatic arts and the use of activities based in drama and theatre have much to offer in ELA classrooms as well. Katherine Macro writes about dramatic methods that offer embodied experiences for use with both literature and writing. These strategies employ drama to explore literature and student identities while strengthening their writing and understanding of texts. Laura Turchi and Pauline Skowron Schmidt's collaboration makes the teaching and learning of Shakespeare active, playful, and thoughtful. The teachers and students in this chapter play with ideas, characters, and relationships. They show how performance and play can help students explore Shakespearean texts.

Several of our contributors address ways to use visual arts in the ELA classroom to facilitate learning. Alisha White shares her experiences with integrating art, composing with images, and embracing creative responses to literature in contexts that require accountability and assessment. She examines a variety of tensions, including reasons why teachers may be hesitant about bringing in an art form that differs from those of the traditional reading and writing curricula. Using specific strategies and illustrations, she speaks to each tension and offers rationales for using creative, open-ended responses. Next, Pamela Hartman, Jessica Berg, Brandon Schuler, and Erin Knauer discuss the way that using artistic response strategies in the ELA classroom can increase students' comprehension of difficult texts and help them evoke, enter, and explore story worlds.

Michelle Zoss's chapter illustrates a variety of activities in which drawings support learning about literature, and then explains the importance of using drawings and large-scale visual projects to connect with students and help them make their own connections to the subject. She also addresses the concerns that critics have about using visual arts integration in an urban high school. Finally, visual arts can also serve as a vehicle for expression of learning and meaning outside the classroom. To that end, Stephen Goss explores urban classrooms that utilized guerilla, public, and conceptual art forms as a means to publish and forefront student writing while giving authentic purpose to the exploration of a district-mandated curriculum and high-stakes test preparation. His work gives concrete ways to incorporate arts-based instruction in an environment without much room for an exploratory curriculum.

Developing this book in the current age of accountability is an imperative for us as teachers, professors, artists, and performers. When the stakes are so high in schools that tests determine passing rates and promotion for students, effectiveness measures for teachers, and soon-to-come effectiveness ratings for colleges of education, now is the time for reinvesting in the passions that brought us into teaching in the first place. This book aims to tap into the enjoyment, thoughtfulness, and excitement of teachers and students alike. Like the studies that find teachers renewed and affirmed when aesthetics and the arts are integral to the curriculum (Augustine & Zoss, 2006; Macro, 2011; Zoss & White, 2011), this book represents a moment to regroup, locate some new teaching tools or dust off some old ones, and find ways to make school more like the place we imagine it could be.

References

Albers, P., & Sanders, J. (Eds.). (2010). *Literacies, the arts, and multimodality*. Urbana, IL: National Council of Teachers of English.

Applebee, A. N. (1996). *Curriculum as conversation: Transforming traditions of teaching and learning*. Chicago, IL: University of Chicago Press.

Arnheim, R. (1969). *Visual thinking*. Berkeley: University of California Press.

Augustine, S. M., & Zoss, M. (2006). Aesthetic flow experience in the teaching of pre-service language arts teachers. *English Education, 39*(1), 72–95.

Banks, F. (2014). *Creative Shakespeare: The Globe education guide to practical Shakespeare*. London, UK: Bloomsbury.

Beach, R., Campano, G., Edmiston, B., & Borgmann, M. (2010). *Literacy tools in the classroom: Teaching through critical inquiry, grades 5–12*. New York, NY, and Berkeley, CA: Teachers College Press and the National Writing Project.

Bogard, J. M., & Donovan, L. (2013*). Strategies to integrate the arts in language arts*. Huntington Beach, CA: Shell Education.

Capelouto, S. (2013, July 25). Georgia the latest state to back out of K–12 PARCC tests [Transcript of audio story]. Retrieved from http://www.npr.org/templates/story/story.php?storyId=205548324

Dewey, J. (1989). Art as experience. In J. A. Boydston (Ed.), *John Dewey: The later works, 1925–1953* (Vol. 10, pp. 1–400). Carbondale: Southern Illinois University Press. (Original work published 1934)

Donahue, D. M., & Stuart, J. (Eds.) (2010). *Artful teaching: Integrating the arts for understanding across the curriculum, K–8*. New York, NY; Reston, VA: Teachers College Press; National Art Education Association.

Efland, A. D. (2002). *Art and cognition: Integrating the visual arts in the curriculum*. New York, NY: Teachers College Press.

Eisner, E. W. (1992). The misunderstood role of the arts in human development. *Phi Delta Kappan, 73*(8), 591–95.

Eisner, E. W. (2002). *The arts and the creation of mind*. New Haven, CT: Yale University Press.

Emert, T., Macro, K., & Schmidt, P. S. (2016). Imagination, creativity, and innovation: Showcasing the "A" in English Language Arts [Special issue]. *English Journal, 105*(5).

Fletcher, R. J. (1993). *What a writer needs*. Portsmouth, NH: Heinemann.

Freire, P. (1970). *Pedagogy of the oppressed*. New York, NY: The Seabury Press.

Georgia Department of Education. (2013, July 22). *Georgia withdrawing from the Partnership for Assessment of Readiness of College and Careers (PARCC) Consortium* [Press release]. Retrieved from https://www.gadoe.org/External-Affairs-and-Policy/communications/Pages/PressReleaseDetails.aspx?PressView=default&pid=123

Goldberg, M. R. (2012). *Arts integration: Teaching subject matter through the arts in multicultural settings* (4th ed.). Boston, MA: Pearson.

Greene, M. (1995). *Releasing the imagination: Essays on education, the arts, and social change.* San Francisco, CA: Jossey-Bass.

Heathcote, D., & Bolton, G. M. (1994). *Drama for learning: Dorothy Heathcote's mantle of the expert approach to education.* Portsmouth, NH: Heinemann.

Holbrook, T. (2010). An ability traitor at work: A treasonous call to subvert writing from within. *Qualitative Inquiry, 16*(3), 171–83.

John-Steiner, V., & Meehan, T. M. (2000). Creativity and collaboration in knowledge construction. In C. D. Lee & P. Smagorinsky (Eds.), *Vygotskian perspectives on literacy research: Constructing meaning through collaborative inquiry* (pp. 31–48). Cambridge, UK: Cambridge University Press.

Macro, K. (2011). *Playing the part: A case study on new literacies and drama* (Doctoral dissertation). Retrieved from ProQuest Dissertations & Theses database. (AAT 3475344)

Macro, K. (2015). Drama as literacy: Perceptions of an interactive pedagogy. *Research in Drama Education: The Journal of Applied Theatre and Performance, 20*(3), 337–39. https://doi.org/10.1080/13569783.2015.1059270

Macrorie, K. (1976). *Writing to be read* (Rev. 2nd ed.). Rochelle Park, NJ: Hayden Book Company.

McDonald, N. L. (2010). *Handbook for K–8 arts integration: Purposeful planning across the curriculum.* Boston, MA: Pearson.

McDonald, N. L., & Fisher, D. (2006). *Teaching literacy through the arts.* New York, NY: Guilford Press.

Morrison, C. (1997). *How to build a long-lasting fire: Writing poems from your life.* Lincolnwood, IL: NTC Publishing.

NCTE Commission on Arts and Literacies. (n.d.). Commission purpose statement. Retrieved from http://www.ncte.org/cee/commissions/artsandliteracies

Network for Public Education. (2016, April 1). *Message from Diane Ravitch about opt out* [Video file]. USA: Shoot4Education. Retrieved from https://vimeo.com/161182196

Office of State Assessment (2014, October 27). About the Office of State Assessment. Retrieved from http://www.p12.nysed.gov/assessment/about-osa.html

Schneider, J. J., Crumpler, T. P., & Rogers, T. (Eds.). (2006). *Process drama and multiple literacies: Addressing social, cultural, and ethical issues.* Portsmouth, NH: Heinemann.

Smagorinsky, P. (2001). If meaning is constructed, what's it made from? Toward a cultural theory of reading. *Review of Educational Research, 71*(1), 133–69.

Wagner, B. J. (1976). *Dorothy Heathcote: Drama as a learning medium.* Washington, DC: National Education Association.

Whitin, P. (1996a). Exploring visual response to literature. *Research in the Teaching of English, 30*(1), 114–40.

Whitin, P. (1996b). *Sketching stories, stretching minds: Responding visually to literature.* Portsmouth, NH: Heinemann.

Whitin, P. (2005). The interplay of text, talk, and visual representation in expanding literary interpretation. *Research in the Teaching of English, 39*(4), 365–97.

Wilhelm, J. D., & Edmiston, B. (1998). *Imagining to learn: Inquiry, ethics, and integration through drama.* Portsmouth, NH: Heinemann.

Zoss, M., & White, A. M. (2011). Finding "my kind of teaching": How a drama project became a teacher's expressive teaching moment. *English in Education, 45*(2), 161–75.

Musical Adaptations and Explorations in English

Timothy J. Duggan, *Northeastern Illinois University*

Integrating the arts into our English language arts classrooms is natural and necessary. After all, we would be hard pressed to justify the term *English language arts* without acknowledging and incorporating the many different ways in which language intersects with other art forms. If we constrict our definition of language arts to poetry, fiction, and creative nonfiction, we lose many relevant, contemporary, and impactful practices that help shape our students' identities. Students come to us saturated by cultural messages received through media images, dramatic stories experienced in cinemas or through television, and musical texts that combine language and sound in ways that stir the emotions and puzzle the will. Often, these cultural messages tell stories using music to influence emotions and privilege particular responses (Jourdain, 1997; Wood, 2016). While many teachers incorporate the arts in hopes of challenging students to develop critical consciousness as consumers and interpreters of these cultural texts, I would challenge us to seek ways to develop students' abilities to produce original artistic texts themselves, through visual art, movement, creative dramatics, and, as this chapter will illustrate, music. Historically, much art derives from stimulus found within the culture, and teachers who consciously connect literary and nonliterary written texts to artistic production will activate student creativity, as well as develop analytical and interpretive skills honored by educational standards.

Several progressive educational thinkers have written about the advantages of opening spaces in the classroom for a variety of student-generated responses to educational concepts. For Eisner (2002), constructing a variety of "modes of response" to concepts allows for a rich and deep consideration of those concepts. For Harste (2001), developing practice that honors alternative "ways of knowing" constitutes what he views as a necessary redefinition of literacy instruction. Gardner (1999) acknowledges that a common curriculum is beneficial, but that "a commitment to some common knowledge does not mean that everyone must study these things in the same way and be assessed in the same way" (p. 152). Contemporary emphases on creative thinking in business and problem-solving

(Levitt & Dubner, 2015; Pink, 2005) have found traction among the reading public, and many teachers seek to make creativity a viable part of their curriculum despite the constraints of the testing regime discussed in the introduction to this book by Macro and Zoss.

Many authors have written about the benefits of including music in the study of literature, most notably Brock Dethier (2003) in his book *From Dylan to Donne: Bridging English and Music*. Special issues of *English Journal* have asked teachers to share practices that include music, and many professional articles show how music may enhance the study of English (see Johnson & Goering, 2016). Teachers can use music to relax or excite students in class (Wood, 2016), they can play songs that share thematic elements with classroom texts (Dethier, 2003; Nutt, Goering, & Gerhardson, 2016; Sewell, 2016), or they can examine how music intersects with other media, such as film (Golden, 2001). Essentially, these uses of music cast the student as witness or investigator, but not as artist–participant. Goering (2016) explains the difference between arts integration and arts enhancement by claiming that true integration incorporates students' own musical ideas and production as opposed to simply enhancing literary study by exposing students to relevant musical selections. I am interested in developing students' ability to produce musical (and other artistic) responses to texts they encounter in English class and in the world.

The M.A.S.T.E.R. Framework

One model to assist teachers in conceptualizing ways to stimulate student musical production in response to classroom texts is the M.A.S.T.E.R. framework (Duggan, 2016). Teachers can use individual elements of the framework during any instructional unit, or they can give students options from the menu of choices offered. Here is a brief overview of the six M.A.S.T.E.R. components:

1. *"M" = mnemonics.* Mnemonics are memory strategies, and musical mnemonics, such as "The Alphabet Song," have been used for generations to help people store terms and concepts in a way that is readily retrievable. While the practice is common in early childhood education and elementary school, it is not as common in the higher grades, but it still may function to help students remember lists, names, processes, or key concepts.

2. *"A" = adaptations.* Students retell stories or concepts they have learned through song. In this strategy, students may recast a story's setting or change certain details, but the goal is to retell the story or re-present the

concepts in an informational text in such a way that the essence is preserved or transformed to meet the needs of the interpreter. Opera composers and popular musicians have been adapting literature to music for centuries, and students can generate their own musical adaptations of the stories they read or the concepts they learn if given the opportunity. Students compose verses and choruses that reflect the structure of the text they have adapted. They can create melodies that reflect the tone of the text. They may also use existing familiar melodies, though building original melodies will add a creative element, which is preferable. Students who understand song structure may tie musical elements to story elements, such as writing in a bridge or a key change at the turning point in the story. The students' adaptations should be faithful to the themes and spirit of the original text (as interpreted by the students). Students may also write essays to explain their artistic process and what they were trying to achieve with the adaptation. They may reflect on how their understanding of the text influenced their musical interpretation, thus adding a metacognitive element to the activity.

3. *"S" = settings.* Settings are, as the name implies, musical renderings of literature that do not change the actual language of the reference text. Setting a poem to music is an example, whether it be a poem written by Shakespeare or by a fellow student in class. Students composing musical settings may repeat or rearrange key lines or phrases from the text, but the language is not changed, thus distinguishing setting from adaptation. As with musical adaptations, musical settings may employ original melodies produced by the students or familiar melodies.

4. *"T" = themes.* Based on the concept of the leitmotif, the task of composing mono- or multi-note themes to represent individual characters in stories, or to represent different events or processes, can inspire student creativity and analytical skills. The same may be done as "background music" for dramatic readings. Students develop these themes using their own musical instruments or using readily available music software, such as GarageBand (Apple Inc., Cupertino, CA) or Minimoog (Moog Music, Asheville, NC). Classes can discuss the musical choices presented in the instrumental (or hummed) themes and defend the musical choices they made to represent a certain character or scene.

5. *"E" = extensions/explorations.* Rather than attempting to recount narrative events in a story, this element of music integration invites students to reflect on the story at a certain point and step outside the progression of

events to reveal an internal state of a character, or to musically portray that state. One example is "Over the Rainbow" (Arlen & Harburg, 1939). The song does not further the action of *The Wizard of Oz*, but it reveals Dorothy's inner state. Students may compose songs that are laments or celebrations based on their understanding of a character's emotions at a given time in a story.

6. *"R" = recital.* Remember to give the students the opportunity to perform their compositions. From a recital approach to an open mic, festival, or competition, recital opportunities foster artistic growth and build community. Follow up with reflective or critical conversations about the performances that examine the connection with material learned in class.

In this chapter, I explore in depth the *adaptation* element of the M.A.S.T.E.R. framework, with examples from teacher and student workshops I have done over the past few years, as well as work done by teachers I've had the good fortune to know. I also offer an example of how one student responded to a text through a musical *exploration*. Along the way, I comment on the activities with suggestions to help teachers find success using these strategies that may transform the culture of individual classrooms.

Virtually any classroom text, whether language based, auditory, or visual, offers the opportunity for students to construct original musical responses. Students do not need to have a musical background or specialized knowledge to engage in the process; however, nearly every secondary classroom will include at least a few students who either play an instrument or sing in choir, or both. In that sense, finding out who the musically inclined students are early in the year will be helpful. Teachers themselves need not be musicians in order to teach students to create musical compositions. They only need to be willing to take small risks by introducing and perhaps modeling the processes and then have the courage to release control over the final product of the students' labors.

The process for including musical adaptations and explorations is simple: read or view classroom texts, invite students to respond musically, work with students to discover how a song might best represent the reference text, and then give students the time and tools to complete their songs. Musical instruments help, as do electronic apps that provide musical sound, but songs may be written and sung a cappella as well. Students may benefit from analyzing a popular song in class to learn how verses, choruses, bridges, and instrumental breaks work, but they can also discover those elements as they build their own songs. A simple graphic organizer may also prove helpful, such as the following (slashes indicate musical beats). Students can write their original lyrics in the spaces between beats:

Verse 1:

_/_____/_____/_____/_____

_/_____/_____/_____/_____

_/_____/_____/_____/_____

_/_____/_____/_____/_____

Verse 2:

_/_____/_____/_____/_____

_/_____/_____/_____/_____

_/_____/_____/_____/_____

_/_____/_____/_____/_____

Chorus: _/_____/_____/_____

     _/_____/_____/_____

Verse 3:

_/_____/_____/_____/_____

_/_____/_____/_____/_____

_/_____/_____/_____/_____

_/_____/_____/_____/_____

Bridge:

_/_____/_____/_____/_____

_/_____/_____/_____/_____

Chorus: _/_____/_____/_____

     _/_____/_____/_____

One thing to watch out for, though, in providing such scaffolds in the process is not to limit students' musical ideas. In other words, students must be allowed to change the structure of the organizer to fit the song they hear in their heads. Writing original songs brings students face to face with rhythm and meter, two important literary concepts. An additional benefit of writing music in English class is the fresh take this process offers on sound-based poetic elements. Through the examples that follow, taken from classrooms and workshops, we will see a variety of strategies to get students involved in musical response building.

Adaptation Activities

One way to use musical adaptation successfully and to introduce the process of musical response is to have students collaborate to write a song *together as a large group*, based on a piece of narrative text. In a workshop with the ARTeacher Fellowship program at the University of Arkansas (see the glossary in the present volume), I used a local story found on the website of Petit Jean Mountain State Park (Arkansas State Parks, 2016), which is near the site of the workshop. The park received its name from the legend of a woman named Adrienne who loved a French explorer named Chavet. When he decided to lead an expedition to the Louisiana Territory, Chavet forbade Adrienne to join him, claiming that he would marry her the next year when he returned. Adrienne disguised herself as a cabin boy and boarded Chavet's ship, accompanying him in disguise and spending an entire summer in what is now Arkansas, just to be near her love. Apparently, she fell ill and her disguise was revealed, and, when she died, the members of the expedition, along with some kind and helpful Native Americans, carried her to the top of the small mountain that now bears her name. On the park's website, the story is told in a series of paragraphs that amount to about 1,500 words. The story fascinated me, and I wanted to see whether these thirty teachers with local knowledge would invest themselves in the process of writing a song together, even though only about one in every five of them had any musical training. Participants were placed in small working groups, and each group was tasked with translating one paragraph into a verse for a song. I offered a simple, three-chord progression on the guitar to give them a sense of possibility, and, in the space of about forty-five minutes, they constructed an entire song. Here is an excerpt from the original text:

> Chavet was engaged to be married to a beautiful young girl from Paris, Adrienne Dumont. When told of his plans, she asked that they be married right away so she could accompany him. Thinking of the hardship and danger on the journey, Chavet refused her request, telling her upon his return if the country was good and safe, they would be married and go to the New World.
>
> Adrienne refused to accept his answer and disguised herself as a cabin boy and applied to the captain of Chavet's ship for a position as a cabin boy, calling herself Jean. The girl must have been incredibly clever in her disguise, for it is said that not even Chavet recognized her. The sailors called her Petit Jean, which is French for Little John. (Arkansas State Parks, 2016)

After reading the passage, the groups set out to write individual verses, based on their assigned paragraph from the history. Here is what the first two groups came up with for verses:

> Verse I:
> Adrienne was to be married to Chavet
> Both exploring souls, but he wanted to pave the way.
> He asked her to wait but she said "No,
> Wherever you will travel, I must go."

> Verse II:
> In love, she couldn't accept his answer
> She longed for adventure
> So a cabin boy she became
> Even to him Petit Jean was her name.

The other groups also contributed verses, sharing the work of adaptation with the common thread being the simple song structure of 1–4–5 (in this case, D chord, G chord, and A chord, in the key of D), typical of popular songs. Even though the melodies varied in individual verses, the basic beat of the song and the simple chord progression provided cohesion. We also took one of the verses and changed the melody and chords, creating what is called a *bridge* in musical terms:

> Verse III:
> Across cold ocean waves she followed him
> So close but never really with her love
> Mountaintop summer but alone in the crowd
> Longing for him and the wedding bells sound

> Bridge:
> Sickness. . .
> She was out of love
> It was soon found out she wasn't who she said she was.
> "Oh baby please. . . forgive me."

> Verse IV:
> So she made her last request,
> Brought to the mountain summer blessed,
> And they laid her there to rest.
> Sweet Petit Jean's Mountain possessed.

Working together, the group composed a short chorus, which would be repeated throughout the song after each verse:

> Chorus:
> Petit Jean did you follow all this way?
> On this mountain, you must stay . . .
> . . . and I will go.

We performed the song together, each group singing its own verse, and everyone singing the chorus. After we performed the song in the seminar, participants discussed how they could implement the strategy in their own classrooms, as the process of songwriting was demystified for them. As they each had a hand in the creative process, even the non-musicians came to see the value of their contributions. According to Goering and Strayhorn (2016), participants became convinced through the process that they could implement the strategy in their own classrooms.

One concern teachers may have about assigning *small groups of students to collaborate* to build a song in class is potential lack of broad participation. To address this problem, the process through which students collaborate to build musical responses to literature can be informed by the creative problem-solving model (Treffinger, Isaksen, & Stead-Dorval, 2006), because building a song from scratch is a problem-solving process. Some students think creatively as *explorers*, generating new ideas, perhaps melody, perhaps language. Other students think creatively as *developers*, taking the ideas generated by the explorers and making them fit the structure established in the opening verse and/or chorus. As explained by Treffinger et al. (2006), explorers think well "outside the box" while developers think well "inside the box" (p. 23). Both skills are valuable for generating a tight, effective narrative song.

First, students need to determine what is most important to include from the text they are adapting, and perhaps generate a few lines taken directly from the text or paraphrased from the text that capture an essence in the work. Using those lines, students construct a verse or a chorus that will provide the foundation for the song's structure. Establishing a melody and building a song structure is part of the process. Verses, a chorus, and sometimes a bridge and/or an instrumental break—these are the building blocks of nearly any song that contains lyrics. Once a group has an idea for a verse, they can work within the structure established in that verse to write more verses. The chorus, typically, says something interpretive about the story told in the verses, assuming the song is a narrative song. A bridge, which has its own musical structure, typically contains a turning point in the progression of the story or situation depicted in the song.

As a song takes shape, the problem to solve is how to fit the language to the music in a way that sounds natural and not forced or trite. Again, explorers and developers working together can find the right mix of innovation and cohesion that makes a song work. If an individual student excels in both creating new structures and shaping a song through verse, chorus, and bridge, that student is the budding songwriter.

Some teachers and students will want to set language to existing songs that are familiar, such as pop tunes or traditional tunes everyone recognizes. I don't want to de-emphasize the value of doing so, but more of the brain is activated when students are attempting to create original melodies, and the ownership will be much deeper once the song is completed (Sousa, 2001). When working with an already familiar tune, the creative work is purely language based. The irony or humor in hearing new words sung to a familiar tune can create a certain delight, but the presence of the reference tune cannot be escaped entirely. With an original melody, on the other hand, both the language aspect of the new work and the musical aspect, with its own signature tones, become part of the new text that is created.

In workshops similar to the one described above, I have used a vignette titled "My Name" from Sandra Cisneros's (1991) popular classroom text, *The House on Mango Street,* to illustrate the M.A.S.T.E.R. framework. In one such workshop, students were asked to work alone or in pairs (their preference) to write a musical adaptation of the story of Esperanza's great-grandmother or to reflect on Esperanza's perspective on her great-grandmother. Marcus, a tenth grader, took the vignette and turned it into a rap song. He performed the rap to a house beat that he had stored on his mobile phone. Here is an excerpt from the original that captures Esperanza's angst:

> It was my great-grandmother's name and now it is mine. She was a horse woman too, born like me in the Chinese year of the horse—which is supposed to be bad luck if you're born female—but I think this is a Chinese lie because the Chinese, like the Mexicans, don't like their women strong.
>
> My great-grandmother. I would've liked to have known her, a wild, horse of a woman, so wild she wouldn't marry. Until my great-grandfather threw a sack over her head and carried her off. Just like that, as if she were a fancy chandelier. That's the way he did it.
>
> And the story goes she never forgave him. She looked out the window her whole life, the way so many women sit their sadness on an elbow. I wonder if she made the best with what she got or was she sorry because she couldn't be all the things she wanted to be. Esperanza. I have inherited her name, but I don't want to inherit her place by the window. (p. 12)

Here is Marcus's adaptation:

Esperanza
Zeze the x or maybe lisandra
just anything but esperanza
my great grandmomma
had the same drama
suffered the same karma

My name is like pin needles and tin
I can't defend
since it's mispronounced even by my friends

In español my name is soft
but in ingles the translation gets lost
probably the cost of immigration
verbal constipation
is what i feel when i hear the mispronunciation,
creation of names didn't favor me
as you can see
my great grandma stared out the window vacantly
probably wishing things were different
the sentiment
of the name that only carries woe

She was abducted by my great abuelo
my name has no flow
she didn't want to go, and i want my name to go
if the sorrow of our hearts were lights, how bright would they glow
i don't know
well, i sleep now, maybe i'll care less tomorrow
looking out my window

Marcus's delivery style was rapid fire, words tumbling out of his mouth like water from a high-pressure hose, and the other participants applauded wildly. An interpretive conversation among participants followed that combined references of Marcus's images with the images Cisneros packs into the vignette. The connection between Marcus as a rap artist and Cisneros the author emerged through his individual colloquialisms, such as "had the same drama" and "name has no flow," and the phenomenon of dual identification, hearing her story through his voice, amplified both voices. The conversation we shared around his performance would not have happened without the rap song as a reference point. This point is germane to the value of arts integration. As Dewey (1934/1980) points out in *Art as Experience*:

> It has been repeatedly intimated that there is a difference between the art product (statue, painting, or whatever), and the *work* of art. The first is physical and potential; the latter is active and experienced. It is what the product does, its working. For nothing enters experience bald and unaccompanied, whether it be a seemingly formless happening, a theme intellectually systematized, or an object elaborated with every loving care of united thought and emotion. Its very entrance is the beginning of a complex interaction; upon the nature of this interaction depends the character of the thing as finally experienced. (p. 162)

With the work of creating musical responses to literary art or texts in the classroom, conversations around the literature have access to formed artistic products, and the work of producing these artistic products, whether they be songs, paintings, or, increasingly, multimedia creations, allows for self-reflection on the part of the creator.

Explorations: An Example

A third strategy for introducing musical adaptations or explorations into English classes is to make songwriting *an option in a menu of possible projects* in an instructional unit. Rather than having the entire class collaborate to write a song or require all individuals to compose music, teachers may throw a lifeline to musical students in their classes by including songwriting as a choice. Doing so encourages students to develop their talents in music while also increasing their attention to the original text read in class. Recently, a student of mine who was student teaching at a Chicago high school included a number of artistic choices for her students to demonstrate ways of knowing (Duggan, 2007; Harste, 2001) related to the class's reading of a contemporary novel. The student teacher, Mimi Cross, is an accomplished songwriter and musician herself, so she was able to model the process effectively. She and her cooperating teacher, Olivia Craig, collaborated to teach the short story collection *Krik? Krak!* by Edwidge Danticat (1995). According to Mimi:

> I wanted to give the students a chance to analyze a character, through their chosen medium. It could be a song, illustration, game design, poem, etc. I wanted to make it a final project by providing a menu they could choose from—each

option included an accompanying essay that was a bit more formal. I included a mini-version of this within the unit as a way for the students to start thinking about whom they could write about in their final essays. Whatever they came up with had to be created from the perspective of one of the characters. This fit in nicely within the scheme of things because they had been practicing analyses of various kinds on Fridays, which I set up as an art-themed day. We analyzed a song or looked at a photograph and answered questions about it. However, what the students enjoyed the most was listening to a piece of music and writing to it, expressing themselves. Almost all the students, including the ones who never raised their hands, were eager to share their pieces. Through this experience, I confirmed that art is still the vessel that can bring students out from their mysterious caves. It provided me with a lot of information about their thought process and grammatical level while bringing a sense of pride and joy to an otherwise humdrum Friday. Hearing the students perform the songs they wrote during my class made my day. It made me think about my high school English teacher who once allowed me to write a song for class and how much it stayed with me and inspired me to love English literature well past my high school years.

Following the *Krik? Krak!* unit, two of the ninth-grade students who wrote original songs were invited by Mimi to record the songs at a professional recording studio, which became a formative event in these young women's educational and artistic lives. One of the students, Shannon, wrote a lament by the female narrator in the opening short story of the collection, "Children of the Sea." This song is a great example of what I call an *exploration* or an *extension* because the song steps outside the narrative progression of the story and comments on the situation in the story, much like "Over the Rainbow" (Arlen & Harburg, 1939). The "Macoutes" referenced in her song were the secret police operating in Haiti during the Duvalier regime. I've included chords for the song in the first verses to give a sense of musical structure. Page numbers cited reflect direct quotes from *Krik? Krak!* (Danticat, 1995).

"Hope"

Verse 1:
Bm
Difficult times now
G
Keep your tapes to have peace
D   A
Even though my heart is breaking

Bm
'Cause of the things I've seen
G
Are you really deceased?
D   A
I'm doubtful scared and shaking

Chorus:
Bm
Hope, it keeps us moving forth
G
When you don't know which way's north
D
When smiles disappear
A   Em
And there's no light anymore

Bm
Faith, it makes you really strong
G
When you don't know right from wrong
D
But truth hits you
A   Em
And your sky grows gloomy

Verse 2:
Beat me and called me names
Really hated him for that
"Wished those Macoutes would kill him" (11)
He judged my adoration
Later I appreciate
"Thank you Papa because you saved my life" (28)

Repeat Chorus

Bridge:
"From here I cannot even see the sea" (29)
Only a black butterfly fluttering by me
Mountains will disappear, dark butterflies gone
But the sea "is endless like my love for you" (29)

Repeat Chorus

This particular use of musical exploration is important not only for what it offers a class, but also for how it creates a culture of talent development within the classroom. Shannon was able to contribute something of value to her classmates' experience with the story collection, and she was also able to develop her talent and interest in songwriting. Furthermore, that song, having been written, recorded, and performed, will stand as an artifact of her high school academic career.

As reflective teachers, we do well to consider how the work of school helps our students to make sense of the world and of their place in it. One tool I've found useful in this regard is the parallel curriculum model developed several years ago (Tomlinson et al., 2002), which conceptualizes *curriculum* as having four parallels: the core curriculum, the curriculum of connections, the curriculum of practice, and the curriculum of identity. Essentially, the *core curriculum* includes key concepts and knowledge in a discipline. The *curriculum of connections* includes knowledge of how a discipline interacts with other disciplines. The *curriculum of practice* examines what kind of work is done in a discipline, how it's done, and how professionals go about furthering the work. Finally, the *curriculum of identity* invites the learner to reflect on her relationship with the discipline. For students in an English class, the connection between studying literature and songwriting will become clearer through the process of adapting stories into songs. In so doing, the students extend their knowledge of the practices of songwriters who take ideas, shape language, build a musical structure, and physically perform their art. Perhaps most important, the students will see that the content of the English class and the process of writing a musical adaptation help to shape an emerging identity as artist/musician. Even students who follow other paths in their careers will understand and appreciate the creative process of artist/musicians through the memory of constructing musical pieces inspired by the texts they encounter in English class. Conscientious teachers can exploit opportunities for students to discuss their various artistic responses to class texts and to reflect on how they see themselves fitting into the world of the artist and literary interpreter.

Adaptation is a sort of transformation, and part of the fun in adapting any story to a different format is to decide what remains rigidly faithful to the original text and what gets transformed. In writing musical adaptations to literature, students cannot include every detail from the source text, so they are forced to solve the problem of how to retell the story (or concept), what is essential, and what must be cut for the sake of a three- or four-minute song. Students may also consider how transforming setting, both time and place, might affect the story they are retelling. Several years ago, I took the story of *Romeo and Juliet* and turned it into a Western ballad. In order to remain faithful to the original, the lyrics in the first and last verses provided a prologue and epilogue (Duggan, 2008). With a 3/4 time signature to create the feel of a cowboy song, the opening lyrics were as follows:

> In the town of Sioux City on the Western frontier,
> Two households grew strong through the prosperous years,
> But the feudin' between them caused trouble and death
> For two star-crossed lovers, Romeo and Juliet

In the song, Romeo's father is a cattle rancher and Juliet's father is a grain dealer and bootlegger. The friar becomes a preacher, the potion Juliet drinks is moonshine, and the Tybalt character shoots Mercutio in a gun battle, though neither is specifically named. The nurse's role is cut, as are those of the other minor characters. Following the deaths of the two lovers, the last verse goes as follows:

> In the town of Sioux City on the Western frontier
> Two households endured many sorrowful years
> Put their feudin' behind them, but they'll never forget
> Those two star-crossed lovers, Romeo and Juliet

The challenge in writing this adaptation of Shakespeare's classic tragedy was to maintain enough of the emotional honesty to affect the listener, while also allowing for a few grins at the absurdity of the transposition to a new time and place. Carefully selected quotes from Shakespeare's text lent authenticity to the lyrics, and an ascending key change following Romeo's banishment helped to build the dramatic tension in the song. I do not want to take a simplistic view of adaptation, as though it is just easy work that allows kids to be creative in class, or to feel as though they are creative, when they are really just being imitative. Composing can be very difficult, and effective revision requires an extensive recursive process until every line in the lyric is valuable. The fun to be found through musical adaptation is in the work itself and the fruits of one's labor. Rather than another school assignment to be forgotten or tossed aside, this work can be remembered through the simple act of singing. In an age when students may negotiate their way through four years of high school and not produce one assignment that they will want to keep forever, it is just fine for them to exercise their creativity and enjoy the artistic products they produce.

One potential problem teachers may face in encouraging students to use music to build their understanding of classroom texts relates to how we assess those efforts. Ironically, perhaps, nonlinguistic manifestations of textual understanding, such as music, art, and dance, don't necessarily free us from the need to use language to assess student performance on those tasks. Teachers may design rubrics with criteria they (and their students) determine to be vital elements of the artistic responses, but those rubrics rely on language to describe what was successfully developed by the student composer.

However, assessment of student musical compositions is not limited to language-based tools, such as rubrics or written feedback from the teacher. In Marcus's case, his rap song written in response to Esperanza's story received applause from the other participants in the workshop when he performed it. This gave him immediate and tangible feedback on his work. Similarly, students who post their musical creations on social media venues will receive feedback through the number of *likes*, the comments made by listeners, and/or the number of *views* tallied. Students who engage in adaptations and explorations of musical signatures and original lyrics build language, intersect it with music, and offer to their classmates and the world the marriage of the two.

Conclusion

Encouraging musical adaptations and explorations of works of literature opens a space in class to have different kinds of discussions about the meanings of literary work—and not just literary work, but also informational texts, such as essays, and even technical or seemingly mundane texts such as instructional manuals. Music is a pure and ancient form of storytelling. This is not a new thing. Teachers who regularly incorporate music into their teaching will be in good historical company, joining the likes of Aristotle and Peter Abelard (Duggan, 2003, 2016).

The case has been made many times by many people how important music is to our interactions in the world, and the degree to which it affects identity. Entire generations are identified through their music. The case has been made that listening to music provides a neural primer for learning (Jensen, 1998; Sousa, 2001). Likewise, the case has been made that creating and performing music activates the brain to higher levels (Costa-Giomi et al., 1999). In a survey of English teachers in one state (Duggan, 2003), over 90 percent of teachers indicated that they incorporate music into their teaching, while very few incorporated songwriting as options for students. I believe practice is ripe for change with the further diffusion of critical theory and cultural studies into our mindset about the world and about school (Morrell, 2004). Many teachers now recognize the significance of arts integration for enrichment, talent development, and establishment of respectful, positive classroom culture. Musical adaptation is about increasing one's attentiveness to the world and then translating that to song.

Taking the step of getting students writing songs in class, setting poetic text to music, or making musical signatures for characters or scenes in a story will expand the dynamism of the classroom. Students will transform from witnesses of art into artists themselves—full participants. Witnessing has value; participation has significance.

References

Arkansas State Parks. (2016). The legend of Petit Jean and French exploration. Retrieved from https://www.arkansasstateparks.com/parks/petit-jean-state-park/about/history

Arlen, H., & Harburg, E. Y. (1939). Over the rainbow [Recorded by Judy Garland]. On *The Wizard of Oz* [Motion picture soundtrack]. Beverly Hills, CA: MGM.

Cisneros, S. (1991). *The house on Mango Street.* New York, NY: Vintage.

Costa-Giomi, E., Price, H. E., Rauscher, F. H., Schmidt, J., Shackford, M., & Sims, W. L. (1999). Straight talk about music and research. *Teaching Music 7*(3), 29, 31–35.

Danticat, E. (1995). *Krik? Krak!* New York, NY: Soho Press.

Dethier, B. (2003). *From Dylan to Donne: Bridging English and music.* Portsmouth, NH: Boynton/Cook.

Dewey, J. (1980). *Art as experience.* New York, NY: Perigree Books. (Original work published 1934)

Duggan, T. J. (2003). *Uses of music in the high school English/language arts classroom in South Dakota: Teacher perceptions and practices* (Unpublished doctoral dissertation). University of South Dakota, Vermillion, SD.

Duggan, T. J. (2007). Ways of knowing: Exploring artistic representation of concepts. *Gifted Child Today, 30*(4), 56–63.

Duggan, T. J. (2008). *Language arts 201* [CD]. Self-published.

Duggan, T. J. (2016). M.A.S.T.E.R.ing the art of music integration. In L. L. Johnson & C. Z. Goering (Eds.), *Recontextualized: A framework for teaching English with music* (pp. 51–62). Rotterdam, Netherlands: Sense Publishers.

Eisner, E. W. (2002). *The educational imagination: On the design and evaluation of school programs* (3rd ed.). Upper Saddle River, NJ: Merrill/Prentice Hall.

Gardner, H. (1999). *Intelligence reframed: Multiple intelligences for the 21st century.* New York, NY: Basic Books.

Goering, C. Z. (2016). Language power: Saying more with less through songwriting. In L. L. Johnson & C. Z. Goering (Eds.), *Recontextualized: A framework for teaching English with music* (pp. 141–152). Rotterdam, Netherlands: Sense Publishers.

Goering C. Z., & Strayhorn, N. (2016). Beyond enhancement: Teaching English through musical arts integration. *English Journal, 105*(5), 29–34.

Golden, J. (2001). *Reading in the dark: Using film as a tool in the English classroom*. Urbana, IL: National Council of Teachers of English.

Harste, J. C. (2001). Foreword. In R. Beach & J. Myers (Eds.), *Inquiry-based English instruction: Engaging students in life and literature* (pp. vii–ix). New York, NY: Teachers College Press.

Jensen, E. (1998). *Teaching with the brain in mind*. Alexandria, VA: Association for Supervision and Curriculum Development.

Johnson, L. L., & Goering, C. Z. (Eds.) (2016). *Recontextualized: A framework for teaching English with music*. Rotterdam, Netherlands: Sense Publishers.

Jourdain, R. (1997). *Music, the brain, and ecstasy: How music captures our imagination*. New York, NY: HarperCollins.

Levitt S. D., & Dubner, S. J. (2015). *Think like a freak*. New York, NY: William Morrow.

Morrell, E. (2004). *Becoming critical researchers: Literacy and empowerment for urban youth*. New York, NY: Peter Lang.

Nutt, T., Goering, C. Z., & Gerhardson, A. N. (2016). It's like when the new stuff we read mixes with the old and becomes one: Pop music and *Antigone*. In L. L. Johnson & C. Z. Goering (Eds.), *Recontextualized: A framework for teaching English with music* (pp. 11–20). Rotterdam, Netherlands: Sense Publishers.

Pink, D. H. (2005). *A whole new mind: Why right-brainers will rule the future*. New York, NY: Penguin.

Sewell, W. C. (2016). Woody and me: Connecting millennials to the Great Depression. In L. L. Johnson & C. Z. Goering (Eds.), *Recontextualized: A framework for teaching English with music* (pp. 65–75). Rotterdam, Netherlands: Sense Publishers.

Sousa, D. A. (2001). *How the brain learns: A classroom teacher's guide* (2nd ed.). Thousand Oaks, CA: Corwin.

Tomlinson, C. A., Kaplan, S. N., Renzulli, J. S., Purcell, J., Leppien, J., & Burns, D. (2002). *The parallel curriculum: A design to develop high potential and to challenge high-ability learners*. Thousand Oaks, CA: Corwin.

Treffinger, D. J., Isaksen, S. G., & Stead-Dorval, B. (2006). *Creative problem solving: An introduction* (4th ed.). Waco, TX: Prufrock.

Wood, W. (2016). Afterword: Broadening the context of music in the classroom. In L. L. Johnson & C. Z. Goering (Eds.), *Recontextualized: A framework for teaching English with music* (pp. 153–159). Rotterdam, Netherlands: Sense Publishers.

2

"I am Arkansas": Social Activism through Protest Songwriting

CHRISTIAN Z. GOERING, *University of Arkansas*

AMY MATTHEWS, *Fayetteville High School*

L et us pretend for a minute that each high school English student in America spent at least some time writing and performing original music and lyrics each year. Consider the possibilities of students collaborating with local songwriters and lyricists and developing their voices and identities by performing in front of their peers. Classrooms, for two or three weeks each year, become laboratories for collaboration as students construct knowledge and ability together, an effort that highlights the assets with which students arrive in classrooms. Students are artists, collaborators, thinkers, creators, and it is easy to scan the student population of any given high school today to see the ubiquity of earbuds and Beats headphones. They are immersed in music—but are they creating it? What if every American high school student—some twenty million strong—contributed to a new song each year? As Eisner (2002) asks about school, "In what forms of representation are students expected to become 'literate'?" (p. 9). We believe the world—and school—would be a better place if students were provided the opportunity to represent their ideas, passions, visions in an art form of some kind, if not specifically songwriting.

The title of our chapter begins with the phrase "I am Arkansas," which also starts a group's protest song that they wrote, played, and sang for the class during a unit on writing protest songs (Fuller & Montgomery, 2017). The refrain still echoes in our individual psyches—"We hate your hateful policies / Just like the thirteen Colonies / We are not anomalies / We won't make apologies"—because the writers represented members of society who have recently felt attacked and were speaking out in protest. As coauthors Kennedy and Danny played the ukulele and sang, the rest of the class sang along, and one of those magical moments that one can't plan for as a teacher was realized (Zoss & White, 2011). While Danny brought some musical background to the equation, we suggest that what the class as a whole accomplished—especially including how—is worthy of repeating here and in more classrooms. In this chapter, we provide a practical approach to employing the art of songwriting to teach concepts of protest and social activism and songwriting itself in the context of a high school

English class. This work is grounded in our view of students as actors in their own learning and as capable builders of skills and knowledge when given the opportunity and support to interact, explore, and create understanding together. Thus, our approach to teaching and learning is anchored in social constructivism most closely associated with Vygotsky (1978).

In 2016, we—Chris and Amy—collaborated on a month-long arts integration songwriting unit, one in which we used elements that Chris had practiced in other places (Goering & Strayhorn, 2016) and that Chris and Amy had experienced together (Duggan, 2016); specifically, elements of Duggan's M.A.S.T.E.R. framework (see Chapter 1 in this volume) aimed at moving students toward writing songs. While working in small chunks to ultimately help students get to a point where they felt comfortable performing an original song in front of the class worked on many levels, the songs that students wrote and "performed" were still very much a collective work in progress. In short, we tried everything in our thirty-five or so combined years of working around the teaching of secondary English to attempt to extract enthusiasm and well-performed original songs from the class. For one reason or another, this didn't happen (see more in Goering, 2016), but we reflected carefully about those results as we were planning for the follow-up experience. In 2016, we were teaching the concepts surrounding "saying more with less" (Goering, 2016, p. 169) or language power. We focused on social activism for our 2017 foray into songwriting. We took up the John F. Kennedy Center for Performing Arts' definition of *arts integration*: "an approach to teaching in which students construct and demonstrate understanding through an art form. Students engage in a creative process which connects an art form and another subject area and meets evolving objectives in both" (Silverstein & Layne, 2010). In our class, the objectives were to create authentic songs that were personally meaningful but also addressed a targeted audience. We wanted students to socially engage with an issue important to them and do so while learning about song structure, technique, and approaches frequently used in protest songs. By having two teaching artists share songs and provide feedback, students were given evolving objectives to meet as songwriters, while the nature of writing for an audience and receiving multiple opportunities for performance and feedback provided evolving objectives for growing as writers more generally as well.

Arts integration works. That said, we are quick to side with Chemi (2014) in our shared concern that "it is easy to imagine the downside of the exploitation of learning potential, where [the arts] role becomes rigid and ancillary and expected to serve purposes other than artistic" (pp. 375–76). Our perspective was that songwriting in English class is valid and valuable on its own merits, not because our students would necessarily become better test takers or score higher on state exams. Because it "works," arts integration is often proffered as an education reform strategy, a saving grace for children of poverty. It's not that simple, and, while we acknowledge the record of positive results for arts integration programs around the country, we follow Maxine Greene's (1995) and Elliot Eisner's (1992) perspectives first and foremost when they observe that the arts are essential to the human experience and have wide benefits that cannot be measured. The art of songwriting in the context of English class in particular appears to be a less well-utilized approach, as Duggan (2003) found in a statewide survey of English teachers in South Dakota. We have reason to believe that students' opportunities to create original songs as part of class may have decreased, if anything, in the fifteen years since Duggan's study, given the rise of standardization and pressures of testing. Informally, we've seen almost none of it in the classrooms with which we are familiar.

In establishing the partnership that led to this work, we drew upon our previous co-teaching experiences along with several common professional endeavors, including working together to prepare teachers: Chris worked at the university in the teacher education program and Amy served as a mentor for teacher education students in the field. We also both experienced the 2009 Invitational Summer Institute of the local National Writing Project site, as well as the ARTeacher Fellowship program, a collaborative effort in the state to prepare high school teachers to be experts in arts integration. While wearing many hats, Chris was positioned as a teaching artist, a singer–songwriter who visited classes and helped students develop their own songs. Amy was positioned as their teacher, a role she'd served all year. As such, we asked students to complete a questionnaire in advance of the unit so that we could calibrate lessons and experiences to the students' strengths (see Appendix 2A). To an extent, we wanted to know what songwriting experiences students had in advance of the unit in hopes that we could provide appropriate support to move the individuals and class forward as much as possible.

Day One: Social Protest in America

Our unit began with a discussion of social activism and the art of protest songwriting, specifically by examining the events surrounding the Kent State University Massacre on May 4, 1970. We selected this event in part because the song written about it, "Ohio" (Young, 1970), is one of the most immediately recognizable anthems of protest, and in part because the social protest phenomenon that inspired the song was so well documented. "Ohio" changed the politics of the day and altered how people viewed then-President Nixon. It is considered a "vital historical document of a time when politics felt like a matter of life and death" (Lynskey, 2010, para. 18). For some of our students, politics felt the same way in early 2017. Additionally, we connected the events at Kent State University, Ohio, to those of our state of Arkansas, which had recently passed legislation to allow pretty much anyone (twenty-one years old with a carry permit and extra training) to carry guns on college campuses and almost everywhere else, a fact that makes us shudder to think about in relation to the Kent State shootings. Prior to delving into the events surrounding Kent State, we posed the following question to our students: "What does protest or social action look like in America today?" "What forms does it take?" Students generated this list of examples through their conversation:

rally	social media gathering
forming a committee	media
Twitter/Facebook	letter-writing campaign
legislative office visits	hunger strike
school or business walkout	false participation (e.g., signing up as Muslim on a Muslim registry)
march	riot
purposeful arrest	physical blocking
boycott	songs

We then turned to local examples of social protest, including two issues that had recently made national news from Arkansas: (1) a town hall meeting with Senator Tom Cotton in nearby Springdale, and (2) the guns on campus issue—specifically, a picture of a room full of activists holding targets in front of their bodies during a legislative forum. Students contributed their own experiences with walking out of school on President Trump's inauguration day to protest alongside other community members. We believe that all opinions and perspectives were valued in this classroom, though we admit that many of the students held more progressive or liberal perspectives. From that point forward, we asked students to begin to personalize a list of causes that they were interested in or saw others taking up around them. Following the creation of a list individually and then as a class, we invited each student to write about one cause for five minutes, in the hope that we would be able to access their interests in the forthcoming days of the unit.

We shared several pictures and stories from the *Slate* piece, "Personal Remembrances of the Kent State Shootings, 43 Years Later" (Rosenberg, 2013), as a way to begin the conversation about social issues that resulted in protest songs. We then asked students to consider other texts and accounts of the events as well, including a piece from *Ohio History Central*:

> Eventually seventy-seven guardsmen advanced on the protesters with armed rifles and bayonets. Protesters continued to throw things at the soldiers. Twenty-nine of the soldiers, purportedly fearing for their lives, eventually opened fire. The gunfire lasted just thirteen seconds, although some witnesses contended that it lasted more than one minute. The troops fired a total of sixty-seven shots. When the firing ended, nine students lay wounded, and four other students had been killed. Two of the students who died actually had not participated in the protests. (Ohio History Connection, n.d., para. 8)

Finally, we listened to Neil Young's (1970) "Ohio," studied the lyrics, and started a brief conversation about the structure of this protest song. Students identified the repetition, unfamiliar structure (the third and fourth stanzas repeat the first and second in reverse order), and first-person account as three elements of "Ohio" that grabbed their attention. For homework, we asked students to review the "Ten Best Protest Songs of All Time" (Greene, 2014), as ranked by *Rolling Stone*, to provide a bit of context of what historically popular protest songs were like, in an effort to continue to build knowledge about the genre. We also invited students to bring in a protest song that they enjoy or have listened to recently. From the *Rolling Stone* list, only songs by Rage Against the Machine and Bob Dylan were brought forward for further examination.

Structure Sings: What's in a Protest Song?

Day Two of the unit began with students grouping up to share and analyze the various contemporary protest songs that they brought to discuss. As small groups looked at the structures of their chosen protest songs, a few additional ideas began to surface. In some cases, like Marvin Gaye's "What's Going On" (Cleveland, Benson, & Gaye, 1971), the music and message seemed to be a mis-match, but, in most of the cases of the examples students brought along, the music and lyrics supported each other. "Hurricane" by Bob Dylan was a story of stories, but was delivered musically like a barrage of fists in a hurricane (Dylan & Levy, 1975). A singable chorus was another concept surfaced by the group. We asked the students next to take a look at the structure of the song stanzas in an effort to understand if there was repetition or other concepts available through an examination of the lyrical structure. Indeed, students identified that almost all of their examples used syllable patterns that were consistent within different verses (e.g., line one, verse one has the same number of syllables as line one, verse two; rhyming patterns were consistent throughout songs, etc.). Another concept that students generated about protest songs is that they often were more literal than other music, hitting issues directly instead of through figurative language or obfuscation. Finally, ideas and language were distilled to their purest form in the examples. Taken together, the list of techniques, approaches, and structures of protest songs generated by the students were then used as an anchor chart for protest songwriting. Students chose an eclectic mix of artists, ranging from Green Day and U2 to Marvin Gaye and Bob Dylan, giving the students a sense that there are some common threads of protest music that might be different from other subgenres of popular music.

Next, Chris performed a protest song that he'd written for the then newly confirmed US Secretary of Education, Betsy DeVos, called "Hey Betsy" (Goering, 2017). Following the performance, students examined the lyrics and structure of that song in an effort to find additional patterns or structures worth repeating—specifically, examining the structure of the song without lyrics using a sheet that had the syllables and verse structures (see Appendix 2B).

The song structure of "Hey Betsy" was used to demonstrate and reinforce a few concepts about protest songs that the students had highlighted previously, specifically the repetition of the syllable counts in the verse and rhyme patterns. We also provided the "Hey Betsy" handout as a song template or scaffold for students to use in their composing process. They could write new lyrics to the melody and/or structure of "Hey Betsy" or go their own way. Students were then given an opportunity to choose groups and begin writing their own protest songs, with a verse due at the end of the hour. Table 2.1 describes each of the groups and their chosen protest topics.

TABLE 2.1. Groups and Protest Topics

Group Members' Names	Protest Topic
Martin, Cole	Criminalization of marijuana
Kennedy, Danny	Anti-othering of minorities
Bia, Rachel, Natalie	Love over hate/feminism/environmental issues/gay rights
Katherine, Zach, Ricardo	LGBTQ
Dane, Erica	Child abuse
Tanner, Gemma, Price	Poverty, war, preserving planet Earth
Atiana, Eric	Government incompetence

In that first day, the group consisting of Tanner, Gemma, and Price was able to generate a truly singable and memorable chorus as well as a verse of their song that they ultimately submitted at the end of the unit. The chorus is melodic, simple, and musical, while the verses are delivered through spoken word.

Chorus:
This rock is so damn cold
We are growing, growing old.
I can feel it in my soul.

Verse Two:
We've got bombs in the backyard
People starving, kids working too hard.
We need a relief, a release and
A chance to be free.
Put your weapons up,
Hold a light in the dark.
Turn your hate to love.
Why is loving this hard?

Not all of the groups were to the point on Day Two that they could share lyrics, but most of them were at least able to read aloud a portion of what they had started to write. Tanner, Gemma, and Price didn't use the structure or melody of "Hey Betsy," but, rather, created their own. Other groups used parts of the structure we provided. We felt it was important to invite the students to begin crafting lyrics and working with the structure we provided early in the process so that they could get used to the process of collaborating to write, sharing with one another. By hearing other students' processes, the entire class had the opportunity to gain ideas and insights, and to see possibilities for approaches that they may not have otherwise considered.

Evolving Objectives: Local Songwriter Shannon Wurst

In the spirit of the Kennedy Center's definition of arts integration, we invited local songwriter Shannon Wurst to visit the class, perform, and talk through a new song, and to provide feedback to each of the groups as they continued to work to develop lyrics and ideas on Day Three. Shannon frequently works with younger students to write songs alongside curricula in math, science, social studies, and language arts, and performs nationally. Students responded well to her songs and feedback, and spent the majority of the day continuing to work on lyrics, melodies, and music. She embodied a sense of evolving objectives, providing in-the-moment instruction (Zoss & White, 2011) for the students in her performance, mini-lesson, and feedback. In those moments, we also saw what was possible for the students, providing us with an expanded sense of the potential of the protest songwriting unit. Individual songs continued to develop and we sensed that the peer pressure in the room to write a good song and outdo one another was palpable. When Tanner's group, for example, took the limelight at the end of Day Two, other groups took notice and realized that they had to step up their protest songwriting game.

Writing Is Never Finished, Only Due

The first due date for this songwriting challenge was on Day Four and, following an opportunity for the groups to continue to work to finalize their words and music, each group performed or read a portion of their song in front of the class. Groups were reluctant to share but all did, gaining written and verbal feedback from the class. Just as helpful to each of the groups as the feedback about their songs was the feedback being provided for all of the other songs, which provided an opportunity for students to continue to raise expectations of one another.

While the response forms we used are fairly commonplace in teaching English—forms that asked the students what they liked, what questions they had, and what suggestions they could offer—what makes formative assessment truly work in the context of creating art is the fact that progress happens out loud. In this case, each of the groups performed drafts of their songs and thus shared ideas with one another through the models and the brief discussions that followed each performance. This multimodal feedback, we informally observed, led to students holding higher expectations for one another and for themselves. Students received verbal feedback, including artists' critiques from Shannon and Chris and written feedback on the form from classmates, and performed models of completed drafts for one another as well.

Day Five: Performances, Reflection, Analysis

Walking into the classroom on performance day was like walking into a performance hall. Amy had the desks pushed to the windows and positioned the chairs facing a stage space. Danny and Kennedy were first up, and they shared their lyrics on a slideshow while Danny played the ukulele and both sang "I am Arkansas." The bar was set high, but the other groups weren't reluctant to perform their songs. The day progressed and each group presented their lyrics and a version of their song. Tanner played guitar for Bia's group, which didn't have their music in place. Cole rapped a song protesting the criminalization of marijuana, perhaps with less flair than originally planned as his partner, Martin, was absent that day. A pair of students who shared abuse in their pasts wrote, played guitar, and provided a spoken word song tackling that serious subject and how to interact with people who have been abused. President Trump and Vice President Mike Pence each had songs protesting against them and some of their ideas. Three of the songs centered on protests concerning the treatment of LGBTQ members of our society. We've highlighted several of the groups up to this point, and, in the sections that follow, continue to share their ideas and lyrics in order to provide the fullest possible picture of what they created.

Progress on Social Activism

To understand the extent to which protest songwriting and studying elements of songwriting can help students identify an effective avenue of social protest, we can look at the processes followed and the products created. Eric and Atiana brought their love of musical theatre to protest songwriting and created a skit that surrounded their song, adding layers of meaning to what they composed. President Donald Trump and his policies were their chosen object of protest, a song featuring a staccato delivery not too dissimilar to the effect tweeting has on discourse:

> T-t-tweety tweety tweeting our doom
> I'd say impeachment's waiting for you
> Firing missiles at everyone with glee
> T-tuh tweeting tweeting no tweet can redeem
>
> "Bombing Iraq or was it Syria?"
> "Yeah, yeah, yeah. It's the same thing."
> Too busy stuffing face with cake
> Or at a golf course for twenty-one days

The group picked up on a recent interview with President Trump in which he became confused about which country he'd recently bombed but kept talking about eating chocolate cake. They found this problematic and wanted to direct criticism toward the president. The next group—Bia, Natalie, and Rachel—touched on Trump and Vice President Mike Pence, and offered a message of hope while also directly addressing a common criticism of Pence:

> Pence we see you, what are you gonna do
> When you realize gays are human too
>
> Chorus:
> Come together come come together
> Maybe one day it'll get a bit better
>
> And someday soon when we link arms
> We'll lie down our firearms
> We could do more good than we do harm
> So take some time and think about
> How we have this giant cloud
> And how together we could take it down.

This song stands out because it was a struggle for the group to develop. One member wrote lyrics to a song, a second member wrote different lyrics, and ultimately they attempted to fit together disparate ideas and structures. Natalie reflected after the workshop, "We thought of highly debated topics and threw lyrics together until they worked." All three group members were surprised at how well their song turned out, each also lending praise to Tanner who provided a rhythm guitar and vocal addition to their presentation of it.

Cole and Martin took on a different topic, the decriminalization of marijuana. Their songwriting process looked different too as they found a beat online and then developed all of their lyrics as they listened to that beat. The first draft that they presented for peer response was, perhaps, more of a pro-marijuana rap versus the draft they presented, which took on additional socially relevant issues, specifically through this verse relayed from the perspective of a corrupt police officer:

> This is how it's going, this is how it's going down
> Hands up in the air and everybody on the ground
> You have the right to keep it shut so don't you make a sound
> You want to play it tough then we can go a couple rounds
> I can shoot a couple rounds and this badge gives permission
> To pick you up, to beat you down, and leave you with the fishes
> I can really make your life a hell if you don't listen
> A murder on a gram of weed it doesn't make a difference

The song concludes with the narrator jailed and getting the experience of spending time with his father, also imprisoned for marijuana charges.

> I just kept on thinking, this is what they did to dad
> Twenty-five to life man I ain't seen him since the past.
> Well, I guess I'll get my chance, finally get some one on one
> Ain't nothin' like a cell to make a bond of father–son

Martin and Cole harnessed elements of the social unrest in America in the context of their song. While other lyrics are hopeful, providing lyrical images that create a sense of being in it together, the systemic racism that members of our society experience ends here with a father and son in prison.

Scaffolds for Songwriting: Arts Integration, Family, Groupings, Structures, and Deadlines

As we put our heads—still spinning from the final projects—together to sort through what worked well and why during the protest songwriting unit, we returned to several ideas. In an effort to understand what the experience was like for the students, we again solicited feedback (see Appendix 2C) and held a reflective discussion following the final performances. Chris remarked to the class on the last performance day, for example, that they should consider getting their songs copyrighted through a performing rights agency like Broadcast Music Incorporated (see https://www.bmi.com/creators) because there were elements of them and entire songs that someone could potentially financially benefit from.

First and foremost, Amy deserves credit for the success of this group of young people because of the productive and safe learning environment she'd created prior to Chris's appearance. Students knew one another on deep, personal levels. They knew each other's strengths and weaknesses. They had experienced a plethora of previous guest teachers. The class was diverse in multiple ways, including racial and ethnic backgrounds and gender and sexual identities, with two members of class openly identifying as transgender. These students thrived in each other's company and felt positive peer pressure to perform. Amy recognized this community as different compared to her other classes over the years, offering that she believed that the fact that she picked this group as her pilot class for a three-year intensive arts integration fellowship in which she was participating was directly or indirectly responsible for the cohesive community atmosphere and their willingness to tackle "any crazy challenge" without hesitation. Having experienced a number of art forms in the context of their Creative Writing class—creative writing being a collection of art forms itself—her students were adept at working in different and unfamiliar creative formats. Eisner (2002) suggests that schools "function as cultures" in that they make possible a "shared way of life" and a "sense of belonging and community" (p. 3). These experiences throughout the year created a learning environment ready to embrace any new idea with open arms.

Perhaps the strongest scaffold we provided to students through this process was one another (Vygotsky, 1978). Students were encouraged to work in groups of two or three, which built on the family-like bonds they shared in the classroom and allowed for students with talents in different areas to accentuate the talents of their peers, to construct meaning collaboratively. It's easier to get up in front of a group of students when in a group versus as an individual.

The addition of a single structure and additional teaching artist—in the form of Chris's protest song example and in Shannon Wurst—served their respective purposes of providing a starting point from which to get going and individualizing scaffolds along the path of writing a song. Most of the groups chose to go in a different direction from the example provided in the songs presented, but all groups followed a pattern in their song composition. Shannon's presence in the classroom lasted only ninety minutes, but that didn't stop her influence being felt the rest of the time, as songs were shaped by her feedback, example, and encouragement.

Finally, the abbreviated nature of this workshop led to at least some of its success. Multiple students commented in the final discussion about the fact that having songs due in a short period of time forced their hand on decisions over which they might otherwise have labored. For example, by the end of Day Two, some groups had already completed portions of their songs, and, while it took others until Days Four or Five to get to that point, there were deadlines each day and ultimately a short amount of time to write a song. Chris expressed to the students on the last day that it has sometimes taken him seven years to finish a song, making their accomplishments in only a couple of weeks even more impressive.

"And How Together We Could Take It Down"

Taken individually, these projects represent good work by talented high school students who self-selected into a creative writing course. While songwriting isn't often utilized in any classwide form (research that Chris is currently conducting suggests that, if at all, songwriting takes the form of an individual project option for students in high school English courses), we are convinced that it should be, but it presently represents an opportunity lost from multiple perspectives. As we audaciously asserted earlier in the chapter, we believe every student in America in every English class should write a song each year, or at least create something in an art form that accesses their identity and views on the world. Following Eisner (2002), we feel that "work in the arts enables us to stop looking over our shoulder and to direct our attention inward to what we believe or feel" (p. 10). Taken together, we argue there's potential for this to mean much more than whatever else could be happening in school.

Songwriting matters, one of our students, Dane, observed, because:

> All through high school, I've wished for a class that shows me there is more out there....The style of the writing made it easier to get down on paper emotional topics that were hard to talk about in poems and stories.

We believe that songwriting in the classroom makes the class relevant, and it does so through the collaboration between students and the building of understanding around issues and art forms. Like Holden Caulfield in *The Catcher in the Rye* (Salinger, 1951), so many of our students struggle to express themselves, and they yearn to have someone truly listen to them. With this experience, students enjoyed the freedom to explore and express deeply personal and pressing concerns with original and sophisticated language. They knew all along they would be heard.

After spring break, many senior-level classes become just a process of jumping through hoops to Advanced Placement exams, finals, and getting high school firmly placed in the rearview mirror. The songwriting workshop intrinsically engaged students in learning and thinking. They were forced out of their comfort zone, succeeded, and boosted their skills and confidence as writers. They inspired each other to care more about issues, their peers, and about life. Multiple students have expressed a desire to minor or major in Creative Writing in their future college careers and to pursue the dream of being professional writers. This songwriting workshop nurtured those aspirations by pushing the students to take risks and grow as writers within a structure that allowed them to succeed in a supportive atmosphere.

Conclusion

Will one of these songs become viral and gather millions of followers? That's not a metric that concerns us, but we also happen to think it's possible. After all, as Sun Records producer Sam Phillips said, "I always knew that the rebellion of the young people, which is natural as breathing, would be a part of that breakthrough" (Associated Press, 2003, para. 3). These songs are socially relevant and speak to certain sections of our society—their universality and appeal beyond the immediate lives of these particular teenagers impressed us. To say that all members of a state belong and should be considered by representatives of that state is to say "I, too, am Arkansas." We believe that the social nature of creating these songs, along with the various scaffolds we provided and that the students provided each other, was the chief reason that this group of students found success in the genre—and in all likelihood became better English students at the same time.

Appendix 2A: Preworkshop Questionnaire

1. What's your favorite song?

2. What about that song makes it your favorite?

3. Do you have a favorite songwriter(s), someone who has written several songs you admire? Any particularly reasons why you like that person or group?

4. How much do you listen to music? How would you describe your favorite music?

5. Have you written a song before or attempted to (not required)? If so, how many songs have you written?

6. Do you play an instrument? Do you play in front of others? Are you in a band? Do you sing to yourself in the car?

7. Do you have any experience with audio recording or programs like GarageBand?

8. What is a goal or two you have for yourself as a writer as a whole? What could help you improve as a writer?

9. What does your typical writing process look like for bigger/more important school assignments?

10. Is there anything else that you want me or our guest to know?

Appendix 2B: "Hey Betsy" Song Handout

Title:
Capo 2

Intro
Am C Am F
Verse One

Am	C	
		10
Am	F	
		10
Am	C	
		12
F	Am	
		8
Verse Two		
		10
		10
		12
		8
Chorus		
C	G	
		12
F	Am	
		9
F	G	
		6
Am →	C	
		10
C	F	
		11
		10
		10
		12
		8
(Chorus)		
Outro		
Am	C	
		9
Am	F	
		9 (repeat/fade)

Appendix 2C: Post-workshop Questionnaire

1. As a piece of writing, how do you feel about the final song you wrote with your group? Why?

2. As a performance, how do you feel about performing your final song for the class? Why?

3. What was the song writing process you and your group used to write your song? Explain.

4. What did you learn about songwriting and yourself as a writer during this unit? Explain.

5. If you could change one aspect of the songwriting workshop, what would it be? Why?

6. What did you learn about songwriting from seeing and hearing other groups' songs? Explain.

7. Was this fun for you? Explain.

8. Did this unit help you improve as a writer? Explain.

9. What else would you like us to know about the songwriting unit?

References

Associated Press. (2003, July 31). Legendary producer Sam Phillips dies. *Billboard*. Retrieved from https://www.billboard.com/articles/news/69753/legendary-producer-sam-phillips-dies

Chemi, T. (2014). The artful teacher: A conceptual model for arts integration in schools. *Studies in Art Education*, 56(1), 370–83.

Cleveland, A., Benson, R., & Gaye, M. (1971). What's going on [Recorded by Marvin Gaye]. On *What's going on* [Record]. Detroit, MI: Tamla.

Duggan, T. J. (2003). *Uses of music in the high school English/language arts classroom in South Dakota: Teacher perceptions and practices* (Unpublished doctoral dissertation). University of South Dakota, Vermillion, SD.

Duggan, T. (2016). M.A.S.T.E.R.ing the art of music integration. In L. L. Johnson & C. Z. Goering (Eds.), *Recontextualized: A framework for teaching English with music* (pp. 51–64). Rotterdam, Netherlands: Sense Publishers.

Dylan, B., & Levy, J. (1975). Hurricane [Recorded by Bob Dylan]. On *Desire* [Record]. New York, NY: Columbia.

Eisner, E. W. (1992). The misunderstood role of the arts in human development. *Phi Delta Kappan, 73*(8), 591–95.

Eisner, E. W. (2002). *The arts and the creation of mind*. New Haven, CT: Yale University Press.

Fuller, K., & Montgomery, D. (2017). I am Arkansas [Lyrics]. Unpublished song.

Goering, C. Z. (2016). Language power: Saying more with less through songwriting. In L. L. Johnson & C. Z. Goering (Eds.), *Recontextualized: A framework for teaching English with music* (pp. 169–84). Rotterdam, Netherlands: Sense Publishers.

Goering, C. Z. (2017). Hey Betsy. New York, NY: Broadcast Music, Inc.

Goering, C. Z., & Strayhorn, N. (2016). Beyond enhancement: Teaching English through musical arts integration. *English Journal, 105*(5), 29–34.

Greene, A. (2014, December 3). Readers' poll: The 10 best protest songs of all time. The greatest activist anthems from artists like Bob Dylan, Neil Young and Rage Against the Machine. *Rolling Stone*. Retrieved from https://www.rollingstone.com/music/music-lists/readers-poll-the-10-best-protest-songs-of-all-time-141706/country-joe-and-the-fish-i-feel-like-im-fixin-to-die-rag-173632/

Greene, M. (1995). *Releasing the imagination: Essays on education, the arts, and social change*. San Francisco, CA: Jossey-Bass.

Lynskey, D. (2010, May 6). Neil Young's Ohio: The greatest protest record. *The Guardian*. Retrieved from https://www.theguardian.com/music/2010/may/06/ohio-neil-young-kent-state-shootings

Ohio History Connection. (n.d.). Kent State shootings. In *Ohio History Central* [Online encyclopedia]. Retrieved from http://www.ohiohistorycentral.org/w/Kent_State_Shootings

Rosenberg, D. (2013, May 4). Personal remembrances of the Kent State shootings, 43 years later. *Slate*. Retrieved from http://www.slate.com/blogs/behold/2013/05/04/may_4_1970_the_kent_state_university_shootings_told_through_pictures_photos.html

Salinger, J. D. (1951). *The catcher in the rye*. Boston, MA: Little, Brown.

Silverstein, L. B., & Layne, S. (2010). What is arts integration? In L. Silverstein, A. L. Duma, & S. Layne (Eds.), *Arts integration schools: What, why, and how*. Washington, DC: The John F. Kennedy Center for the Performing Arts/Changing Education through the Arts (CETA) Program.

Vygotsky, L. S. (1978). *Mind in society: The development of higher psychological processes* (M. Cole, V. John-Steiner, S. Scribner, & E. Souberman, Eds.). Cambridge, MA: Harvard University Press.

Young, N. (1970). Ohio [Recorded by Crosby, Stills, Nash & Young]. On *So Far* [Record]. Hollywood, CA: Atlantic.

Zoss, M., & White, A. M. (2011). Finding "my kind of teaching": How a drama project became a teacher's expressive teaching moment. *English in Education, 45*(2), 161–75.

3

Exploring the Art of Spoken Word Poetry with Students: A Sample Unit

WENDY R. WILLIAMS, *Arizona State University*

Standing in front of the group, Stacey clutches a journal. She hardly looks up from the page as she reads her poem. At one point, she rotates the journal ninety degrees to read something she has written in the margins. Stacey looks terrified as she performs. Her voice shakes, yet she pushes through and makes it to the end of the poem.

Nicole reads a poem from her phone, scrolling through the text with the same hand that holds the device. Although she looks back at the poem occasionally, she also takes time to stop and gaze into the eyes of those who are listening. Nicole gestures now and then with her free hand, and her voice is steady and strong. She uses a lot of emotion and delivers the words with varying speed and volume to emphasize her points.

Jorge has memorized his poem, which sets his whole body free to perform it. Like Nicole, Jorge varies his voice, controlling the sound of his poem. However, he also uses a range of gestures that complement his words and bring them to life. The three minutes or so of this poem are like a dance or a dramatic monologue. This poet becomes the poem.

Stacey, Nicole, and Jorge, who ranged in age from fifteen to nineteen when I studied them (Williams, 2018), are youth spoken word poets (all names are pseudonyms). As we can see in the vignettes above, they are at different levels as performers, from the novice struggling to get through a reading to the advanced poet whose piece is memorized and then enacted for an audience using the poet's whole body. A growing area of research has shown that spoken word poetry can benefit writers of all levels and help young people identify with literacy (Fisher, 2007; Jocson, 2008; Sutton, 2008; Weinstein, 2010). Films like *Louder Than a Bomb* (Jacobs & Siskel, 2010) have documented the power of this poetry for young people. Increasingly, teachers around the country are finding ways to use spoken word poetry in their classrooms (Beach, Appleman, Fecho, & Simon, 2016; Coval, n.d.; Reyes, 2006; Weiss & Herndon, 2001).

A spoken word poem is performed with attention to volume, rhythm, facial expression, and gesturing. It is "a multilayered art form" (Weiss & Herndon, 2001, p. xix) that turns a written composition into a vocal and physical performance. Spoken word poetry is not unlike other multimodal compositions used in English classrooms, such as the illuminated text project, in which a poem is animated, set to music, and illustrated using technology (Williams, 2014). However, spoken word pieces put youth voices front and center, which also helps young people cultivate public speaking skills and confidence. As this poetry is performed, audience members respond by snapping and making utterances in reaction to particularly powerful or well-written lines. These responses serve as immediate feedback, prompting poets to commit even more energy to the performance. Audience members may benefit from these performances as well, sometimes learning that they are not alone in their experiences.

Studies have shown that poets from a range of cultural, linguistic, and socioeconomic backgrounds have used spoken word to communicate powerful messages about themselves, their communities, and society (Fisher, 2007; Jocson, 2008; Sutton, 2008). Youth poets may view their work as art, as therapy, or as a form of activism (Williams, 2015). In fact, many youth poets experience personal growth through this art form (Weinstein, 2010). In one yearlong study of an out-of-school poetry organization, youth poets reported developing empathy and openness to emotional vulnerability, experiencing healing, and improving their confidence and leadership skills through their use of spoken word poetry in a supportive space. They also reported becoming more comfortable participating in school and becoming writers who use poetic devices, explore a range of topics, and care more about revision (Williams, 2018). It is no wonder that this medium may appeal to those who have not previously enjoyed writing in school (Mahiri & Sablo, 1996), as spoken word poetry honors all voices. Students from groups that have been historically marginalized can use spoken word to speak out, those from groups that have been historically privileged are confronted with the realities of structural inequities, and all students can start to envision a more just society together through these artistic works.

In this chapter, I present a justification for using spoken word poetry with adolescents. Then I provide some suggestions for bringing this art form into the English classroom with a unit for secondary students, which I currently share with the preservice teachers at my university.

Why Should Teachers Use Spoken Word with Students?

Spoken word poetry has much to offer the secondary English class. For teachers committed to using arts-based pedagogies, spoken word is "multimodal, inquiry-based, and interpretive" (Emert, Macro, & Schmidt, 2016, p. 11). These works encourage "creative expression, writing, and performance" (Weiss & Herndon, 2001, p. xxii) as poets share meaningful stories in their own words and write for authentic purposes and audiences. We know that students need opportunities to develop their creativity (National Council of Teachers of English, 2007) and to work with a range of creative forms, including "fiction, poetry, drama, visual art, music, and dance" (Macro & Zoss, this volume, p. xvi). Through poetry, students can write about their lives, critique their worlds, and "unveil hidden truths" (Kinloch, 2005, p. 98).

This art form can also support culturally relevant (Ladson-Billings, 1995), responsive (Gay, 2010), and sustaining (Paris, 2012) pedagogies in secondary English classrooms. Through spoken word poetry, we can honor students' cultures, languages, and experiences. Young people can also build academic skills and learn about one another as they write, perform, and listen to these works. Poets may draw on multiple languages and dialects as they compose (Jocson, 2006; Kinloch, 2005), making this medium a great fit for students who are English language learners (Berg, n.d.). English education must keep pace with the needs of our increasingly diverse student population and an increasingly connected world (National Council of Teachers of English, 2007).

Rather than viewing spoken word as one more demand on an already-packed curriculum, busy teachers can use spoken word poetry to support several English language arts goals. Spoken word aligns to many of the Common Core State Standards for English Language Arts (Common Core State Standards Initiative, 2016). For example, writing spoken word poetry encourages students to consider audience, to conduct research, to engage in revision, and, in the case of poetry videos, to use technology. Sharing personal stories through this poetry can involve narrative writing and writing for multiple purposes (W.3–8, 10). Spoken word can also help students advance their speaking and listening skills. As students listen to poems, they may "evaluate information presented . . . orally" and "a speaker's point of view, reasoning, and use of evidence and rhetoric"; moreover, performing these poems may require poets to "adapt speech to a variety of contexts and communicative tasks" (SL.2–3, 6). Writing and analyzing poems can lead to discussions about figurative language (L.5). Finally, reading these texts involves making sense of inferences, themes, word choice, text structure, and point of view. Students may also compare texts and read complex literature as part of a spoken word unit (R.1–2, 4–6, 9–10).

The *Framework for Success in Postsecondary Writing* recommends that students develop the following habits of mind to assist them with the types of writing required in college and careers: curiosity, openness, engagement, creativity, persistence, responsibility, flexibility, and metacognition (Council of Writing Program Administrators, National Council of Teachers of English, & National Writing Project, 2011, p. 1). Composing and performing poems can foster creativity and engagement, and working through multiple drafts can foster persistence, responsibility, and flexibility. In addition, as students listen to poems, they may become more curious and open to others' experiences. Teachers can even help poets develop metacognitive skills by asking them to reflect on their decision making in these works.

In summary, spoken word poetry seems to naturally fit within secondary English education. This art form can be used to cultivate habits of mind that postsecondary writers need in college and careers. It can support multiple writing, listening, speaking, language, and reading standards. Spoken word can also be used to honor students' cultures, languages, and experiences and to provide a window into others' experiences. Finally, teachers can use this art form to encourage creativity throughout the writing process.

Suggestions for Teaching: A Sample Unit

Fortunately, there are many ways to integrate spoken word poetry into the secondary English classroom. Teachers can build full-length units that engage students in writing and performance while also examining cultural and historical aspects of spoken word poetry. Some teachers might simply show a video of a spoken word poem and discuss it as part of a thematic unit on bullying, equality, or social media. Still others might ask students to write a spoken word poem after they have composed traditional research papers or persuasive pieces in order to communicate findings to a larger audience. Teachers who enjoy collaborating could design cross-disciplinary units with history, speech, theatre, or media teachers. Other teachers might organize a schoolwide slam. In the sections below, I offer some suggestions as I reflect on the spoken word unit I have used with my students.

Writing and Performing alongside Student Poets

When I use spoken word poetry with preservice teachers, I model what I would do with secondary students. Typically, I begin by performing a poem. I do not preface the piece or explain that we are starting a new unit. Instead, I simply count down from ten to one, take a second, and then launch into my poem. This grabs their attention.

The piece I share is about my mother dying of cancer, and it is my most painful memory. I am not a very good poet or performer. The piece is not memorized, which limits my physical performance of it. However, the poem is honest and based on a real experience. Students seem to appreciate this display of emotional vulnerability from a teacher, and it paves the way for us to start sharing the stories that really matter to us. Barriers start to come down.

By beginning this unit with a poem of my own, I am also demonstrating to students that I write. Some teachers may feel reluctant to share their writing with students, believing it must be absolutely polished and perfect. However, I would argue that these are exactly the kinds of pieces our students need to see, our works in progress. We need to model the writing process with all of its ups and downs as we write alongside our students. Kinloch (2005) has had success going a step further and asking students for their feedback on these works as well.

Defining Spoken Word Poetry Together

After I perform my poem for students, we attempt to arrive at a definition of spoken word poetry together. I will usually show at least three videos of poets performing and ask students to jot down distinguishing characteristics of this art form while they watch. For the secondary classroom, teachers might select some of the "25+ Slam Poems" videos from the Teacher Off Duty blog (Wolz, 2017). Teachers might also be interested in viewing Taylor Mali's (2006) "What Teachers Make," Sarah Kay's (2011) TED Talk about spoken word poetry, and multiple Brave New Voices videos (Youth Speaks, n.d.) before designing a spoken word poetry unit. Many poems that are available online contain mature content and language, so teachers are advised to preview poems before showing them in class.

After students have viewed examples of this art form and made some notes about distinguishing features, we have a class discussion in which we define *spoken word*. Typically, these discussions will address topics, voice, body movements, facial expressions, imagery, word choice, and timing. Throughout our discussion, I prompt students to refer back to specific examples from the mentor texts to support their points.

Exploring History and Culture

Teaching spoken word poetry creates opportunities for students to learn about history and culture. Teachers could have their students explore spoken word history by giving them the names of poets, groups, places, and movements to research, and then everyone could come back together to share information, co-construct visuals (e.g., timelines, maps), and reflect on class findings. Students may be interested to learn that the Nuyorican Café in New York has hosted poets since the 1970s (Jocson, 2008) or about Marc Smith's role in creating the poetry slam as a contest (Eleveld, 2003, 2007). Perhaps English and history teachers could work together to oversee these activities.

It is important to examine spoken word poetry's connections to culture. Students could consider how Langston Hughes's poems—with their jazz and blues sounds—are similar to spoken word poems. After all, there is a strong musical component to this poetry (Fisher, 2007). They could also examine how "the recitation style of the poetry slam in the United States is heavily influenced by the oral poetry traditions of the Harlem Renaissance, the Beat Poets, the Black Arts Movement and especially hip hop" (Rivera, 2013, p. 116). Indeed, exploring spoken word's relationship to hip-hop (Beach et al., 2016; Weinstein, 2009) and rap (Bradley, 2009; Chang, 2005; Smith, 2010) will likely interest many adolescents in the secondary classroom. Students could research groups like the Last Poets and the Watts Prophets (Weinstein, 2009; Weiss & Herndon, 2001). They could also think about spoken word poetry's relationship to the Civil Rights Movement, perhaps using documentaries such as those from the series *Eyes on the Prize: America's Civil Rights Years 1954–1965* or the Martin Luther King Film Project's film *King: A Filmed Record . . . From Montgomery to Memphis*, as Weiss and Herndon (2001) recommend. It would make sense to address today's Black Lives Matter movement as well.

Poetry slams borrow from several African American and religious practices. For instance, they involve *testifying* and *witnessing*, a set of practices in which a speaker shares an epiphany or a personal story while audience members serve as witnesses (Hill, 2009; Smitherman, 1977; Weinstein, 2009). *Call* and *response* is another set of practices that are often at work during a poetry slam. This involves a call by a speaker and a response by the audience. When I spent time with a youth spoken word poetry group, I found that the host of the slam would call, "What time is it?" and the audience would respond, "Time to put the bun in the oven and turn it up!" (Williams, 2018). For an example of call and response, see the video link for *Nappy Hair* in the resources section of this book. In general, there is a great deal of interaction between poets and the audience at a poetry slam. Audience members snap to lines that move them and make comments and other utterances in response to poets' words. Listeners might remark "Mm-hmm" or "Oh." When poets forget lines or become overwhelmed with emotion, audience members might shout out words of encouragement like "Come on" or

"You got this." Acknowledging the cultural and historical roots of spoken word can give students a deeper appreciation of this art form.

Writing: Getting Started

To help students get started with the writing process, I like to set up brainstorming stations around the room. At each station, I place a large, twelve-inch-by-twelve-inch piece of cardstock (e.g., different colored scrapbook pages) with a topic written in the center and room for students to brainstorm around that word or phrase. Some of our topics have included the following: your home or neighborhood, love, the challenges of being a student, a person of importance, a painful experience, something funny, an injustice, something beautiful, a current event or issue, something unexpected, the state where you live, a question you have, or other topic ideas (students come up with their own). Although I give students some starting points, I also honor the right for young writers to choose their own topics. As Kinloch (2005) reminds us, "Writing about what is real means that students are free to exchange, explore, create, write, and revise ideas" (p. 100). Students need opportunities to exercise their creativity and to make decisions throughout the writing process.

Prewriting could also take the form of lists. Students list everything they can think of for a given topic, and they have about thirty to sixty seconds before the next topic is introduced. Recently, teaching artists Kevin Coval and others from Young Chicago Authors (the organization that hosts the *Louder Than a Bomb* contest) conducted a spoken word workshop in my state. They asked participants to make lists for the following topics: favorite fruits, favorite people, favorite cultural or religious traditions that are not mainstream, things you like or love that are not 100 percent good for you, and things you love to wear. The teaching artists emphasized that this method of prewriting helps adolescents find a topic to write about, and it is such a low-stakes activity that anyone can do it.

Quick writes (Kittle, 2008) are another form of prewriting that can help students explore a topic before they sit down to write a spoken word poem. Students might draw a heart, fill it with people and items they love, and then write about one of them. Another possibility is for students to draw a map of their neighborhood, sketch in significant memories, and then choose one to write about. Scar stories work well also: Draw an outline of a human figure, mark any places with scars, and then choose one and tell that story. We use these quick writes at our local National Writing Project site, and readers may already be familiar with these common journal prompts (if not, see Nelson, 2004). Of course, if students have already completed multiple short quick writes in a writer's notebook, they can turn there for ideas (Kittle, 2008).

Current events can also serve as inspiration for poems. Students could spend some time scanning newspapers and magazines for stories and quotes that stand out. Perhaps the original clippings or printouts could be posted around the room for students to visit in "gallery walk" style after they have heard the poems performed. This would give students a chance to read about the real stories behind the poems they heard.

Considering Content

As students are considering possible topics for their poems, this is a good time to clarify expectations for the assignment in terms of content. In my classes, we talk about selecting content and language with an audience in mind, and we discuss how a piece might change depending on whether it will be performed for this particular audience versus that one. Secondary teachers should be upfront about any language or topics that are off limits and explain the reasons for these limitations. I also recommend that teachers speak with administrators and social workers to get clarification about what they are required to report (e.g., abuse) and to learn about the full range of resources available to students who are facing serious challenges. As with other forms of personal writing, spoken word encourages honest reflection, which may lead to revelations a teacher cannot ethically or legally ignore.

Imagining the Performance

When writing a spoken word poem, it is hard *not* to think about audience. In fact, awareness of audience may encourage poets to engage in more careful revision throughout the writing process (Jocson, 2006; Smith, 2010). I remind students to start thinking about performance while they are finishing their drafts at home. Reading the piece aloud will likely prompt early revision as poets hear the places where a word or phrase sounds awkward. Practicing in front of a mirror will also reveal how their poems look. These days, poets who have smartphones can even video-record themselves and critique their performances before going public.

Sharing Drafts

When rough drafts are due, I put students in pairs so they can give each other feedback. One person performs a poem while the other completes a Peer Review Form (see Appendix 3A). This sheet asks the listener to comment on both the poem and the performance. Students then reverse roles and repeat the process.

It is not uncommon for students to have powerful emotional responses when they are performing a poem for a partner. After all, spoken word involves "sacrifice" and "truth-telling" (Rivera, 2013, p. 119). I make it a point to visit these poets and praise them for taking a risk and sharing something meaningful.

Performing in Small Groups

On the day that final drafts are due, I ask the poets to perform in small groups (i.e., three to four people per group). As each person performs, the others listen and write supportive comment cards. I typically ask that listeners comment on three things: (1) the ideas in the poem, (2) the sense of voice in the poem, (3) the performance. Group members then give their completed comment cards to the performers, who will read them before turning in these comment cards along with all of their other materials documenting the writing process.

After group members have shared with each other, I offer a sign-up sheet for those who would like to participate in our class's open mic event. Typically, poets are more eager to sign up for this after they have performed for a small group and realized that performing was not as scary as they thought it would be. It seems that the small group sharing serves as a useful form of scaffolding, helping students prepare for the challenge of performing for the whole class.

Experiencing a Poetry Slam or Open Mic

I make performing for the whole class optional. I am a shy person myself, so I understand that students may not feel comfortable embracing vulnerability in front of a room of peers. Smith (2010) writes that "public arenas, such as poetry slams, can be both dangerous and exhilarating for adolescents, whose identity development continues to evolve" (p. 207). I sometimes give students an incentive for participating, such as entering their names in a drawing for books I have brought back from a National Council of Teachers of English conference.

I like to have a student emcee our event. This person welcomes each poet to the front of the room and afterward says something about each poem. For a full-blown poetry slam, a deejay should play music between poems, and three to five students who are not competing should serve as judges, typically scoring poems in the 7.5 to 10 point range. Rivera (2013) writes that the mood of a slam sometimes becomes "carnivalesque" as audience members react to judges' scores (p. 116). In my classes, I tend to forego the judges and deejay, an adaptation that technically makes our event an *open mic* rather than a *slam*. Teachers who have the luxury of not having to worry about volume—those with access to an auditorium or a room away from other classes—should consider including judges and a deejay, though, because they bring great energy to the event.

Before the event, I share the following ground rules, which I learned from a youth poetry group I studied in Arizona: (a) be brave, (b) be respectful, (c) your voice matters (Williams, 2015). We also talk about slam norms such as clapping people to and from the "stage" and snapping and making utterances in response to powerful lines. At this point, I turn things over to the host, who runs the event while I sit with my students, snapping and commenting alongside them in response to the poets. It is an amazing feeling to let them take over the event. Students testify, and together we witness and celebrate the power of their voices.

Reflecting on the Unit

After our class poetry slam, I ask students to reflect on the unit (see Appendix 3B). They comment on the ideas and voice in their poems, changes made between the rough and final drafts, and the performance experience. Secondary students could indicate whether they are interested in follow-up activities such as future spoken word workshops and slams or even a spoken word club. Students attach several papers to the reflection sheet to document the writing process, including the rough draft, peer review form, comment cards, and final draft. At this point, we typically have a short discussion reflecting on the unit, and, with preservice teachers, this includes exploring their own ideas about teaching spoken word poetry.

Unit Assessment

At poetry slams, it is common to hear the following expression: "The point is not the points; the point is the poetry." In other words, assigning scores to poems may make for a fun game, but this game should not be confused with what actually matters in a poetry slam: the poetry. Is the poet speaking a truth? Has the poem helped the author heal? Is an audience member moved to tears? These things are far more meaningful than a poem's scores. Therefore, when I use spoken word in my own classes, I reward students for going through the process of writing a poem, engaging in peer review, revising the piece, sharing it with a small group, and reflecting on the experience. My own opinion is that determining whether a poem—and the poet's performance of it—would be an A or a B or a C misses the point of this work, and it perpetuates unfair distributions of power in the classroom, rather than using spoken word to break down barriers and value all voices.

When poets perform their pieces for an audience, they receive line-by-line feedback. Audience members respond to poets throughout their poems to let them know how they are doing. A funny line will get laughs. A sad line will get reassuring utterances. Audience members smile, frown, snap, clap, and gesture in response to poems. These authentic reactions are a form of informal assessment tailored to each poet, each poem, and each performance. For poets who wish to be formally scored and ranked, poetry slams have this feature built in. Just to be clear, though, I would never take poetry slam scores and use them for a grade in a course.

Extension Activity/Alternative: Creating Poetry Videos

As an extension activity, or even in the place of a slam, students could create poetry videos. Prince Ea's (2014) "Can We Auto-Correct Humanity?" is a beautifully constructed video that combines spoken word poetry, cutaways, animated text, and music. This video takes poetry to another level, revealing yet another way students can bring poetry to life in the classroom. Students' finished videos could be shared in class or with a wider audience online. Perhaps school and district poetry contests could even have a category for poetry videos. While a live performance can be rewarding, making a video offers benefits as well, including opportunities to work with technology. Jocson (2011) points out that poets can take a poem "from the page to the stage and onto the screen" (p. 158). This is certainly true, whether poets are simply recording and posting unedited performances or carefully constructing videos like Prince Ea's.

Spoken Word on Campus: Poetry Clubs

After experimenting with spoken word, secondary students may express interest in participating in a school poetry club. These clubs could meet informally (Mahiri & Sablo, 1996) or have a set structure, meeting weekly and holding regular events. When I studied a spoken word club at a high school, I saw that having two cosponsors significantly helped teachers manage the workload. Also, delineating clear roles for sponsors, officers, and members is essential. School clubs might even look for ways to connect to professional poets in the area. The best place to start when organizing a school club is to ask students what kind of club they would like to be a part of and go from there.

Conclusion

Exploring spoken word poetry with students will take different forms in different classrooms. Some teachers may be comfortable integrating a day of viewing or writing poems, some may use a unit like the one presented in this chapter, and others may pull from Brave New Voices or the *Louder Than a Bomb* curricula (Coval, n.d.; Weiss & Herndon, 2001). Spoken word poetry's flexibility is also one of its strengths. When considering its potential in the classroom, I believe we are limited only by our own creativity. Teachers can bring this art form into schools in a myriad of ways to inspire, challenge, and honor students.

Appendix 3A: Peer Review Form

Poet:_____ **Reviewer:** _____

Directions:
The poet will perform his/her poem while the peer reviewer listens and watches. The reviewer will write comments on this page. If time allows, the reviewer should also read the written draft of the poem and make additional suggestions directly on that draft.

1. What did you *hear*? Did the words flow well? How was the timing? Was the emphasis well placed in this poem?

2. What did you *see*? Did the gestures make sense? What suggestions do you have?

3. Think about the poem's *organization*. Would it benefit from rearranging sections? Which ones?

4. Was an *idea repeated* unnecessarily? If so, could the weaker of the repeated ideas be cut?

5. Was there an *extended metaphor* in this poem? If not, do you have suggestions for one? Was other figurative language at work?

6. Can you see possibilities for *juxtaposing ideas* (i.e., placing two different ideas side by side)? Explain.

7. Were the *details concrete and vivid*? Which details were too general or vague?

8. What *questions* do you have for the poet? Was anything unclear?

Appendix 3B: Spoken Word Performance Reflection

Name: _____

Poem Title: _____

Directions:

Reflect on your spoken word poem and the experience of performing it. Please include specific examples in your responses.

1. Comment on the *ideas* in your poem.

2. Comment on the *voice* in your poem.

3. Comment on the *changes you made* between the rough and final drafts.

4. Comment on the *experience of performing your poem*.

5. Comment on your interest in *additional spoken word opportunities on campus* (e.g., workshops and slams in our class, a spoken word club, a school-wide slam).

Please attach the following:

1. Rough draft

2. Peer Review Form

3. Comment Cards

4. Final draft

References

Beach, R., Appleman, D., Fecho, B., & Simon, R. (2016). *Teaching literature to adolescents* (3rd ed.). New York, NY: Routledge.

Berg, D. (n.d.) *Crossing boundaries through bilingual, spoken-word poetry*. Retrieved from http://www.readwritethink.org/classroom-resources/lesson-plans/crossing-boundaries-through-bilingual-30525.html?tab=5#tabs

Bradley, A. (2009). *Book of rhymes: The poetics of hip hop*. New York, NY: Basic Civitas.

Chang, J. (2005). *Can't stop won't stop: A history of the hip-hop generation*. New York, NY: Picador.

Common Core State Standards Initiative. (2016). *English language arts standards*. Retrieved from http://www.corestandards.org/ELA-Literacy

Council of Writing Program Administrators, National Council of Teachers of English, & National Writing Project. (2011). *Framework for success in postsecondary writing*. Retrieved from http://wpacouncil.org/files/framework-for-success-postsecondary-writing.pdf

Coval, K. (n.d.). *Louder than a Bomb film curriculum*. Retrieved from https://www.slideshare.net/AnnaFesta/ltabfilmcurriculum-49918294

Ea, P. (2014, September 29). *Can we auto-correct humanity?* [Video file]. Retrieved from https://www.youtube.com/watch?v=dRl8EIhrQjQ

Eleveld, M. (Ed.). (2003). *The spoken word revolution: Slam, hip hop, and the poetry of a new generation*. Naperville, IL: Sourcebooks MediaFusion.

Eleveld, M. (Ed.). (2007). *The spoken word revolution redux*. Naperville, IL: Sourcebooks MediaFusion.

Emert, T., Macro, K., & Schmidt, P. S. (2016). Celebrating the arts in English classrooms. *English Journal, 105*(5), 11–12.

Fisher, M. T. (2007). *Writing in rhythm: Spoken word poetry in urban classrooms*. New York, NY: Teachers College Press.

Gay, G. (2010). *Culturally responsive teaching: Theory, research, and practice* (2nd ed.). New York, NY: Teachers College Press.

Hill, M. L. (2009). *Beats, rhymes, and classroom life: Hip-hop pedagogy and the politics of identity*. New York, NY: Teachers College Press.

Jacobs, G., & Siskel, J. (Directors) (2010). *Louder than a bomb* [Motion picture]. United States: Siskel/Jacobs Productions.

Jocson, K. M. (2006). "The best of both worlds": Youth poetry as social critique and form of empowerment. In S. Ginwright, P. Noguera, & J. Cammarota (Eds.), *Beyond resistance! Youth activism and community change: New democratic possibilities for practice and policy for America's youth* (pp. 129–47). New York, NY: Routledge.

Jocson, K. M. (2008). *Youth poets: Empowering literacies in and out of schools*. New York, NY: Peter Lang.

Jocson, K. M. (2011). Poetry in a new race era. *Daedalus: Journal of the Academy of Arts & Sciences, 140*(1), 154–62.

Kay, S. (2011, March). *Sarah Kay: If I should have a daughter* [Video file]. Retrieved from https://www.ted.com/talks/sarah_kay_if_i_should_have_a_daughter

Kinloch, V. F. (2005). Poetry, literacy, and creativity: Fostering effective learning strategies in an urban classroom. *English Education, 37*(2), 96–114.

Kittle, P. (2008). *Write beside them: Risk, voice, and clarity in high school writing*. Portsmouth, NH: Heinemann.

Ladson-Billings, G. (1995). Toward a theory of culturally relevant pedagogy. *American Educational Research Journal, 32*(3), 465–91.

Mahiri, J., & Sablo, S. (1996). Writing for their lives: The non-school literacy of California's urban African American youth. *The Journal of Negro Education, 65*(2), 164–80.

Mali, T. (2006, October 24). *Taylor Mali on "What teachers make"* [Video file]. Retrieved from http://www.youtube.com/watch?v=RxsOVK4syxU

National Council of Teachers of English. (2007). Globalization and English education. Retrieved from http://www.ncte.org/cee/2007summit/globalization

Nelson, G. L. (2004). *Writing and being: Embracing your life through creative journaling*. San Francisco, CA: Inner Ocean.

Paris, D. (2012). Culturally sustaining pedagogy: A needed change in stance, terminology, and practice. *Educational Researcher, 41*(3), 93–97.

Reyes, G. T. (2006). Finding the poetic high: Building a spoken word poetry community and culture of creative, caring, and critical intellectuals. *Multicultural Education, 14*(2), 10–15.

Rivera, T. (2013). You have to be what you're talking about: Youth poets, amateur counter-conduct, and parrhesiastic value in the amateur youth poetry slam. *Performance Research, 18*(2), 114–23.

Smith, A. M. (2010). Poetry performances and academic identity negotiations in the literacy experiences of seventh grade language arts students. *Reading Improvement, 47*(4), 202–18.

Smitherman, G. (1977). *Talkin and testifyin: The language of Black America*. Detroit, MI: Wayne State University Press.

Sutton, S. S. (2008). Spoken word: Performance poetry in the black community. In J. Mahiri (Ed.), *What they don't learn in school: Literacy in the lives of urban youth* (pp. 213–42). New York, NY: Peter Lang.

Weinstein, S. (2009). *Feel these words: Writing in the lives of urban youth*. Albany: SUNY Press.

Weinstein, S. (2010). "A unified poet alliance": The personal and social outcomes of youth spoken word poetry programming. *International Journal of Education and the Arts, 11*(2), 1–24.

Weiss, J., & Herndon, S. (2001). *Brave new voices: The Youth Speaks guide to teaching spoken word poetry*. Portsmouth, NH: Heinemann.

Williams, W. R. (2014). New technologies, new possibilities for the arts and multimodality in English language arts. *Contemporary Issues in Technology and Teacher Education, 14*(4), 327–55. Retrieved from https://www.citejournal.org/volume-14/issue-4-14/english-language-arts/article1-html-3/

Williams, W. R. (2015). Every voice matters: Spoken word poetry in and outside of school. *English Journal, 104*(4), 77–82.

Williams, W. R. (2018). *Listen to the poet: Writing, performance, and community in youth spoken word poetry*. Amherst: University of Massachusetts Press.

Wolz, J. (2017, March 22). 25+ slam poems appropriate for middle school and high school [Blog post]. Retrieved from http://teacheroffduty.com/20-slam-poems-you-can-use-in-your-classroom-tomorrow/

Youth Speaks. (n.d.). Brave new voices international youth poetry slam festival [YouTube Channel]. Retrieved from https://www.youtube.com/playlist?list=PLGWDDcCZS9wJzN6rvvy29RyvfUCfeUkbv

Dadaism, Found Poetry, and Close Reading in English Language Arts

4

TOBY EMERT, *Agnes Scott College*

A line of poetry is a chance to get rid of all the filth that clings to this accursed language.

—HUGO BALL, *Dada Manifesto* (Sterling, 2016)

The Dadaists, members of an early twentieth-century arts movement, promoted the concept of *anti-art* and questioned the modes, methods, purposes, and effects of art (Ratliff, 2016, para. 2). The aggressive technological revolution of the First World War, epitomized by its military machinery, forever altered the scope of human destruction and mayhem. The Dadaists wished to represent the social and spiritual disfigurement they were witnessing as a result of the war and sought to create artwork that *intended* to deconstruct, decompose, and manipulate. They declared that art can be whatever the artist produces or assembles. "Dada doubts everything," claims Tristan Tzara (1989, p. 92), one of the movement's central figures. Their aesthetic greatly influenced subsequent avant-garde movements, such as surrealism, as well as our contemporary understanding of the definition of artistic effort. Dada's style, which celebrates chance, eschews individual authorship, and urges imaginative re-creation, provides us with practices that can be mined for application in the English language arts classroom.

Translating Dada's Aesthetic for the English Language Arts Classroom

In this chapter, I share a text-based response strategy that derives from the Dadaists' inclination to repurpose and reinterpret: the found poem. Tzara (1989, p. 92) provided the following instructions for writing a found poem:

To Make a Dadaist Poem

Take a newspaper.

Take some scissors.

Choose from this paper an article of the length you want to make your poem.

Cut out the article.

Next, carefully cut out each of the words that makes up this article and put them all in a bag.

Shake gently.

Next, take out each cutting—one after the other.

Copy conscientiously in the order in which they left the bag.

The poem will resemble you.

And there you are—an infinitely original author of charming sensibility, even though unappreciated by the vulgar herd.

"The literary equivalent of a collage, found poetry is often made from newspapers, articles, street signs, graffiti, speeches, letters, and even other poems" (Academy of American Poets, 2004, para. 1). It encourages remixing, allowing the poet to appropriate language and construct new meaning from existing text. This style of writing gained prominence in the twentieth century, several decades after the emergence of Dadaism, and it has been employed by a range of authors, including such luminaries as T. S. Eliot and William Carlos Williams. As a classroom activity, the process of generating a found poem privileges individual expression and invites iterative transactions with class texts; students selectively collect words and phrases from their reading and rearrange them to compose poems that illustrate key themes and motifs. The exercise emphasizes the conditional and multifaceted nature of language and works to accomplish one of the objectives of the anti-art movement: questioning "the sanctity of the written text—the very possibility of its *possessing* any final signification" (Sayre, 1989, p. 15). The strategy asks students to consider language's inconstancies and to be playful in their interpretive work. It also encourages them to think both critically and creatively, to purposefully decode and infer.

I have used the found poem strategy to assist students across grade levels—from middle school to graduate school—as they develop inventive responses to the texts they read. For many students, examining readings in an unfamiliar way can, at first, seem daunting—perhaps even confusing—but the strategy promotes re-reading and critical engagement with language and ideas, skills that are fundamental to reading mastery. Approaching analysis from this perspective requires students *and* teachers to expand their definitions of text-based response and to imagine an instructional ethos that privileges unconventional expressions of comprehension.

Theory behind the Found Poem-as-Response Strategy

In his book about the contingent nature of literacy, *Changing Our Minds: Negotiating English and Literacy*, former executive director of NCTE Miles Myers (1996) claims that the truly literate of the twenty-first century see texts as constructed and negotiable, "not as an immutable set of information and procedures" (p. 11). To illustrate his point, he employs an example from industry. He describes a General Motors plant that, because of an evolving work environment, required employees to develop a more flexible skill set and to be willing to problem-solve in teams, rather than play the discrete role of "specialist." As a result, the plant revised its expectations for managers, asking them to "see themselves as part of the negotiation of solutions, not as sole owners of information and the sole producers of answers, solutions, and directions" (p. 10). Myers argues that literacy, similarly, requires adaptability and the capacity to "translate data into different representations" (p. 12). This ability to transpose information into new forms exhibits mastery of the information. Asking students to respond to texts by creating found poems, which reconstruct the ideas within classroom texts, builds on Myers's ideas. The strategy also draws on William Pinar's (1975) *currere* method of generating what he calls *biographical "data"* about interaction with a text. Whereas Myers posits that literacy is evidenced by students' capacity to translate ideas from one mode to another, Pinar suggests that interpretive work is influenced and aided by an explicit focus on the reader's autobiography, which guides her or his interpretation of any text.

In developing research about the role of readers in reading, Pinar recorded himself musing as he read a text and later analyzed the recordings. Like Rosenblatt (1969), he believes that autobiography plays a leading role in any reader's transaction with texts and proposes that we acknowledge and leverage this natural tendency as we teach and learn. Socorro Herrera (2010) echoes both Myers and Pinar in her exploration of using biography-driven curricula, especially with culturally and linguistically diverse learners:

> We are beginning to depart from a conceptualization of "literacy" as text-driven and move toward a view of literacy as the active transformation of texts. In the past, meaning was thought to be derived from the text; however, new ways of thinking find that meaning is created through interactions of the reader with the text. (p. 40)

When we encourage students to deconstruct the texts they encounter in the English classroom and then to compose a new *companion text*—in the case of the activity described here, a Dada-inspired found poem—we offer them an intellectual and creative challenge, as well as an enticement to develop a close relationship with the ideas in the text. We ask them to make choices about interpretation, to explicitly acknowledge the personal perspective they bring to that interpretation, and to practice flexibility and adaptability, which, as Myers (1996) reminds us, are requisite attributes for twenty-first-century learners.

Process of Creating the Found Poem

When I first began using this activity with students, I worked to develop a process that would allow them, ultimately, to create pieces that felt both substantial and considered, as well as resonant of the text we were reading together. I thought it important for the students to understand the artistic reference for the exercise and to engage in a progression of steps that demanded close reading. I specifically wanted them to understand that, though the activity involved creative response, those responses were not capricious or inconsequential. "The authentic avant-garde . . . was always properly formalist," art historian Henry Sayre (1989) points out in his overview of twentieth-century art movements (p. 8). Without a discussion of the premises of the avant-garde, students may misunderstand its intentions, thinking of an artistic effort that dismisses established views of what constitutes art as suspect, perhaps even the domain of the unskilled and unthoughtful. Sayre uses the word *authentic* purposefully; those artists whose work delves into unexplored territory—as the Dadaists' work did—comprehend the specific histories of the aesthetic they are questioning. Their efforts are at once referential and forward thinking.

Take, for example, a painter like the French Neo-Impressionist Georges Seurat, known for juxtaposing small strokes of contrasting and complementary colors, a technique that came to be called *mélange optique* (optical mixture). Seurat disregarded both the classical subject matter and techniques that were most highly respected at the time, but he had a full understanding of the tradition he was resisting. Science interested him, and he began to speculate about color and investigate its formal properties. This examination ultimately led him to devise a painting method that arranged small individual dots of color on the canvas in a precise relationship so that the eye of the viewer perceived them as blended, rather than as distinct. The technique, later called Pointillism, was conceptually formal—it represented a new set of *rules*, which, while experimental, were based on the science of color and vision. Furthermore, it embodied a disciplined method of working. The technique could be studied, emulated, and reproduced. I wanted to create a similarly formal method for the found poem assignment for my students, a scaffolded procedure that inspired not only curiosity and invention, but also serious reflection and deliberate wordplay.

Like Pinar, I began by studying my own process. I practiced the activity with a text I was reading at the time: Jamaica Kincaid's (2000) *A Small Place*. I marked passages as I read, but purposefully chose not to take notes during the first reading. Later, I reviewed the passages I had highlighted, looking for connections, similarities, and themes. Then I began fiddling with the words and phrases, attempting to arrange them into lines that expressed a metaphor I found implicit in the passages I had marked: that colonialism is like tourism. My poem collaged Kincaid's words and phrases to create a piece that was inherently related to her writing, but that was indisputably my own, and it represented the critique of colonialism she makes in the text. Reading the draft, I realized that it served as a creative synopsis of an important concept—an aesthetic response to the book. I could also have written an essay or a reflection that explored the theme, but the poem represented a distilled and memorable (for me as a reader) rendering of my interaction with Kincaid's writing. I titled the poem "Thematically Speaking, Colonialism Is a Lot Like Tourism," using the title as a functional frame for the metaphorical language of the lines.

Translating my own experience to create an assignment for students allowed me to categorize and codify the phases of the process: (1) noticing, (2) note-making, (3) questioning, (4) composing, and (5) publishing. In the following section, I explain each of these phases. My objective is to describe the process sufficiently so that teachers can adopt or adapt it for texts they are bringing to their own students. The steps are designed to be intentionally supportive to students in their initial efforts to create found poems.

Steps in the Process

Step 1: Noticing

As students read a text for the first time, they simply mark any passages that they notice. There are a variety of reasons for noticing, and, in this first interaction with a reading, students should be liberal in identifying connections with the language of the text. They can either underline or highlight the passages (which can be individual words, phrases, sentences, or paragraphs) or mark the text with self-adhesive notes. In this initial step of the exercise, the students do not need to do any interpretive work. They only notice and highlight. Pinar (1975) likens this kind of noticing to the "psycho-analytic technique of free association" (p. 2), which encourages random, and perhaps inexplicable, connections.

Step 2: Note-Making

Once the students have marked the text in their first interaction, they begin the analytical work of note-making, which asks them to identify themes in the language they highlighted. This phase includes a preliminary examination of the ideas expressed in the text and spotlights the extraordinarily individual interpretations we all make of the ideas we encounter. In these early analytical musings, students posit tentative interpretations of the authors' meanings and identify thematic links, but they are not working to state a definitive thesis. Rather, they are purposefully delaying the objective of assigning meaning in an effort to disrupt more traditional methods of deciphering texts. As Rosenblatt (1969) has suggested, readers are naturally guided in their transactions with texts by what Keene and Zimmerman (1997) categorize as *text-to-self connections*: past experiences with reading, personal histories, and prior conceptions of ideas represented in the text. Each of us, as readers, develops a "relationship with the text" (Rosenblatt, 1969, p. 35), which can be uniquely personal. This phase of the exercise emphasizes personalization and demonstrates "the exuberant multiplicity among individual readings" (Harkin, 2005, p. 412). For example, students who have selected the same passages in the text may identify quite divergent themes. A goal of this step in the process is to create a short list of themes for further exploration.

Step 3: Questioning

To continue the process of analysis, in the third step of the exercise, students develop questions to ask of the text. The students' queries can emanate from any number of conceptual stances toward the reading. For example, the questions might have thematic frames ("What big ideas is the author attempting to convey in this text?"); interpretive frames ("How does this text promote or disrupt dominant cultural values?"); investigative frames ("Why does the author make certain choices about the characters or the plot?"); or autobiographical frames ("What excites me, confuses me, or angers me about this text?"). Because the focus in this kind of dismantling and remixing exercise is on both decomposing and recomposing, the students can be deliberately mischievous in the construction of their questions. The Dadaists' aesthetic embraced a style of intentional mockery as a mode of questioning norms, condemning bourgeois attitudes, and rousing consciousness. Adapting elements of that aesthetic for responding to texts invites a range of question types—from the obviously humorous (e.g., "Why should every American be a little in love with playwright Tony Kushner?") to the appreciably earnest (e.g., "How do you domesticate love?").

Step 4: Composing

Dada popularized collaging as an art-making technique for both written and visual pieces, pushing against traditional creative practices that included careful planning. The Dadaists, instead, incorporated chance and improvisation to produce work that provoked questions about the nature and purpose of art, as well as the role of the artist more generally. They developed a variety of techniques to foster this kind of expression of randomness, including a collaging activity they referred to as *exquisite corpse*. For this exercise, a small group would collaborate to craft a piece of art. They would, for example, sit in a circle, draw or write something on a piece of paper, then fold the paper to conceal their contribution and pass the paper to another member of the circle who would repeat the process until all members had contributed to the "finished" piece. The collaged work represented their notion that the world was disconnected, random, and, ultimately, not understandable. Once the students have developed questions for the text they are reading, they generate responses to one of their questions by collaging together language from the text. They begin with the passages they identified in the first step in the process, which will now have significant resonance, because they have reviewed the notes they made several times: they have scoured them for themes, sifted through them for answers to their thematic questions, and reviewed them for selection as possible lines in their drafted poems. In some iterations of this activity, I have asked the students to use the question they were attempting to answer as the title of the poem; in other instances, the students have drafted alternative kinds of titles, but the poem is always generated as a response to a question the student is asking about the text.

Step 5: Publishing

Artists need an audience, and, in the classroom, the act of "publishing" finished drafts of writing is especially important, because it honors students' work and provides authentic feedback. For this activity, publishing includes having the students share their poems in class with their peers. I have orchestrated the publishing phase of the assignment in a number of ways, but, most often, I have the students conduct a reading circle in which the writers simply read their poems aloud and the rest of the class listens and then thanks the author for sharing. In their manual on providing feedback to writing, *Sharing and Responding*, Peter Elbow and Pat Belanoff (2000) provide an overview of useful strategies designed to encourage revision; their first suggestion is to say, "Thank you for sharing your writing." It is a gracious acknowledgment of the writer's courage to present her or his work in a public setting. To prepare students for the reading circle, I occasionally divide the class into small groups of four to six and ask the students to bring enough copies of their poems to share with the group members. I want the listeners to read along with the author; having the text in front of them encourages closer attention and minimizes distractions that might detract from the author's experience of the reading circle. If the whole class is serving as a large reading circle, which I have encouraged for some courses, I often project each student's poem on a screen during the reading, which eliminates the need to have a copy of the poem for every student. I always ask the students to read their own work, however.

The reading circle serves as yet another opportunity for the class to interact with the text we have read together and to consider varying perspectives, interpretations, and creative responses. Often, the readings reveal connections among students' ideas about the text—repeated words, phrases, and lines underscore themes in the reading. It is also common for students to have marked the same passages as they read, but to have organized the passages quite differently when they draft their poems, so the class observes how one phrase from the text, for example, can engender multiple interpretations. The shared reading of the poems acts as a conclusion to the multistep thinking and writing activity and offers the opportunity for the class to continue their discussion of the text, having now examined the author's use of language from sundry perspectives. The students often comment on the repeated lines in the poems, noticing how the mere fact that several students excerpted the same language from the text suggests significance. This kind of interpretive work is inherent in the process; when the students see and hear the same passages repeated in the poems, they naturally recognize the motifs embedded in the passages. And the themes they have intuited as they drafted their poems are explicitly tied to the language of the text. By extension, this creative interaction with the author's ideas emphasizes the importance of providing text-based evidence for literary analysis and interpretation.

Notes about Evaluation and Assessment

Since the emphasis for this kind of imaginative close reading assignment is on students' interaction with the text from a dramatically personal perspective, I do not typically evaluate the individual poems they create with traditional assessment tools. I do not use a rubric or assign a percentage grade, for example. I do coach the students to focus their attention on the language of the text and to note dominant themes, and, as part of the class discussion, I comment on those elements of their work during the group reading. I praise interesting uses of repetition and point out unexpected juxtapositions of lines and words or especially clever titles. I also require the students to reference the page numbers for each phrase they appropriate, which reinforces the importance of providing credit for source material and allows me to gauge some measure of their involvement with the author's ideas. I want the students to think of this assignment as unorthodox and rule breaking, in keeping with the Dada philosophy that underpins it, so "grading" the writing could negate the inventive impulse I am working to elicit. The poems, however, are often submitted as part of a writing portfolio, and the students are offered the opportunity to revise after participating in the reading circle. As part of the assessment strategy for the portfolio, I ask the students to contextualize the writing samples they include and to reflect on their experience of creating the piece of writing, as well as their sense of its value in helping them think about the reading that inspired it.

Example Application of the Found Poetry Strategy

I have used the strategy described in this chapter in multiple educational settings and have adapted it for a variety of student audiences and reading assignments. In this section, I share one experience of using the strategy and provide an example of the poem one student wrote as she read and responded. I have several times taught a seminar for first-semester college students that focuses on contemporary American drama. The course aimed to teach recent high school graduates how to engage with advanced texts, how to prepare for threaded group discussions, and how to think critically and write reflexively. In the course, the students were introduced to a range of provocative award-winning scripts from the last fifty years of American theatre, including Wendy Wasserstein's (1991) *The Heidi Chronicles*, August Wilson's (2010) *Fences*, Edward Albee's (2003) *The Goat or, Who Is Sylvia?*, and Tony Kushner's (2013) *Angels in America*. Wasserstein's script is an episodic history lesson on feminist ideals; Wilson's family drama examines the mislaid dreams of an African American father in mid-century America; and Albee's absurdist comedy explores the aftermath of a husband's unforgivable trespass. Each of these plays offers a complex portrait of family, relationships, and personal aspirations. Kushner's two-part epic drama also addresses those topics, but he frames his fantastical plot with history, philosophy, and politics, which makes it less immediately accessible than the other scripts read in the course. Students tended to have little familiarity with the philosophical underpinnings of the play and often struggled to translate Kushner's grand ideas, even when they grasped the narrative arc of the plays. The language of *Angels in America* is also richly poetic and metaphorical, adding to the elegance of the script, but complicating the text for younger readers. I asked the students to develop found poems that appropriated language from the script and that demonstrated their capacity to interpret, personalize, and relate to Kushner's themes.

The students followed the steps as described here, at first simply marking language in the plays that stood out or affected them and later mining their notes for possible thematic questions. Finally, the students drafted found poems that used only Kushner's (2013) words, collaging their selections in ways that resulted in an imaginative representation of each reader's experience of the plays. During this phase of the assignment, the students could make any artistic choice as they composed: repetition, rearrangement, punctuation—no expressive technique was prohibited. The only rule was that they had to draw all source language from the plays. After the initial work on the assignment, I presented a lesson on the Dadaists and a short history of found work. I did not want the students to approach the first interaction with the text with the expectation that they would later be developing a poem, because that frame for reading would likely influence their choice of language. They may have been tempted to search for "poetic" lines in the script. Instead, I shared the history lesson after they had generated their list of questions. At that point in the unit, they had already done a preliminary analysis of their notes and had filtered out themes for examination, so, as they reviewed their note-making and the plays to draft a poem, they could focus on highlighting motifs they had each intuited.

Each student chose a question to serve as the organizing principle for the poem and developed a creative reply to that question with the repurposed lines from the play. Kushner (2013) interrogates the construct of American democracy in the script, and one student crafted a question that acknowledged that theme and echoed Kushner's intimation that the world is still waiting for a less corrupted, less American incarnation of democracy, titling her poem "How Long Do We Have to Wait for Democracy to Come?" (the numbers here refer to the pages in the play from which the student selected the lines):

How Long Do We Have to Wait for Democracy to Come?
(With appreciation to Tony Kushner)

Nowadays:
People in a boat, waiting, terrified (48)
Underneath all the tolerance is intense, passionate hatred (96)
We're just a bad dream that the real world is having
And the real world is waking up (168)

There are so many laws; find one you can break (116)
You want to keep your eyes where the most powerful enemy really
    is (159)

Unequal distribution of goods on this earth, or, (189)
Addiction to being alive? (267)

The Great Question before us is:
Can we change? In time? (148)

Sound of energy, sound of time (181)
Big Ideas are all you love (228)
Not the idea with blood in it. (96)
When we think we've escaped
The unbearable ordinariness and untruthfulness of our lives,
It's really only the same old ordinariness and falseness rearranged
Into the appearance of novelty and truth (38)

You do not live in America (16)
He set the word "free" to a note so high nobody can reach it (228)
It's all too much to be encompassed by a single theory (278)
You understand me? It ain't all so much mechanical as they think (268)

You can cry but you endanger nothing in yourself (217)
Water won't ever accomplish the end
No matter how much you cry (233)

Let's just go home (233)
To face loss. With grace
But not letting go deforms you so (253)
Listen to the world, to how fast it goes, (181)
Don't be afraid to live in the raw wind, naked, alone (64)
Naked he will be in the world, prey to the forces of chaos (148)

The only cure: to keep moving (24)
Show me the words that will reorder the world, or else keep silent
   (148)
Maybe the door will hold (24)
In that struggle, fierce and unfair (55)
You can't wait for a theory, but you have to have a theory (278)
Go Now (278)
I want to be around to see it, I plan to be, I hope to be (280)
I'll send postcards with strange stamps and tantalizing messages on
   the back:
"later maybe." (23)

She asks in her poem a question Kushner includes in the play: "Can we change?" In the script, this line is repeated in several contexts and it serves as both a provocation and a critique. The student's poem appropriates the line, as well as the invitational impulse she interpreted. She makes the choice to position the question within the first few lines of her poem, connecting it to her title and using it to frame the lines that follow. Then she develops a litany of complaints: "It's really only the same old ordinariness and falseness rearranged," "It's all too much to be encompassed by a single theory," "You can cry but you endanger nothing in yourself." The poem repositions itself after this litany though: having acknowledged the difficulty of the task of being a citizen (a term Kushner uses in the play to denote awareness, consciousness, and responsibility), the student expresses a quiet sense of optimism about the future. She collages together a series of dovetailed lines intentionally structured as points and counterpoints: "Don't be afraid to live in the raw wind, naked, alone / Naked he will be in the world, prey to the forces of chaos." This juxtaposition of competing ideas, as well as the repetition of selected words (*naked*, in this case), mimics Kushner's writing style, especially lines he assigns to one of his characters, Harper, the pill-popping Mormon wife trying to reconcile her worldview with the realization that her closeted husband struggles with internalized homophobia. In fact, the voice of the poem the student wrote has a cadence and tone that simulates Harper's voice in the play. The student may not have been intentional in rendering a speaker that echoes Harper's voice, but the poem demonstrates that she intuited Kushner's rhythms and that they had affected her interpretation of the text. Other students in the class selected some of the same passages, but they generated divergent questions and responses. I find this individuality of expression one of the fortes of the assignment; it illustrates Rosenblatt's (1969) assertion that each of us, as readers, develops a unique relationship with the words and the ideas we encounter in a text.

To conclude the assignment and one phase of our class discussion, the students shared their final pieces in a reading circle. After everyone had read and we had thanked them, we remarked on the lines that appeared in more than one found poem, noticing the impact of certain phrases, the beauty of Kushner's (2013) writing, and the compelling themes in the plays. I do not typically evaluate the poems formally, because I think of them as formative rather than summative work. Instead, my students submitted their poems as part of a portfolio of work for the course, which required them to return again to the language and themes in the play, since they had the opportunity to revise any work included in their portfolios.

As with any creative effort, the students generated poems that invited a range of responses: some poems shimmered with the same elegance that Kushner (2013) achieves in the language of the plays; others explored a straightforward question in a direct way. Every student, however, engaged with the ideas in the text iteratively. It is impossible to complete this assignment without revisiting the text the students are reading, as well as revisiting their own notes about the text. For me as a teacher, this is the instructional strength of the assignment. It requires students to re-read, which encourages not only a developing sense of connection to text-based ideas, but also a consideration of the author's rhetorical uses of language. Effective reading skills are naturally embedded in the structure of the exercise. The assignment does more than assist students to practice academic skills though; it also invites them to question (like the Dadaists) their assumptions about the world as it has been constructed for them, especially the world of school and schooling and the kinds of activities that constitute reading. The English classroom too often ignores the aesthetic core of our discipline's content. We teach literature and the art of language, and invite students to respond to the texts we offer them. Using practices and tools of artists widens their expectations about the possibility of human expression and encourages the kind of intellectual flexibility that Myers (1996) believes is an attribute of the truly literate. The Dadaists valued freshness, possibility, and self-reflexivity (Kuspit, 2006, para. 30). Adapting this ethos for the English language arts classroom has the potential to bolster students' engagement, comprehension, and sense of themselves as inventive critical thinkers.

References

Academy of American Poets. (2004, September 14). Found poem: Poetic form. Retrieved from https://www.poets.org/poetsorg/text/found-poem-poetic-form

Albee, E. (2003). *The goat or, who is Sylvia? (Notes toward a definition of tragedy)*. New York, NY: Dramatists Play Service.

Elbow, P., & Belanoff, P. (2000). *Sharing and responding* (3rd ed.). New York, NY: McGraw Hill Higher Education.

Harkin, P. (2005). The reception of reader–response theory. *College Composition and Communication, 56*(3), 410–25.

Herrera, S. G. (2010). *Biography-driven culturally responsive teaching*. New York, NY: Teachers College Press.

Keene, E. O., & Zimmerman, S. (1997). *Mosaic of thought: Teaching comprehension in a reader's workshop*. Portsmouth, NH: Heinemann.

Kincaid, J. (2000). *A small place*. New York, NY: Farrar, Straus and Giroux.

Kushner, T. (2013). *Angels in America: A gay fantasia on national themes* (Rev. ed.). New York, NY: Theatre Communications Group.

Kuspit, D. (2006). *A critical history of 20th-century art.* Retrieved from http://www.artnet.com/magazineus/features/kuspit/kuspit1-10-06.asp

Myers, M. (1996). *Changing our minds: Negotiating English and literacy.* Urbana, IL: National Council of Teachers of English.

Pinar, W. F. (1975). The method of "currere." Paper presented at the annual meeting of the American Research Association, Washington, DC. Retrieved from http://files.eric.ed.gov/fulltext/ED104766.pdf

Ratliff, B. (2016, July 8). Dada was born 100 years ago. So what? *The New York Times.* Retrieved from https://www.nytimes.com/2016/07/10/arts/dada-100-years-later.html

Rosenblatt, L. M. (1969). Toward a transactional theory of reading. *Journal of Literacy Research, 1*(1), 31–49.

Sayre, H. M. (1989). *The object of performance: The American avant-garde since 1970.* Chicago, IL: The University of Chicago Press.

Sterling, B. (2016, July 11). Hugo Ball's Dada manifesto, July 1916. *Wired.* Retrieved from https://www.wired.com/beyond-the-beyond/2016/07/hugo-balls-dada-manifesto-july-2016/

Tzara, T. (1989). "Seven Dada manifestos." In R. Motherwell (Ed.), *The Dada painters and poets: An anthology* (2nd ed., pp. 75–98). Cambridge, MA: Harvard University Press.

Wasserstein, W. (1991). *The Heidi chronicles, uncommon women and others, and isn't it romantic.* New York, NY: Vintage.

Wilson, A. (2010). *Fences.* New York, NY: Samuel French.

Integrating Drama: An Embodied Pedagogy

5

KATHERINE J. MACRO, *SUNY Buffalo State College*

Leaning against the doorframe of Room 230, I watch my students standing in small groups and talking excitedly. One group is engrossed in deciding on a noise to make and trying to connect movement with it. Another group is huddled together with a piece of text and working to create an image with their bodies that accompanies the text. A different group gathers around a desk and collaborates to write some lines of text, pens in hand. Still another is laughing off to the side as they rather conspiratorially plan their version of a scene. There is laughter, there is activity; there is discussion of thunder, of lightning, of rain. There is talk about feeling, intention, and the meaning that is conveyed by the words, actions, and sounds they are about to share with their peers.

This is a different kind of English classroom from the one described in the opening page of this book's introduction. It is a classroom infused with drama. A classroom where students are actively involved in learning, in deciphering text, in writing pieces of their own, and in making meaning. They are interacting with one another in embodied ways. They are embarking upon an inquiry into themselves, the texts they are reading, and the meaning they are making with their bodies as well as their minds as they play, interact, and react to the class around them. Integrating drama offers students opportunities to physically experience texts, and they learn to reflect upon ways people interact with the world. Drama in an English language arts (ELA) class is an opportunity to educate the whole student (Dewey, 1938).

As a classroom teacher for many years, I used drama to approach many different texts and topics. When we read anything from Shakespeare to Frank McCourt, we explored and experienced the language physically. We made meaning by making connections to our own lives and worlds. We wrote about the things that we'd seen happen during the dramatic exercises, the things we thought might happen, or the things we thought the characters might be thinking. We explored texts by doing, moving, and being, and it gave students the freedom to express all sorts of learning. The embodiment present in this pedagogy was an integral part of the learning and the community we built together. Students began to look forward to doing and feeling rather than sitting and listening as they did in other classes. They began to ask for more personal writing topics, and for ways to connect the texts we were reading to their lives, to other texts, and to other contexts. As a classroom community, I think we inspired one another. We supported each other, and we pushed each other to new places of interacting and meaning making. The key component to our community was drama.

There were many ways I used drama over the years, so it was difficult to select one or two experiences to write about for this chapter. When using drama in the classroom—that is, when exploring creative drama—my goal was always to allow students to be active and to play, or, as Banks (2016) puts it, to allow the students to be "creative interpreters." I have found year after year that drama helps students to understand, remember, and connect to other texts and their own lives in ways that simply never materialized when they were just reading and writing analytical essays while sitting at desks. In this chapter, I explore strategies such as sculpting, throwing the ball, role-play, writing in role, and Crisp Packet Orchestra as different ways to integrate drama into regular instruction for reading and interpreting literature, as well as for writing.

Creative Drama

Before going further, it is necessary to define what I mean by the terms *drama* and *creative drama*. It is easy to confuse the term *drama* with the genre of drama. In an ELA class, teachers often explore the drama genre by reading plays or watching performances based on a script. However, drama is far more than lines written by playwrights. It is the creation of meaning through various types of performance and interaction with texts and with other people; it is the act of placing oneself in an active environment that allows for personal exploration and understanding that cannot be created based solely on observation and passivity. My work in the classroom employed creative drama, which means that I used a variety of activities to explore literary texts and create meaning. Improvisations and exercises such as role-plays and model discussions (students and teachers interacting and discussing topics in character) are all dramatic methods that are part of creative drama. When an actor trains, he does far more than work with scripts and prepared texts. Actors experience and explore what it means to create characters and stories in a variety of ways. Students can do the same thing if they experience creative drama in school. I use the term *drama* in this chapter to refer to all types of creative and interactive exercises from this point forward.

Wagner's (1998) definition of drama in education is also helpful. She says that:

> [d]rama practitioners transform texts, sometimes using them as starting points, but always exploring the spaces between episodes in a story to create an imagined world and change the story into something quite new. . . . Through ritual, dramatic encounters, pantomime, *tableaux vivants* (still pictures made with the bodies of the participants), writing in role, and reflection, participants enter the lives of imagined characters and play out their responses to challenges and crises. (p. 7)

Drama is the use of play and active enterprises that places student and teacher alongside each other as they create meaning that helps to extend learning in both real and imagined worlds (Edmiston, 2000, 2007; Eisner, 2002; Heathcote, 1984; Heathcote & Bolton, 1995; O'Neill, 1995; Wagner, 1998; Wilhelm & Edmiston, 1998). The types of activities mentioned above are ways for teachers to help students transform texts into moments of interaction with their peers. In these moments, students learn, interact, and react to each other, the literary texts, and the emotions and movement associated with the activity.

The concept of creative drama has a long history in America. Ward (1930) writes about her attempts to include drama in curriculum for public schools. In creative drama, a teacher calls upon various methods of instruction, which might include improvised role-play or dramatic techniques like acting games, tableaux, and other creative exercises, to help students interpret a text. The plots are already known; the text being enacted is a scene from a play, novel, short story, poem, film, painting, and so on. Some improvised role-play can be used in creative drama, though it is not the focus or the only technique used. Creative drama helps students to understand and develop literacy skills; students and teachers participate in dramatic exercises that help explore meaning in literary texts, connect those texts to students' lives, and facilitate language understanding.

Cowan and Albers (2006) describe a method in line with creative drama, though they write about fourth and fifth graders, as opposed to the secondary students and teachers we focus on in this volume. They emphasize drama because it aids in "developing richer, more complex literacy" (p. 124). Their study looks at the arts connected to language arts instruction. In it, students dramatized their personal experiences and emotions by reliving an emotion or experience, and they were better able to understand literary terms and ideas. Cowan and Albers ultimately find that "literacy educators can work with students to move them toward a more complex understanding and development of literacy that is explicitly linked to the visual and dramatic arts" (p. 124). This complexity of understanding that students showed stemmed from the embodied nature of drama and their physical interactions with emotions, experiences, and literature.

Several researchers have written about the arts both in school and out of school. Heath (2004) describes the arts in out-of-school experiences, and advocates for more of those opportunities in school. Greene (1988, 1995) writes about making people free through learning; schools and education should be places where teachers care about and are connected to the students. Drama provides a way to do that: a place where conversation supports community so that learning and a sense of freedom go hand in hand. Eisner (2002) talks about the arts as a way to invite youth into the learning process; he says that a "major aim of arts education is to promote the child's ability to develop his or her mind through the experience that the creation or perception of expressive form makes possible" (p. 24). Drama is an expressive form that encourages students to learn through living, thinking, perceiving, interacting, and reacting to the world around them—and the literary texts in their hands.

Most of the research done on drama education shows that drama educators (those who teach theatre) seek to help their pupils develop a sense of individual identity (Hellier-Tinoco, 2005). It seems that when people, young or old, are involved in creative drama workshops or classes, they are able to cross borders or barriers that are otherwise closed to them. The ability to explore other senses of self comes through in drama quite clearly and strongly. In addition to the positive aspects of developing a keener sense of self and one's place in the world, when looking at students' reactions across the curriculum, those involved in drama tend to produce higher test scores as well (Fleming, 2004). The arts helped me to teach the whole student; to educate their bodies and minds, to allow room for thought and expression of opinions, emotions, and critical thinking that the tests often do not measure. Drama affords students the opportunity to be better developed individuals. They can temporarily take on different roles, experience different social and cultural statuses, and, in doing so, explore new meanings about life through drama (Medina, 2004).

Heath and Wollach (2008) write about the kinesthetic nature of theatre and drama in terms of the way it enables students to learn interactively through role-play, among other things, as a method for understanding and developing thinking and identity. Drama allows students to interact with the wider community and themselves. It allows for fine-grained interpretations that in turn encourage students to examine and explore issues and ideas outside of the text at hand. Drama supports students making text-to-world connections and text-to-self connections through embodied activities.

Principles of a Drama-Based Pedagogy

I grounded my pedagogy based in creative drama in a few basic principles. I define the three principles—embodiment, identity, and multimodality—briefly here, and show them in greater detail with classroom applications later in the chapter.

1. *Embodiment principle.* Learners are immersed in what they are doing. They are active participants in the learning and are thinking critically about what they are doing based on their environment, their peers, and their instructor's guidance. Students become part of the learning by moving their arms, legs, torsos, hands, and faces, and physically explore and express meaning through embodied exercises.

2. *Identity principle.* Learning involves taking on and playing with identities; learning is set up in such a way that learners come to think consciously about who they are and their places in the world. Students become active participants in building skills and exploring interests and ideas, which allows them to customize their learning experiences and to take ownership of their learning.

3. *Multimodality principle.* Teachers help students move back and forth between texts and embodied experiences. In addition to embodied textual experiences, they also provide context for meaning making through the use and creation of images, symbols, interactions, and sound.

The principles outlined above create a shift in the learning environment from a passive to an active one; they are building blocks for a pedagogy that addresses the bodies and minds of students. The application of these principles is accessible to both skilled and novice teachers through drama. Through the action and interaction that dramatic exercises entail, students can have embodied experiences that shape their identities in multimodal ways that also connect them to the ELA content.

Embodiment and Drama

The embodiment principle gives teachers the means to employ exercises, games, and discussion techniques that allow learners to be immersed in what they're doing. Students are physically active in the learning space, and participate in critical thinking about their actions as well as the environment and the people around them. They do these activities with the guidance of their teachers. They become a part of the learning by doing and thus engage in experiences that are truly embodied. Drama is a natural and even logical end to kinesthetic learning.

Sculpting Activity

Any actor or drama teacher will tell you that there are a myriad of exercises teachers can use in order to better understand a character or a text. These activities all create opportunities for embodied experiences. One example is an exercise commonly known as *sculpting*. In this activity, students create visual pictures with their bodies based on a word, an action, an emotion, or a character. This works best when breaking the class up in two so that one group functions as sculptors, while the other functions as the clay, or the statues in a gallery.

For example, a student may desire to depict the sadness felt in *Angela's Ashes* when Frank McCourt's (2003) younger siblings die. The sculptor might position their clay partner to strike the pose of a young child lying in a coffin, or a parent wracked with grief, head in hands. As other students look at the statues created, discussion begins based on what they see and the feelings or ideas this sculpture invokes. Students describe the positions of their peers' bodies and comment on the roles the sculptures seemed to portray. The statues' facial expressions reveal pain, sadness, grief, and even guilt. Through this exercise, students are given the opportunity to show what they know about the story by physically depicting a moment or an emotion. The sculpting activity fulfills the requirements of the embodiment principle because students begin to think critically about what they both saw and did. Positioning each other's bodies is an action tied to analysis and response. Students show understanding through body positioning and facial expressions that have to register with the cultural experiences of their peers. It is not enough to say the parent is grieving; rather, they have to arrange their limbs, eyes, and trunk to personify grief in a way the character might have felt.

This activity can be used in many situations, both with or without a literary text. I often began our work with Shakespeare with sculpting to allow students to enact the way they felt about Shakespeare with their bodies. Students created statues that reflected all sorts of emotions and perceptions. There were excited statues jumping for joy with arms and legs outstretched, bored statues with heads propped up on hands and eyes closed, confused statues with perplexed facial expressions, and even some more creative ones that showed writers, actors, and bits of story lines or characters.

I also used this exercise as a relatively quick way to address different aspects of a topic or theme within a piece of literature. For example, when I wanted students to explore themes within a text, sculpting gave them an opportunity to represent those themes in different ways and to literally see a topic from more than one perspective or angle. In terms of formative assessment, this activity helped me see who understood different parts of our reading. It gave us an opportunity to talk about literal interpretations and basic reading recall as well as more insightful and figurative representations of characters, moments, and topics within a literary text. Perhaps the best thing about this activity is that it only needs to take about five minutes, if time is tight. Thus, sculpting is a short yet meaningful way to look at scenes and topics from a literary text in an embodied way.

Throwing the Ball: Embodied Writing

As a classroom teacher of twelfth graders for many years, I typically began each year with a unit on writing college application essays. I wanted my students to do well with these, but, more important, I wanted to give them the chance to write creatively and thoughtfully about themselves, which was something they had not been allowed to do much as high school writers.

We studied the art of writing these essays; we explored different kinds of prompts and the ways to best approach them so that their pieces stood out from others. It became apparent early on that many of them had no idea how to tell stories in writing. Not about themselves. They all could answer the questions and list their activities and achievements, but they struggled to craft anything that was original or interesting to read. They did not know how to make connections between experiences in their own lives and the things they were being asked to answer about themselves. I read many drafts about an important game they played or moment they had, but they described these experiences with stiff academic language and phrases like "from this I learned," "for example," "I am a leader because," and more. The problem as I saw it was how to get them to create vivid and interesting pieces of writing that revealed something about who they were after years of little creative writing and narrative exploration in secondary classes. We began by exploring the questions of how to use words, how to frame a snapshot, how to show instead of tell—and we did this exploration using drama.

One day, I began class by playing catch with a soft squishy ball that we tossed around the room. We used this ball sometimes to take turns in discussions or to warm up for a lesson in which I was going to ask students to use their bodies to express ideas. But, on this day, I used the ball to demonstrate as we talked about words. I began to throw the ball to different students around the room and we talked about what was happening while we did it. How did I throw the ball?

How did the student catch it? What words would you use to describe what just happened? They began describing the way I threw the ball by saying things like I tossed it, whipped it, or lobbed it, instead of saying I threw it.

The next step of the process was to have one student get up and stand at the back of the room to play catch with me. It would be possible to use two students for this as well, so that the teacher then acts only as director and discussion facilitator, but this is a personal choice. We began to play catch and got a rhythm going. Once that rhythm was established, we began to vary our throws. The class acted as audience, watching the players and the exchange of the ball back and forth for about three minutes. Next, the audience began to discuss and debrief what they had seen. They talked about the looks on our faces as we played catch, they used different kinds of verbs and adjectives to describe the way we threw, and they used language to describe the mood and tone of the moment as well.

My final questions for them were, "What did you learn from watching the two of us play catch?" and "What did you notice about these moments?" To my surprise and delight, they talked about how the game of catch showed our relationship to each other, that it showed there is more than one way to do things, and that words matter to create a vivid picture. Then I asked them to write. I told them to start by writing about the game of catch they had just watched or participated in, and to show the reader what happened and what it represented with the words they chose. It was only a quick write, but their responses revealed that they got it. I did not get one response back that said, "She threw the ball" or "This shows that they have a good relationship because . . ." Instead, they told stories. One student wrote about a friendly game of catch in which one born leader showed a friend how to handle the ball. He wrote about the things he inferred from the scene by saying that the two characters were friends, and that one had leadership qualities based on the way she threw and the way she interacted with her partner. It was a transformative moment for me as a teacher because I saw the way that drama helped them to write more clearly, convey ideas in vivid ways, and infer meanings about the way people interact in the larger world.

Throwing the ball became an exercise I used to help illustrate the importance of word choice and telling a story, but there was more to it than that. Students were connected to their writing after doing drama work; their voices were louder and clearer on the page. My students wrote college application essays that told stories and showed qualities that admissions officers sought in applicants. They wrote about important games, mission trips, heroes, parents, teachers, struggles, and triumphs. Their writing stood out, and many of them did indeed get into the colleges of their choice.

Identity and Drama

Drama gives students the opportunity to learn in a way that involves reflection about who they are, who they wish to be, and who they are in relation to others. Integrating drama into ELA classes gives students opportunities to think consciously about who they are and their place in the world. Being an active participant in the learning process enables students to customize their learning experiences because they inquire and learn about themselves and their own interests through dramatic activities. These activities help students to make links between their lives, the literature they read, and the writing they produce. Students begin to take ownership of their learning as they build skills and make progress toward their own goals. One way to explore the identity principle is through role-play and writing in role.

Role-Play

When teaching literature, there are obvious connections to the identity principle in that each character represents a different persona a student might "try on." It is easier to understand someone's motivation if you have spent a moment in their shoes. Therefore, one excellent activity to address this principle is role-playing.

Role-playing in a dramatic context simply involves students taking on different roles in a given scenario. When teaching a piece of literature, I gave students situations that reflected issues in the play before reading it. Situations that arise in everyday life, such as two people who secretly like each other but cannot get along, parents and children at odds with each other, people struggling to fit in, rise above, or make difficult choices, are all experiences students can relate to. When a group of students role-play these scenarios and others watch, they begin to think about what it would feel like to be in the characters' positions.

The discussion and reflection generated by performing and watching role-plays allows students to begin to think critically about issues of right and wrong, good and evil, love and hate, justice and injustice, and more. They can also see what they might do in a similar situation. Role-plays are one example of a way to get students to make learning personal. Through selecting different roles, students explore characters from the inside out and focus on the things that interest them or that they want to learn more about, thereby customizing their learning experience. Teachers can focus on what students identify as important about characters in relation to texts and themselves. This strategy, then, offers teachers a tool for assessing what students know about the nuances of a text in ways that writing essays might not.

Writing in Role

Role-play is an exercise that can be used with writing as well as literature in an English classroom. Writing in role requires that students take on a different persona in written form to explore characters or story lines based on a literary text. Writing in role includes letters, monologues, dialogue, Facebook posts, or tweets. These writing activities are all great ways to get students to explore what they know about the way a character thinks and feels. It also allows them to go beyond the text a bit and connect to literary material in a more personal way.

Writing in role activities do not have to be long formal assessments. It is the thinking and the practice that matters in this instance. Students can write a tweet or a series of tweets from one character's perspective about the events of the day, a text message to a friend responding to something that was part of the class discussion, or a simple, brief reflection before the end of class. I gleaned a lot from a quick in-class exit ticket in role, just as I learned a lot from an extended scene or monologue assignment my students produced. Shorter writing in role pieces were good formative assessments to check understanding in a fun way. The longer pieces like monologues and letters allowed for more creativity and an exploration of characters and relationships that could serve as summative assessments too. Students enjoyed doing both kinds of writing, and, as a teacher, I found both to be useful assessments of different kinds of thinking and analysis as well.

Multimodality and Drama

Finally, as a teacher, it was important to me that students could move back and forth between texts and embodied experiences. That is why the multimodality principle is essential. This principle required that I use more than print-based texts in my class. Multimodality is achieved when activities and texts incorporate more than one modality, semiotic system, or way of making meaning. Drama by its very nature is multimodal. A drama-based activity incorporates movement, language, sound, and visual representations so that students and teachers can successfully tie embodied experiences and text together.

One successful activity often used in acting classes that involves the use of sound to tell a story works excellently for teaching Shakespeare, among other things. I learned the game while studying with Globe Education at Shakespeare's Globe Theatre in London. Known as the Crisp Packet Orchestra, the game involves the use of everyday objects to make noise. A group of students use objects such as an empty potato chip bag (crisp packet), a half-full tin of breath mints, a noisy pair of shoes, or a spiral notebook and a pen to create a series of sounds that tell a story using only those objects and their voices. No words are involved in this activity, but, when a group of my students attempted to create a scene from a horror film using creaks, loud noises, and whistling, the eerie effect was aptly achieved. This use of sound directly translated to creating the mood for a piece of literature. Students then used sound more effectively as they worked with the literary text to help convey emotion and intensity.

In *Macbeth*, characters talk about the unrest and chaos in Scotland in particularly vivid speeches filled with sounds and description. Students used this speech to portray a scene that extended beyond the words on the page; they created audio during the Crisp Packet Orchestra exercise that added to the meaning, the atmosphere, and the fervor. When watching the whole scene, the rest of the class served as the audience and had a visual representation of the embodied action in the scene as well as the sound and text that all contributed to the storytelling and understanding. It was a truly multimodal endeavor.

The Crisp Packet Orchestra activity allowed students to explore a mode of expression they might not normally address when reading. They reflected upon the way sound contributed to meaning, and did so multimodally by moving, touching, seeing, and hearing a scene all at once. This strategy further served as a community-building activity and helped students sharpen their interpretation skills.

Reflection and Drama Integration

Integrating drama into both the study of literature as well as writing instruction offers students new possibilities for expression. One thing that any dramatic activity must also have is reflection. The process of talking about what was done and what was learned after the lesson is essential. Reflection offers students an opportunity to notice the world around them by commenting on what they see happening, as well as to debrief regarding the exercise and how it applies to the text they are working with.

At the end of any type of drama exercise, I began our reflection with the questions "What did you notice?" "What stood out to you?" "How or what did you feel during the exercise?" Most of the time, students began by recalling what they saw or heard. That recall usually moved into how they felt during the activity. The students liked to talk about feeling funny, confused, or awkward, as well as feeling powerful, happy, or confident in a moment; sharing what they emotionally experienced as part of the exercise was an integral part of the learning. Sometimes, even without prompting, they connected our drama work back to the text. These connections applied meaning or context to what we were reading together, based on the dramatic experience. If students did not make this link themselves, I simply addressed it by asking, "How does this connect to the text?"

Using drama to explore literary texts helps to make worlds that are strange to students more tangible. Banks (2016) says that it makes texts more real and shows them that the situations encountered on the page can "resonate strongly with our lives" (p. 205). Reflecting upon what each drama activity means and helps to illustrate about a text is essential because, as Banks (2016) observes:

> Students feel safe discussing a character's situation and exploring their feelings because they belong to the specific world of the play, yet in doing so they are enabled to reflect on their own feelings and response to such a situation. (p. 205)

These moments of questioning and reflecting that follow each dramatic activity help to tie the embodied experience to the literature and connect to students' lives as well. In these moments, drama is a powerful learning tool.

Discussion

Being a teacher who uses an arts-based pedagogy does indeed affect my opinion about drama and its use and value in teaching. I used drama in my high school classes because it worked well. I used it because students learned more about what I was teaching. I used it because students had fun while doing it, because they could discuss issues from our readings from different sides based on their experiences in the dramatic activities. My students had stronger opinions about things because they had experienced them with their bodies. Drama engaged my students in ways of thinking and being that were not available to them through simply sitting at their desks and reading or talking about a piece of literature. I continue to use drama in my graduate and undergraduate courses with prospective teachers to set an example of what an arts-based pedagogy means in action, and to show the opportunities it affords students at all levels.

It is true that teachers with a background in drama may take on these activities without much difficulty, while those who do not know much about theatre and drama may feel apprehensive about entering into tasks with their students that are new to them. To that end, Darling-Hammond (2006) and Langer (2001) argue for professional training programs and/or development opportunities that encourage and prepare teachers to tackle the problems faced in today's schools. Educating teachers about methods that allow for imagination and creativity will make them better prepared for the real world of the classroom and its pressures (Eisner, 2002; Greene, 1988). Teachers need opportunities to take classes that foster growth and development in arts-based pedagogies.

The ELA classroom is a place with more freedom than other disciplines since the content is not what drives instruction. ELA is driven by literacy skills and practices. Teachers help and encourage students to make meaning, foster higher-order thinking skills, shape analysis of literary texts, and facilitate expression of ideas in spoken and written form. This is a space that can be energized by a drama-based pedagogy. Drama gets students involved in class discussions, in group presentations, in talking about the things they really believe, desire, feel, love, hate, and so on. It provides a positive and embodied learning environment for students and teachers alike. Drama connects students to texts, their own lives, and the wider world both in and beyond the ELA classroom.

References

Banks, F. (2016). *Creative Shakespeare: The Globe education guide to practical Shakespeare.* London, UK: Bloomsbury.

Cowan, K., & Albers, P. (2006). Semiotic representations: Building complex literacy practices through the arts. *The Reading Teacher, 60*(2), 124–37.

Darling-Hammond, L. (2006). Securing the right to learn: Policy and practice for powerful teaching and learning. *Educational Researcher, 35*(7), 13–24.

Dewey, J. (1938). *Experience and education.* New York, NY: Simon and Schuster.

Edmiston, B. (2000). Drama as ethical education. *Research in Drama Education, 5*(1), 63–83.

Edmiston, B. (2007). Mission to Mars: Using drama to make a more inclusive classroom for literacy learning. *Language Arts, 84*(4), 337–46.

Efland, A. (2002). *Art and cognition: Integrating the visual arts in the curriculum.* New York, NY: Teachers College Press.

Eisner, E. (2002). *The arts and the creation of mind.* New Haven, CT: Yale University Press.

Fleming, M. (2004). The impact of drama on pupils' language, mathematics, and attitude in two primary schools. *Research in Drama Education, 9*(2), 178–97.

Freire, P. (1970). *Pedagogy of the oppressed.* New York, NY: The Seabury Press.

Greene, M. (1988). *The dialectic of freedom.* New York, NY: Teachers College Press.

Greene, M. (1995). *Releasing the imagination: Essays on education, the arts, and social change.* San Francisco, CA: Jossey-Bass.

Heath, S. B. (2004). Learning language and strategic thinking through the arts. *Reading Research Quarterly, 39*(3), 338–42.

Heath, S. B., & Wollach, R. (2008). Vision for learning: History, theory, and affirmation. In J. Flood, S. B. Heath, & D. Lapp (Eds.), *Handbook of research on teaching literacy through the communicative and visual arts* (Vol. II, pp. 3–11). New York, NY: Routledge.

Heathcote, D. (1984). *Collected writings on education and drama.* (L. Johnson & C. O'Neill, Eds.). Evanston, IL: Northwestern University Press.

Heathcote, D., & Bolton, G. M. (1995). *Drama for learning: Dorothy Heathcote's mantle of the expert approach to education.* Portsmouth, NH: Heinemann.

Hellier-Tinoco, R. (2005). Becoming-in-the-world-with-others: Inter-act theatre workshop. *Research in Drama Education, 10*(2), 159–73.

Langer, J. (2001). Succeeding against the odds in English. *The English Journal, 91*(1), 37–42.

McCourt, F. (2003). *Angela's ashes: A memoir.* New York, NY: Scribner.

Medina, C. (2004). The construction of drama worlds as literary interpretation of Latina feminist literature. *Research in Drama Education, 9*(2), 145–60.

O'Neill, C. (1995). *Drama worlds: A framework for process drama.* Portsmouth, NH: Heinemann.

Wagner, B. J. (1998). *Educational drama and language arts: What research shows.* Portsmouth, NH: Heinemann.

Ward, W. (1930). *Creative dramatics.* London, UK: D. Appleton and Company.

Wilhelm, J. D., & Edmiston, B. (1998). *Imagining to learn: Inquiry, ethics, and integration through drama.* Portsmouth, NH: Heinemann.

Arts-Based Pedagogy: Exploring Shakespeare Study in the Classroom

LAURA B. TURCHI, *University of Houston*

PAULINE SKOWRON SCHMIDT, *West Chester University*

Using an arts-based approach in teaching a Shakespeare play means that visual arts, music, and especially theatre practices can give our students processes, experiences, and skills to advance their development as readers and as human beings. This chapter looks closely at the intentional pedagogical choices a teacher can make with the arts to help develop students as more sophisticated meaning makers. Arts-based instruction emphasizes the choices that create performances. English teachers can use iterations of *performance* to foster important critical perspectives in students. As students enact scenes and become players themselves, they learn to see the alternatives and options that actors and directors explore in professional settings. Teachers can guide students to recognize visual arts and music as complementary performances, and new adaptations can deepen their perspectives on complicated texts. These explorations in turn open doors for powerful and important student reflection and dialogue about identity and why/how the plays are relevant to their twenty-first-century lives.

This chapter draws on our parallel work in teaching Shakespeare and helping new teachers find ways to be successful with complex texts. As members of the Commission on Arts and Literacies, we have engaged in discussions about our work with others who are excited about bringing the arts to English language arts classrooms. In this chapter, we explore some playful performance aspects of teaching Shakespeare, we describe some key strategies and activities, and we explain how this kind of work fosters students' expressions of identity through creative choices. In our own work, we see arts-based approaches to Shakespeare as essential for students to engage with complex and sometimes intimidating texts.

The foundational works in our field by Maxine Greene (1995) and Elliott Eisner (2002) explore and value play as an educational strategy in theory, but play is typically relegated to elementary classrooms in practice. We are very interested in the artistic experiences of secondary students *playing* Shakespeare, and we want to encourage new teachers to emphasize that the *play's the thing* in their classrooms. This means active, creative, and reflective learning opportunities. Eisner and Greene both see that "helping students understand that artists have something to say—and that they themselves have as well—is a fundamental aspect of learning in the arts" (Eisner, 2002, p. 51) and is likewise a goal of education. They both advocate for hands-on, authentic, and diverse learning experiences that promote critical and innovative thinking. Greene (1995), in her essays on aesthetic education, likewise states, "We need to have and to teach self-reflectiveness originating in situated life . . . engaging one another in dialogue" (p. 126). By bringing performances into secondary English, students can gain deeper understandings of texts and experience reflective, dialogic learning that is too often left out of classroom experiences with Shakespeare.

Jeffrey Wilhelm and Brian Edmiston (1998) advocate for drama as appropriate and even mainstream for elementary and middle school students, and we believe the benefits are important for high school students as well. Wilhelm (2002) further makes a case for *enactments*, or teaching strategies that motivate students to express their ideas and interpretations in movement and gestures. Wilhelm explains how students who bring texts to life through these activities gain deeper understandings. He offers ways that teachers can use this kind of play as they model and support expert reading strategies (prereading, during-, and post-reading activities). These approaches, like the ones we advocate in this chapter, are designed to be social, so that students are constructing meaning together.

Edmiston (2014) describes engaging secondary students through active and dramatic approaches that he developed with teachers in an education collaborative between Ohio State University and the Royal Shakespeare Company. He describes opportunities for transforming learning for both teachers and students by tapping into dramatic practices in the classroom and opening up new ways of communicating, especially among peers. Both Wilhelm (2002) and Edmiston (2014) offer practical means for creating experiences for students to hone their skills for dialogue and express their ideas through play with literary texts. By applying these ideas, secondary teachers can effectively engage their students, who, in turn, can benefit from such play and become more skilled and sophisticated readers.

As one of us, Pauline, discovered in her dissertation research (Schmidt, 2008), there is a variety of ways to teach secondary students using creative, dramatic, and playful techniques, and, moreover, these dramatic activities tend to remain in the long-term memories of focal students because the teacher guided them through embodied experiences. Similarly, Laura coauthored *Teaching Shakespeare with Purpose: A Student-Centred Approach* with Shakespeare scholar

Ayanna Thompson, and their chapter therein on embodiment (Thompson & Turchi, 2016), especially, offers teachers theatre-based techniques that focus students on meaning making through informal classroom performances. The present chapter builds on each of our findings, emphasizing how drama can inspire a wide range of responses and reflections from students.

To support a secondary English language arts teacher's adoption of a play or performance approach to teaching Shakespeare's work, we offer strategies for engaging students in meaning making that are active and that utilize the literacy dimensions of speaking, listening, viewing, and visually representing—all crucial to twenty-first-century learners. We see all of these approaches as ways into close reading. We offer example assignments and activities for Shakespearean plays that include performance decisions and writing processes, small group exploration of scenes and themes, and multimodal creative expressions of interpretation. Significantly, it is our intention to illustrate how these arts-based approaches and embodied experiences with Shakespeare texts open up opportunities for student reflection, writing, and dialogue about who they are as adolescents in their own time and place.

Exploring Interpretations of Shakespeare and His Characters

For us, arts-based pedagogy is engaging and essential for developing all aspects of literacy in students. Literacy, according to the National Council of Teachers of English (2013), includes listening, speaking, viewing, and visually representing, in addition to reading and writing. Visually representing information can be done with students' bodies through tableaux, mime, or other body language exercises. It can be done with artistic techniques like collage, painting, or sketching; we leave those options open for teachers and students. In classrooms, teachers who promote the *play* in Shakespeare plays are not being silly—they are firing up literacy dimensions that are not strictly on the page. Student work of invention and creation, and of making meaning collaboratively, requires activity and engagement beyond silent consumption of texts.

The Globe Theatre in London is a center for professional Shakespeare productions, and their education outreach work is dedicated to the idea of learning the text through active engagement in it. As Globe Education Director Fiona Banks (2014) writes of her extensive programs with schools:

> The aim of all activities is to enable students to engage in an active process which mirrors that used by actors creating a play for performance; to put them into a

> position where they begin to experience a play from the inside as a creative in-
> terpreter—a player in all senses of the word—rather than stare at it from without.
> (p. 8)

English language arts teachers know that students need to learn to *be* writers, and arts-based pedagogy can help students *be* players in dramatic interpretations. As Banks and other theatre artists know, Shakespeare plays are enacted in countless ways. Our students can also experience interpretive choices: teachers can lead them in active theatre techniques so that students explore, rather than just receive, meanings in these complicated texts.

In addition to theatre-based opportunities for learning and developing important literacy skills, there are rich Shakespearean references and resonances in visual arts, music, and dance. All of these arts reflect an extensive history and continuing tradition of creative responses to iconic characters and scenes. We want students to experience the satisfaction of recognizing allusions and being in on the joke or aware of "hidden" meanings.

It is a well-established and valuable teaching practice to help students understand "who's who" in a Shakespeare play from the start, which draws from the performance practice of offering a dramatis personae in a playbill. And beyond listing, naming, or presenting a group of unfamiliar characters to students at the start of a unit, teachers can capitalize on student knowledge of contemporary cultural sources and skills for searching. Why not begin with students finding multiple examples of Shakespearean characters everywhere? For example, even a student's quick Google search of portrayals of the character Ophelia from *Hamlet* yields results that span centuries of artifacts. The multiple portrayals can open a robust discussion of who Ophelia is and what she wants—a central concern of the play. At the same time, the variety of creative expression can help students understand that there is no single correct perspective, and that they, too, are invited to acts of creation and interpretation.

For example, the song "Ophelia" written and performed by Natalie Merchant (1998) metaphorically depicts her character as a rebel girl, demigoddess, and even a tempest cyclone. Yet another song also entitled "Ophelia," written and performed by The Lumineers (Schultz & Fraites, 2016), describes the character's impact with similes implying she is like a drug to the singer. As a prereading strategy, students could examine this song pairing and contemplate what sort of character Ophelia might be. This could be an especially effective activity since there are conflicting interpretations in these two songs.

Beyond the references to her in popular music, there are several works of art depicting the character of Ophelia as well; perhaps, most notably, John William Waterhouse's (1894) painting shows Ophelia sitting near a pond filled with lily pads, and John Everett Millais (1852) painted Ophelia lying on her back floating in a body of water. Students can be encouraged to look for historical and contemporary images and use these to expand and interrogate their own understandings.

Beyond looking at individual characters, students can consider the choices and decisions that are embodied in different productions. Shakespearean plays may be produced in ways that represent "original practices" or avant-garde adaptations, and both ends of this spectrum can lead to useful discussion about what is the "real" Shakespeare (Banks, 2014). Sometimes, theatrical productions are available online, and film versions are widely available for most of the plays that are typically found in the secondary English curriculum. Depending on geographic location, there are often locally produced plays for field trips, interaction, and full-theatre immersion. All performances, however captured or experienced, are worthy of examination and consideration by students. In an arts-based classroom, visual arts, music, theatre, and film engage secondary students in multiple literacy modalities and invite them to join in the conversation as players and creators.

Safe Spaces

Before we describe further teaching strategies, we need to point out our assumptions about classrooms as *safe spaces* for students to explore their identities. Safe spaces require teachers to articulate some explicit norms and be consistent in their expectations. Just as teachers need to demand that interpretations are supported by evidence, they need to remind students about the power of words. Students may use lines or gestures to make inside jokes or be unkind (or worse), and then claim that they assume that everyone in the classroom knows that "we're just playing" and that their choices are "nothing personal." We have found that preservice and new teachers may need mentoring and advice to be able to experience talking about "touchy" issues in the increasingly public arena that is the classroom, and we know that veteran teachers understandably worry about controlling these discussions too. Our goal is to have all teachers feel comfortable wading into the waters of controversial subjects while empowering their students with the tools to engage in critical and reflective dialogue.

In research interviews and discussions with expert teacher Matt Seymour (now a PhD student at Ohio State University), Laura heard about his strategies for creating safe dialogue spaces with his students (Thompson & Turchi, 2016). Teaching at a charter high school, where many of his students had spent their elementary years homeschooled by their evangelical families, Matt found he had to prepare his students to not only acknowledge but also discuss difficult topics. They were studying *Much Ado about Nothing* and later *Othello*, and he did not want their understanding to be diminished because they were reluctant to name, to say nothing of express, the evil and rage, prejudice and betrayal that marked the characters they were portraying. As a teacher, Matt chose to ask the best from his students. He chose to be explicit about the challenge of enacting ugly expression and behavior. He asked his students to act as the adults that they wanted to be perceived as, demonstrating they were capable of forthright conversation, with gravity instead of being giggly or coy.

Matt believed in discussing difficult topics and acknowledged that our culture does a poor job teaching people how to have conversations about race, sex, and many other topics that are salient but taboo. His insistence that students act "serious" was an effort to get them to set aside strategies—for example, humor, anger, silence—that shielded them from the vulnerability we can all feel when discussing difficult but important topics. It becomes easier to have good discussions when the risk of openly discussing difficult topics is made explicit. He directly asked, rather than assumed, that the students be serious about the topics in the texts. For instance, he pointed out the veiled racism of Brabantio and insisted that the students recognize what was being said as well as what was being implied. Later, the class was able to discuss the overt racism of Claudio when he said he would marry Hero's cousin even if she were an "Ethiop." His classroom became a safe space because he framed the performances and conversations about the texts as serious.

In support of safe spaces, we want to encourage teachers to be serious about play. And, as we noted above, if a student is the brunt of criticism or the butt of a joke based on a role he or she agrees to play, the teacher will have to decide when a statement like "I'm not offended, we're just playing" requires commentary. Teachers can serve as role models who mediate these sorts of situations: "How do we explore what could be offensive to a peer?" "How do we effectively advocate for ourselves if we are seen as the outsiders?" Students may need support in saying lines and expressing emotions that seem alien to their lives. They also need opportunities to *know* the lines more deeply as they are helped to recognize themselves (and their peers) in socially complex situations. As a result, the teacher's role in an arts-based Shakespeare classroom may feel daunting at first, and not just for the necessary tolerance of more noise—it is play, after all. For classrooms to be safe spaces, teachers need to have the will to step forward and claim at least some of the teachable moments that will arise exactly because students are making sense of the Shakespearean text. Especially through performances and other arts-based interpretive examples, students are going to recognize the real expressions of misogyny, anti-Semitism, and unjust use of power found in Shakespeare's work. With the help of arts-based teaching, students can become more attuned to the relationships of power and status, the inequities that characters suffer or exploit, without feeling threatened about making and sharing their interpretive discoveries.

Classroom Explorations of Casting Shakespeare's Plays

As our discussion of safe spaces should make clear, while Shakespeare's plays have been around for centuries, it's important for us as educators to be aware of the contemporary context in which we are teaching, and the students who are supposed to make sense of these seemingly distant and irrelevant works. Arts-based pedagogy gives teachers and students new tools for making connections between modern lives and old texts. However, Shakespeare, so well established in the curriculum, is often taught as "universal" literature, as if Renaissance England's cultural norms—including slavery, misogyny, and anti-Semitism—were equally valid today. We argue that it is limiting, even inappropriate, to study the plays, and performances of the plays, as if we were color blind and the plays culturally neutral. English classrooms can and should incorporate student collaborative explorations of complex texts without ignoring identity: race, class, gender, ability, sexual orientation, and so on. By discussing fundamental human relationships and passions, we broaden the appeal and connection to our students.

Gloria Ladson-Billings's (1995) landmark work "But That's Just Good Teaching! The Case for Culturally Relevant Pedagogy" reminds us that our teaching needs to nurture academic success for *all* students, that our classroom activities should develop students' cultural competencies, and that students should grow in critical consciousness even as they hone their literacy skills. Representation matters, so we encourage students to consider how Shakespeare's works afford windows and mirrors into humanity over time. One way to engage our students in this reflective practice is to focus on casting choices; this serves as a scaffold that helps classrooms become culturally relevant places for all students.

Arts-based approaches to Shakespeare's plays can explicitly draw on the diversity of our students and the identities they bring and develop. When the focus is on performance, characters are no longer only on the page. Casting the players can mean discussing, analyzing, and interrogating student choices, and these are great opportunities for identity exploration. For instance, casting and performance choices can be an initial topic for individual student reflection. Students can scrutinize professional productions and interpretations and *then* articulate why they chose the portrayals that they did or felt who "was right" for different parts or best fit a particular role. Teachers may want to reflect on which students volunteer to read or play a role, or why we as teachers select particular students. For example, in Pauline's seminar, her students examined the heteronormativity in Shakespeare's story lines and pondered what would happen if we removed gender roles to present more inclusive narratives. Many Shakespeare plays include men and women hiding their identities or cross-dressing, and most students know or learn that the companies of players who initially performed Shakespeare's plays were male. Explicit teaching about casting means making these choices a topic in the classroom through taking advantage of teachable moments as well as through thoughtful instructional design.

Classroom conversations can also be about the challenges of reading Shakespeare aloud, and include the ways students group themselves and divvy up parts for informal work on scenes or preparation for performance. We advocate that teachers experiment with more deliberate and purposeful casting, sometimes with student preparation for specific roles. For example, some teachers post character names on the board and students randomly sign up for a role as they enter the classroom. While that approach might save a few moments in a forty-five-minute class, when students are struggling to understand a scene for the first time, they will not be able to read with any fluency. In contrast, a teacher can expose students to a variety of prereading activities that examine characters—backgrounds, personalities, conflicts—and have them scan the scene prior to volunteering. Similarly, students should never have only one encounter with important scenes, even if time is short. Some teachers manage multiple groups all working on the same scene at the same time, and include brief performances to allow students to see the multiple interpretations that are possible.

Preparation is important to any performance, including student preparation to read aloud or perform. Student reflections on ad hoc as well as preplanned casting decisions can thus become teachable moments worth attention and class time. Some students may feel that their choices for roles are self-evident, or they may defer to classmates who are more willing to risk being goofy or exposed in some way. The teacher can ask how these decisions reflect their understanding and their interpretation.

It may seem easier for teachers to just say that Shakespeare's roles are universal. We argue instead that casting and performance choices need to be made explicit in order for the teacher to signal that discussions about difference "are not separate from the practice of Shakespeare" (Thompson & Turchi, 2016, p. 79). When a male plays a female role, what assumptions is the class making about gender roles? Can adolescents articulate what it means to them to play an old man? What about the role of a buffoon? We ask that teachers and students become willing to take their choices seriously and take a risk, exploring, for instance, the subtle differences between caricature and character in playing a villain/victim such as Shylock. In this way, the practice and the performance of a Shakespeare play become relevant to our students. Through articulating performance choices, classrooms become better attuned to the critical literacy demands of listening and speaking in new and personally connected ways. Students can dialogue about how it feels to say specific words, perhaps in rage or sorrow. They can learn to express how speaking certain lines in different ways can draw from both what they understand about a character and who they are as individuals with complicated and valued lives. They can recognize that these same performative choices are the work of actors and directors, and, more broadly, a key component in making art.

Arts-Based Approaches to Shakespeare Plays in a Culturally Responsive Classroom

Here are five arts-based opportunities, within a Shakespeare teaching unit, wherein emphasizing choices in performance can enable adolescents to explore identity and foster their sense that the classroom is culturally responsive to their lives:

1. performance approaches for getting students started in a Shakespeare play, helping them become familiar with plot and character, and using rather than avoiding Shakespeare's language;
2. performance approaches that give students opportunities to embody key themes and explore identity and status relationships among the characters;
3. contrasting multiple productions of the play through performance choices;
4. performance choices and writing assignments; and
5. multimodal projects for creative expression.

The point here, in addition to sending a teacher in the direction of these rich arts-based strategies, is to suggest that, whatever approach a teacher chooses, there is added value if classroom activities include serious play that explores identity and connects student lives to the text (Wassermann, 1992). Arts-based pedagogy, especially theatre-based practices, offers our students processes, experiences, and skills that support their development as advanced readers and writers.

Performance Approaches for Getting Started in a Shakespeare Play

Many teachers start Shakespeare units with students throwing Shakespeare insults aloud to each other in order to practice with unexpected diction, unusual vocabulary, and the energy of a battle of words. This is a good hook for giving students confidence with language. However, teachers should probably mention that such wordplay usually has consequences, and might reveal more than a character intends. Shakespeare's characters are wittier, more provocative, more dissembling than we may be ready to teach, if we're not careful. Both the Friar and the Nurse in *Romeo and Juliet* offer the young lovers advice that is humorous and mature, and strategies that prove deadly. Everyone needs to know what is going on, and this means knowing the plot and not worrying about spoilers. Part of helping students to be in on the jokes is to make sure they have a solid understanding of the plotlines and characters in the play from the beginning. The remainder of the present section suggests several strategies for helping students develop a broad understanding of the texts.

The 30-Minute Shakespeare series produced by Nick Newlin (2015), in conjunction with the Folger Shakespeare Library (see the resources section in this book) in Washington, DC, offers texts that effectively get students out of their seats and take a familiar strategy like readers theatre and move it to the next level, adding movement and other stage directions. The script is condensed and can succinctly guide students through the whole play in a class period. Pauline used this during her seminar for undergraduate preservice teachers that focused on how Shakespeare gets taught; students had about thirty minutes to read through and rehearse and then thirty minutes to present the play. We discussed how this might play out differently with secondary students compared to undergraduates who all want to become English teachers. Secondary teachers could use such a text in a prereading strategy, giving students the broad strokes of characters, theme, and plot before expecting them to analyze the intricacies of the language in key scenes.

Another good prereading approach originated with the Royal Shakespeare Company (2012a) and its *whoosh* exercise, intended to help students know just enough about the roles they are choosing or casting, but not enough to bias them in any particular interpretation. The Royal Shakespeare Company has an excellent website for finding teaching resources online (see Royal Shakespeare Company [2013], as well as the resources section in this book). The players—ideally the whole class—stand in a large circle. The teacher reads from the synopsis. As each new character is mentioned, the next person in the circle steps forward, assuming a pose or making a gesture to represent what the teacher/narrator has just spoken about. A witch in *Macbeth* might begin to stir an imaginary pot, or a female student asked to step forward as Romeo might begin to swoon over a male Rosaline. At specific times in the synopsis, usually aligned with the ends of major scenes, the teacher says "whoosh" and clears the circle of players. She then continues the story with the next players in the circle. Notice that there is *no* casting decision or choice here: gender does not matter, nor any other aspect of how a character should be played. In fact, a teacher can highlight the circle's random assignment of players, asking students to notice how different class-mates enact the same character through their individual poses or gestures. This whoosh strategy is introductory; getting into the text itself can be an even more powerful experience after starting with a whoosh.

Another powerful performance exercise to open the study of a play has been created for *A Midsummer Night's Dream*. Master teacher Julia Perlowski of the Boston Public Schools utilizes a single speech—Egeus's rant against his daughter Helena, her rejected suitor Demetrius, and her forbidden love Lysander. One student has the speech to speak as Egeus, and she or he is surrounded by four students playing the three lovers and Theseus the Duke. Each of these play-ers creates a gesture that captures who they are as a character (pleading, brave, bold, noble). Each time Egeus says the name *or refers by pronoun* to one of the oth-ers, Egeus must point to that character. In response, the lovers or the duke must make the gesture (again and again). Students must listen and respond even when they do not have to speak. All players must know what is going on at all times. The job of the audience is to make sure all players are referred to correctly and react accordingly. The scene previews much of the dramatic conflict ahead. After multiple runs through the speech text (an important strategy in any active work), the entire class has a visual image of the multiple relationships enshrined in the play and something about the temperament of each of the characters.

Each of the above-suggested arts-based introductions to a Shakespeare play enable teachers to immediately engage their students in the characters and con-flicts of the work. From the start, students can explore ideas and experiences of identity, which will foster their sense that the classroom is responsive and relevant to their lives.

Performance Approaches Where Students Explore Status and Power

Teachers who have been trained in theatre, or enjoy improvisation games, will recognize why status play can be a meaningful, active Shakespeare strategy. A game of *status*, for which there are many variations, challenges players/students to recognize and articulate with their bodies the ways that humans respond to each other based on their perceptions of rank or power. Students might begin by brainstorming ways they feel social standing or occupational prestige are communicated. Things can really get interesting when they are assigned a status level to portray in relation to others. For example, Laura employs a deck of cards and students who are dealt kings are at the top of the social order. Those in the middle have more complex relationships to navigate. Students can see one another's status (cards) and, through silent gestures and expressive poses, some students discover they must bow to others, while others find they can sashay through the crowd and everyone else will make room. The teacher's instructional strategy here is to highlight the decisions students are making in order to portray and assert their status through movement. Then the teacher asks the players to explain themselves. Acclaimed British actor Adrian Lester (personal communication, May 2015) described working with students using a variation on the status game. He asked each student to approach an empty chair based on a level of status. Who is comfortable enough or has the status to sit down in the chair? Who kneels before it? Who sneaks up from behind? Since so many of Shakespeare's plays tackle a power dynamic among characters, this is a very useful activity for students to explore when considering casting.

These exercises are intended to give students insights into the kinds of decisions that directors and actors make in portraying a Shakespearean character. It is not unusual for students to recognize that status is an important matter in Verona and Rome and in their own cities. A teacher may be able to have students draw out connections to what they experience in their out-of-school lives and the power dynamics that may be at play in their families or among their friends. Even if individuals do not want to share or discuss in detail the parallels they see to their own lives, they may nonetheless recognize themselves depicted. Within the safe space of a classroom, this approach to studying the plays promotes affective connections to the text and supports students in meaning making that echoes their lived experiences.

Having explored relationships in this physical way, even students who proclaim they "can't act" can recognize and understand Shakespeare characters with more confidence. Teachers can reference in-class informal performances to help students tease out different interpretive options for a scene. Watching Juliet's parents announce that she will marry Paris, students can see Lord and Lady Capulet divided or united in their anger. Students can depict what it feels like to be obedient or rebellious. They can share their own aggravations and desires for independence, not necessarily by telling all, but certainly by assuming the poses and gestures that communicate these feelings, and then by explaining the choices they made to convey these emotions.

Teachers need instructional strategies that prompt their students to share, in writing or discussion, how they know what characters are feeling and which words matter most. As a result, students can feel the tensions and bonds between the cultures depicted in each play and the cultures in which they live. With a teacher's guidance, they can learn to articulate complex connections among status, power, and emotions, and use literacy skills of comparing, contrasting, and evaluating to process multiple performances.

Interrogating the Performance Choices of Multiple Productions

It is also appropriate to explore identities vicariously through interpreting the performative choices of others, just as students explored notions of status and power from a distance. Film offers tremendous opportunities for interrogating a variety of performances. Mary Ellen Dakin (2013) argues the value of film adaptations in her book *Reading Shakespeare Film First*. She points to specific scenes and film versions worthy of analysis in classrooms. Two of her suggested activities proved quite useful with preservice teachers. In the first, we look at a scene and then analyze it through literary, dramatic, and cinematic lenses. We talk about what's effective and what could be changed to reach a more inclusive audience. In the second, we take different versions of the same scene—for example, the balcony scene from *Romeo and Juliet*—in the Franco Zeffirelli (1968) version, the Baz Luhrmann (1996) version, and the musical iteration in *West Side Story* (Wise & Robbins, 1961). Students return to the literary, dramatic, and cinematic analyses, digging deeper into those particular scenes, but then we also talk about creative license. Students who have experience seeing and talking about multiple interpretations and adaptations in productions will notice and can critique with increasing confidence.

Film adaptations are a particularly helpful tool here, but films require time and access to projectors, screens, and other digital tools. Graphic novels can also provide a way to view the plays that allows for lingering over particular images. Students can look at a scene from a static image and still glean ideas about point of view, character, status, power, and setting. We find that the graphic novel adaptations of Shakespeare plays like those created by Gareth Hinds (2013) are particularly useful. *Kirkus Reviews* (2013) refers to Hinds as "director, set designer and writer," which is a helpful lens when students need to understand the art represented in a graphic novel. We can guide the conversation to consider interpretations of the original texts by asking students to reimagine the characters with varying ethnicities, abilities, or even gender preferences. Further, as Zoss (2009) argues, "to include visual art in a literacy classroom as a text for analyzing and composing is to expand literacy practices to include the multimedia of language and images that adolescents encounter in their everyday lives" (p. 188). For example, Hinds's (2013) version of *Romeo and Juliet* portrays the Montagues as African and the Capulets as Indian. Teachers and students can have powerful discussions about why Hinds made this choice. Students need to talk about how any versions of the plays represent particular choices and visions about characters and relationships, thus adding an extra layer to the rigorous reading of the play. Students can imagine and discuss what they might do as the set designer, writer, and director of a graphic novel adaptation. They can further discuss how they might illustrate the play's larger themes, such as the nature of desire, the power of fate, the burn of ambition, and the exasperations of family, in the depictions of characters and scenery. Hinds's graphic novel has been praised for adding the layer of racial identity to *Romeo and Juliet*, while film critics today are not as kind with regard to casting decisions for *West Side Story* (Wise & Robbins, 1961). *West Side Story*'s film production emphasized the dark complexions of the actors playing the Puerto Ricans by adding layers of brown makeup to Rita Moreno, for instance, despite her being from Puerto Rico. These actors all contrasted with Natalie Wood, a white woman playing the starring role as the Puerto Rican Maria/Juliet. Students might discuss why the director and film producers chose to underscore the Hollywood notions of glamour, which required that the leading female actor have pale skin. Students can further reflect on the ways they might update the contexts to illuminate their own twenty-first-century concerns.

Teachers who incorporate film and graphic novels can guide students to look for production decisions that reveal a director's vision and at the same time illustrate particular social contexts that surround a work of art. For example, a good instructional strategy is to send students to find critical or historical sources to more fully understand what has influenced a particular production. Utilizing a performance perspective on works that interpret or complement Shakespeare plays can develop student abilities to recognize and articulate artistic choices—conscious or not. With any of these suggested strategies, we hope for curiosity on the part of the student and the teacher—and we hope to avoid what Gallagher (2009) refers to as *readicide*. Put simply, readicide occurs when teachers overanalyze a text, to the point where students have disconnected from the learning. The key notion here is that the classroom remains student centered and that these extended inquiry pieces grow from classroom conversation and engagement. Students can come to understand how a work of art is situated in a cultural context, and that their interpretations and evaluations are legitimate expressions of their analyses.

Performance and Writing Choices

Where the cultural weight of centuries of study and traditions of performance can be daunting and distant, it can be a challenge to harness the power of writing processes in support of Shakespeare study. Approaching the plays through arts-based performance strategies such as those already mentioned can help. There are important parallels between writing pedagogy and performance-based Shakespeare study: writing pedagogy asks students to think of themselves as writers, consciously engaged in craft; similarly, arts-based pedagogy asks students to focus on themselves as performers and analyze characterization as a series of choices and communicative gestures. Just as making choices in writing like adding, revising, deleting, and reorganizing affect the quality of writing, students can see the impact of dramatic choices paralleled in their performance.

Student learning will need scaffolding, of course, so that they can become more sophisticated in their writing about performance choices. Teachers can use write-to-learn strategies as write-to-process-experience opportunities. Students can reflect on what it feels like to play a role, making imaginative identification with the character and the scene. This can be especially powerful as they are developing interpretations of particular speeches through writing annotations on the text. Do they know the references to other characters, to mythology or religion, to the historical context of the play? Is an extended metaphor baffling them or can it help them see the shape of a monologue? Puzzling through writing is a good way to find out. Master teacher Mari O'Meara of Eden Prairie, Minnesota, extends this discovery process with art (Thompson & Turchi, 2016). Her students choose a key *Hamlet* character and an associated monologue. The assignment asks students to edit it down, redacting all but the most important twenty words that each student believes reveals or captures who the character essentially is. Students then illustrate this new edited text, decorating it to reveal and display their understanding of the character. The students' products are an important expression of who they believe the individual characters are.

It is worth noting that this instructional strategy has students editing Shakespeare and thus focusing on the text itself. Students interpret the chosen character, but they are grounded in the words on the page. As a result, they demonstrate that they know important things about who the character is in the context of the play. At the same time, each student in effect creates a personal interpretation of the character, depicting motivations and often duplicity or other sophisticated dimensions of what someone might be, or only appear to be. Determining who can be trusted, who has integrity, or who is a scoundrel can be deeply important in our students' lives.

Multimodal Projects for Creative Expression

Making something new—creating—is a powerful expression of play. Students who make decisions about how to perform a character are making *art*. Their actions are not random, especially if their teachers have helped them believe that performances of all kinds are meaningful. Culminating projects and productions as part of the study of a Shakespearean play are important, especially if choices about casting, characterizing, and depicting through performance or artistic products include student reflections and self-assessments. Students can be deeply engaged in creative products that respond to the characters, scenes, and themes in ways that reveal their understanding of the play and of themselves.

In one school Laura studied, an assignment at the end of the Shakespeare unit asked students to create a filmed scene to reveal the connections the students made between their own lives, Shakespeare, and the contemporary world (Thompson & Turchi, 2016). This resulted in multiple variations of *Keeping Up with the ~~Kardashians~~ Athenians* as a way of translating *Midsummer*'s bickering lovers. It was interesting that Puck's magic flower juice appeared unaltered in the student videos—apparently, potions are as obviously powerful now as then. The student scenes gave much more attention to the way characters wanted to explain their feelings to each other. Students who chose to incorporate the original text had more difficulty speaking lines meaningfully, but these productions experimented with different venues indoors and out to try to capture the lovers' adventures lost in the woods.

Creativity and Assessment

Creative projects are inevitably extra work for teachers to manage, but they are so important to students' intellectual and artistic growth. Steve Seidel (2012) explains why such student creation is so important:

> Disconnecting seeing from making, as is the case so often in schools, reinforces a kind of passivity in students—their perception that the message of schooling is that you are supposed to take in what others have done but not create original work. The experience of being both a creator of valuable work as well as a critical, thoughtful audience for the work of others shifts the image of the student in his or her mind to one of an active contributor, highly engaged in the real work of a particular field, even if not quite yet at a professional level. (pp. 156–57)

Having spent a day watching those student videos, it is easy to smile at Seidel's kindness when he describes such student projects as "not quite" professional work.

What Are Reasonable Procedures and Standards for Assessing Student Creative Work?

It is important to acknowledge how ambitious students can be to re-create the rich video texts they consume daily. Especially when they work together, the students clearly have fantastic ideas—some original, others imitative—but they may not yet have the skills to match all aspects of their vision.

Good assessment strategies give students the scaffolding to more fully realize their ideas and articulate their understandings. Teachers can focus on both the dramatic qualities and the literary qualities in student productions. This means that teachers can evaluate acting, costumes, sets, camera use, and so on. And teachers can use their grading of student work to highlight places that student productions honor the original text. Formative assessments can capture choices that students are making and reinforce that these choices matter. After productions, presentations, or other performances, a rubric can emphasize a creative work's focus, supporting detail, and organization. Assessing focus asks students to share a consistent interpretive perspective on characterization, setting, costuming, etc. This focus is then developed through the details they select and the way they organize their production or creation. Students can write reflections about these choices (Thompson & Turchi, 2016). When students find ways to create work that is true to, and consistent with, their own artistic vision of a play, they have truly made the work their own.

Conclusion: Shakespeare Is on Your Side

The time and effort it takes to engage students in discussions and activities regarding performance will be valuable. Shakespeare made the case himself when he wrote, "All the world's a stage." Students get to play in safe spaces by capitalizing on performance strategies, by accessing popular culture and visual art, by focusing on the process of making art, and by examining creative productions. In today's society, we are all performing roles. Who are better drama kings and queens than adolescents? Dramatic explorations open doors for powerful and important student reflection and dialogue about identity and why and how the plays are relevant to their twenty-first-century lives.

Performance poet Kate Tempest's short film *My Shakespeare* (Royal Shakespeare Company, 2012b) offers students a dynamic tour of current idioms and common expressions attributed to the Bard. Inspired by Tempest's video example, we believe teachers can engage students in making meaning with their voices and bodies, and that Shakespeare's words can in fact come out of student mouths with powerful possibilities. We believe students can gain a palpable sense of being capable with and owning complex language through the strategies we have described here. Arts-based approaches to Shakespeare plays invite students to participate in reflection, dialogue, writing, and performances about who they are as adolescents in their own time and place—and who they might want to become.

References

Banks, F. (2014). *Creative Shakespeare: The Globe education guide to practical Shakespeare*. London, UK: Bloomsbury.

Dakin, M. E. (2013). *Reading Shakespeare film first*. Urbana, IL: National Council of Teachers of English.

Edmiston, B. (2014). *Transforming teaching and learning with active and dramatic approaches: Engaging students across the curriculum*. New York, NY: Routledge.

Eisner, E. (2002). *The arts and the creation of mind*. New Haven, CT: Yale University Press.

Gallagher, K. (2009). *Readicide: How schools are killing reading and what you can do about it*. Portland, ME: Stenhouse.

Greene, M. (1995). *Releasing the imagination: Essays on education, the arts, and social change*. San Francisco, CA: Jossey-Bass.

Hinds, G. (2013). *Romeo and Juliet*. Somerville, MA: Candlewick Press.

Kirkus Reviews. (2013, August 14). Romeo and Juliet [Review of the book *Romeo and Juliet* by G. Hinds]. *Kirkus Reviews*. Retrieved from https://www.kirkusreviews.com/book-reviews/gareth-hinds/romeo-and-juliet-hinds/

Ladson-Billings, G. (1995). But that's just good teaching! The case for culturally relevant pedagogy. *Theory into Practice, 34*(3) 159–65.

Luhrmann, B. (Director). (1996) *William Shakespeare's Romeo and Juliet* [Motion picture]. United States: Twentieth Century Fox.

Merchant, N. (1998). Ophelia. On *Ophelia* [Record]. Los Angeles, CA: Rhino/Elektra.

Millais, J. E. (1852). *Ophelia* [Painting]. London, UK: Tate. Retrieved from https://www.tate.org.uk/art/artworks/millais-ophelia-n01506

National Council of Teachers of English. (2013). *Comprehensive literacy: A policy research brief produced by the National Council of Teachers of English*. Retrieved from http://

www.ncte.org/library/NCTEFiles/Resources/Journals/CC/0223-mar2013/CC0223PolicyBrief.pdf

Newlin, N. (2015). *The 30-minute Shakespeare anthology: 18 student scenes with monologues.* Brandywine, MD: Nicolo Whimsey Press.

Royal Shakespeare Company (Producer). (2012a, May 14). Whoosh [Technique]. *Teaching Shakespeare* [Video file]. Retrieved from https://www.youtube.com/watch?v=1ANp0cbRasU&feature=youtu.be

Royal Shakespeare Company (Producer). (2012b, April 7). *My Shakespeare by Kate Tempest* [Video file]. Retrieved from https://www.youtube.com/watch?v=i_auc2Z67OM

Royal Shakespeare Company. (2013). *The RSC Shakespeare toolkit for teachers: An active approach to bringing Shakespeare's plays alive in the classroom* (Rev. ed.). London, UK: Methuen Drama.

Schmidt, P. S. (2008). *Typecasting the ideal woman: The dramatic shaping of students at an urban, all-girls' school* (Doctoral dissertation). Retrieved from ProQuest Dissertations & Theses database. (AAT 3342069)

Schultz, W., & Fraites, J. (2016). Ophelia [Recorded by The Lumineers]. On *Cleopatra* [Digital download]. Nashville, TN: Dualtone Records.

Seidel, S. (2012). "The only thing that will save us from ourselves": The arts, social engagement, and social transformation. In H. R. Kohl & T. Oppenheim (Eds.), *The muses go to school: Inspiring stories about the importance of arts in education* (pp. 147–63). New York, NY: New Press.

Thompson, A., & Turchi, L. (2016). *Teaching Shakespeare with purpose: A student-centred approach.* London, UK: Bloomsbury.

Wassermann, S. (1992). Serious play in the classroom: How messing around can win you the Nobel Prize. *Childhood Education, 68*(3), 133–39.

Waterhouse, J. W. (1894). *Ophelia* [Painting]. Retrieved from https://www.wikiart.org/en/john-william-waterhouse/ophelia-1894

Wilhelm, J. D. (2002). *Action strategies for deepening comprehension: Role plays, text structure tableaux, talking statues, and other enactment techniques that engage students with text.* New York, NY: Scholastic Professional Books.

Wilhelm, J. D., & Edmiston, B. (1998). *Imagining to learn: Inquiry, ethics, and integration through drama.* Portsmouth, NH: Heinemann.

Wise, R., & Robbins, J. (Directors). (1961). *West side story* [Motion picture]. United States: Mirisch Corporation.

Zeffirelli, F. (Director). (1968). *Romeo and Juliet* [Motion picture]. London, England: BHE Films.

Zoss, M. (2009). Visual arts and literacy. In L. Christenbury, R. Bomer, & P. Smagorinsky (Eds.), *Handbook of adolescent literacy research* (pp. 183–95). New York, NY: Guilford Press.

7

Exploring the Possibilities and Tensions of Visual Responses to Literature

ALISHA M. WHITE, *Western Illinois University*

The English language arts (ELA) curriculum focuses on a variety of content and skills, including learning how to read and write, learning through reading and writing, reading content from multiple genres, and composing in multiple genres. The twenty-first-century ELA curriculum also requires speaking and listening, and increasingly includes viewing and creating images and digital texts as integral parts of the curriculum too. In fact, Wilhelm (2004) argues that "visualizing is central to reading and to thinking with what we read" (p. 10). Visualizing strategies "heighten motivation, engagement, and enjoyment of reading," "increase the ability to elaborate on characters, scenes, actions, and ideas," and "improve a reader's ability to share, critique, and revise what has been learned with others" (Wilhelm, 2004, p. 15). While some teachers already assign, view, and evaluate student images, others want guidance in taking a first step toward integrating image-making into their curriculum. In this chapter, I introduce a literature assignment that offers students an assortment of options for using visual art to interpret texts they read, and I offer a discussion of the tensions I've experienced in implementing *arts-based curricula* (Zoss, 2009), in which teachers blend visual literacy skills and visual content with English language arts. Sample student projects from my secondary ELA and undergraduate young adult literature courses illustrate my rationale for teaching students to use creative, visual responses as a form of literary criticism and demonstrate how I experience and counter tensions in these activities.

Supporting adolescents in becoming confident, lifelong readers is an important goal of secondary educators (Gallagher, 2009; Wilhelm, Smith, & Fransen, 2014). When I was a high school English teacher, my students' parents frequently expressed frustration that their teens did not read outside of school and resisted assigned readings, while some of my students expressed frustration with the task of reading anything at all. To encourage independent reading and structure reading instruction, I implemented a reading workshop model (Atwell, 2014) as a time for pleasure reading and an opportunity to further develop reading habits and skills. Many of my students were more than just resistant to reading; they were described as having dyslexia, language-processing disorders, and attention and memory disorders, and they considered any reading a chore. To separate their prior negative experiences with reading, I wanted to remind them of a time before their frustration with academic reading. To do this, I asked them to share book talks about their favorite picture books, and I also shared my childhood favorites. This activity set a tone of play and imagination for our reading workshop (Marjanovic-Shane, 2010; Zoss & Jones, 2007).

Likewise, my young adult literature course introduces undergraduate students to a variety of genres and forms of young adult literature, and continues their understanding and application of literary theory for interpreting texts. I choose the first few novels that we read and students individually choose the last few. The topics and characters in the texts we read include a range of diversity themes, including disability and mental health, culture, race, ethnicity, gender, sexuality, and sexual orientation. For each novel, students apply a different literary theory during class discussions and compose a creative response book project.

Creative Responses to Literature: Tackling Frustration by Encouraging Play

While I wanted to encourage reading for fun and reading widely, I also needed students to take on some level of accountability for the reading they accomplished. I sought an alternative to the boring book report summaries students usually turned in (Gallagher, 2009). I wanted an assignment that prompted students' thinking about what they got out of the text—what Wilhelm et al. (2014) call *intellectual pleasure*. At the same time, I also wanted to inspire students to create something that would entertain their audience, or draw on *social pleasure*. I found a list of prompts online—"91 Ways to Respond to Literature" (Glee, n.d.)—and adapted them to fit my reading workshop for students' independent reading, selecting different writing genres and media forms (see Appendix 7A). The prompts asked students to analyze and represent story elements such as character, setting, plot, and conflict, and to consider social justice issues present in the text. Some options asked students to re-create the text in another form or medium, such as a screenplay or comic strip of a scene, while other prompts asked students to write in more traditional genres, such as letters, diaries, and editorials.

With both high school and college students, I intentionally use an assignment for responding to literature to model *arts-based learning strategies*, which are "methods for explicitly teaching the parallel pathways of visual and linguistic thinking" (Zoss, Siegesmund, & Jones Patisaul, 2010, p. 152). At the beginning of the semester, I describe my arts-based pedagogy and explain how it fits into my teaching philosophy. I introduce resources that explore visual literacy, such as *Picture This: How Pictures Work* (Bang, 2000). We read and discuss a short story and complete a drawing activity in class. I model what I look for in their responses using my own drawing as a think-aloud (Wilhelm, 2004), explaining how I represented my understanding of the story through symbols and scenes. As each student talks through their meaning of the story, I point out aspects of their drawings and statements that reflect what I expect to see in their weekly responses. During class discussions analyzing young adult literature, we talk through ideas students have for representing their interpretations of the text, and then students complete their creative responses outside class. The prompts for the creative response assignment include options for visual design, performance, and written verbal pieces (see Appendix 7A). For this chapter, I focus on the visual response prompts from the list to provide a rationale for visualizing as a literary lens, and describe each visual design option, including composing a sketch-to-stretch, a body biography, a collage, and a drawing. In addition, I show how students use annotations and labels, and the ways that I assess the quality of their work.

When students shared their literature responses with one another, the responses demonstrated connections they made in ways I had not seen previously in traditional book reports. Throughout this chapter, I illustrate how students created responses directly tied to the prompt list; however, my first example is one that shows how a student took a prompt and made it her own. It was important to me to be flexible in this assignment, allowing for engagement with books and creativity in their representations, so I encouraged students to think beyond the list of prompts provided. Students who took art class as an elective at school sometimes worked with their art teacher to brainstorm materials and construction ideas for the project. One student, Lisa, formed a wire sculpture of a hand holding white ceramic pearls to represent the main character's goals and motivation in John Steinbeck's (1947) novella *The Pearl* (see Figure 7.1). The memory of this sculpture stuck with me over the years, because I remember Lisa talking about how, at first, she thought the book was going to be boring, but she was struck by the desperation and obsessive need of the character to find the pearls. Lisa's sculpture illustrates how composing a visual representation of a book provided students with the means for exploring characters' emotions in ways a traditional book report might not. This project changed the way students read the texts and opened new discussions. I present next some of the practicalities of introducing and scaffolding the assignment.

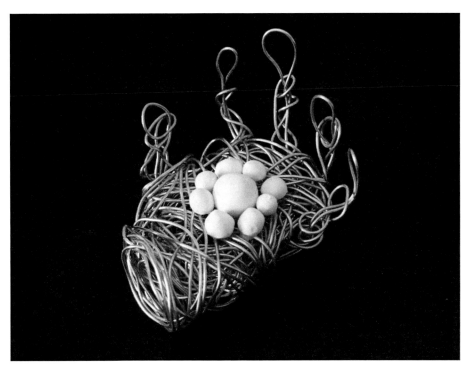

FIGURE 7.1. Lisa's wire sculpture for *The Pearl*.

Visual Responses as Differentiation: Articulating Understanding through Image

I have found that, when woven into course planning, arts-based lessons and assignments add value to students' interactions with texts. In addition to expanding students' visual literacy, including images and image-making in the ELA curriculum provides ways of differentiating instruction by allowing for multiple means of accessing content, multiple ways of demonstrating understanding, and multiple opportunities for choice and engagement, which are three critical elements of differentiated instruction (CAST, 2011; Groenke & Scherff, 2010). Integrating arts-based strategies as methods of differentiation in my English courses has included viewing images to connect to characters and setting, drawing as composition, and creative projects for showing what they learned. The creative response assignment offers choice that allows for autonomy and personal connection with material. In choosing from a variety of options, students can consider the best way to represent their interpretations of what they read and demonstrate what they learned in modes that work for them. The first visual prompt I discuss is sketch-to-stretch, with an example from Amanda. Amanda found sketch-to-stretch helped her articulate her ideas about texts because it allowed her to practice what she wanted to say about the text through drawings before saying them out loud.

Sketch-to-Stretch

Sketch-to-stretch is a method of representing one's understanding of a text through a recursive process of drawing, writing, and talking about the text (White & Zoss, 2015; Whitin, 1996). The process of moving forward and back recursively between composing in multiple modes is called *transmediation* (Suhor, 1984); for instance, translating the meaning found in a piece of artwork through talking or writing about one's impressions, or reading a story and drawing and talking about what it means. To introduce students to sketch-to-stretch, I use science fiction short stories that include vivid imagery, such as "Brandon and the Aliens" (Yolen, 1997) or "All Summer in a Day" (Bradbury, 1960/1990). Students read the story, draw initial impressions, and write about either the drawing or their understanding of the text. When sharing their pieces, they can talk about the text, their drawing, or their writing. Sketch-to-stretch is a technique that helps students visualize what they read (White, 2012) and provides a vehicle for understanding authors' use of literary elements such as tone (White & Zoss, 2015) and symbolism (Whitin, 1996). I have also found sketch-to-stretch works very well with texts that use a lot of metaphoric and figurative language, because students can explore multiple meanings of the metaphors using multiple modes for in-depth analysis. This is illustrated in Amanda's drawing and writing about symbolism found in a text.

Amanda was a student who benefited from well-designed differentiation. While she did not get formal accommodations, she described herself as having trouble focusing and needing more time to process and articulate her thoughts. Amanda created a sketch-to-stretch for Markus Zusak's (2000) novel *Fighting Ruben Wolfe* (see Figure 7.2). In the novel, two brothers set out to make money by joining an amateur boxing syndicate and eventually fight each other. Amanda composed her sketch-to-stretch in the form of a mathematical equation. Moving left to right, she wrote "Wolfe vs. Wolfe" using different colors to represent the brothers, one in light blue and the other in green, plus (+) a pair of red boxing gloves tied together in a blue bow, then equals (=) a pink heart with lips covered by a gray rectangle and a stack of $100 bills in a red circle with a red line through it. On the back of the paper, Amanda wrote about how she represented her meaning:

Wolfe vs. Wolfe—Brother = knot with boxing gloves—unbreakable bond between brothers that fight growing up and as adults, but ultimately, both = (repre-

FIGURE 7.2. Amanda's sketch-to-stretch for *Fighting Ruben Wolfe*.

sent) an unspeakable love between them. The no $ sign indicates, one, the family
has no money, so the boys fight to make money, but by the end of the novel, the
fighting is no longer about money!

Through drawing objects and symbols, Amanda represented several important aspects of the novel. The phrase "Wolfe vs. Wolfe" represents that the boys
fight each other in the ring, but also the different reactions of the boys to their
respective successes or failures in the ring. The boxing gloves knotted together
represent both that the boys are learning how to box, competing, and eventually
fight each other, but also the bond the boys have. Amanda represented the boys'
"unspeakable bond" by drawing a heart with lips covered in a gray rectangle
that I took to be tape covering a mouth. While the mouth being covered literally
means there aren't words for their love, this also represents the silences in the
text we analyzed during class discussions. Using a critical literacy lens (Lewison, Flint, & Van Sluys, 2002), we analyzed this text for power relations, class
struggles, and who was missing from the text or silenced. There were numerous
occasions when the narrator Cameron, who is the younger brother, told the reader what he was thinking, but he stopped himself from sharing these thoughts
with his brother Ruben. We discussed the restrictions society puts on boys when

it comes to expressing emotions with each other and how it impacts their relationships. The money crossed out shows Amanda's analysis of the class struggles evident in the novel, as well as the recognition that, while initially the boys compete to earn money, in the end, it's more about personal power and inner strength. Amanda used the convention of a mathematical equation to demonstrate her understanding of the text. Her analysis went beyond describing characters and plot to interpreting the author's use of symbols and the characters' growth at the end of the novel. By providing students like Amanda opportunities to represent ideas visually, teachers can differentiate the process by which students demonstrate understanding. Students transmediating abstract ideas from a text into symbols and metaphors also shows rigor in the ELA curriculum.

Overall, I saw a remarkable difference in the quality of, and interest in, the responses students produced in comparison to the one-paragraph summaries I usually received. I considered the assignment a success, yet, over the years, have heard a lot of critiques about asking students to produce visual responses to literature. These critiques came from students, parents, administrators, and colleagues. What follows is an exploration of the tensions I see in these critiques and what I have experienced myself.

Considering the Tensions in Visual Responses

While I advocate for the use of arts-based pedagogy, I also recognize that there remain skeptics regarding the appropriateness and validity of such practices in secondary English classrooms. I view the tensions in implementing visualizing as a literary analysis method as opportunities to share my experiences of the importance of arts integration and arts-based pedagogy. The tensions include perceptions of visual composing as less rigorous, arguments that images need language to explain their meaning, discussions with students who are resistant to image-making, and issues around how to assess visual responses.

"Isn't this child's play?" The Perception of Visual Responses as Less Rigorous

While I taught high school, I was occasionally questioned by parents, and even students, who viewed the creative response assignment as a fun project better left in middle school; however, most parents appreciated my goal of getting students to read for pleasure. When questioned about a perceived lack of rigor in the assignment, I used a combination of arguments about how boring traditional book reports are for students and teachers (Gallagher, 2009), and how project-based assignments provide built-in differentiation for students' varied learning needs by offering choices in how students represent their learning (Groenke & Scherff, 2010). Over the years, I have worked to develop a more nuanced rationale for my emphasis on arts-based teaching practices. One theoretical framework I cite is the cognitive model of *dual-coding theory*, which seeks to understand students who have trouble visualizing what they read and verbally expressing their mental pictures, and promotes the development of instructional methods for teaching students how to create mental pictures and verbally describe them to improve reading comprehension (Sadoski & Paivio, 2004). A sociocultural model I cite is John-Steiner's (1997) concept of *cognitive pluralism*, which describes the diversity of modes for representing one's thinking as well as expressing ideas. Understanding a variety of theories about how we make meaning from texts and express that meaning to others helps me articulate the complexity inherent in creating images as interpretation of text (White & Zoss, 2015). I continue to have conversations with those who perceive image-making as less rigorous, and hope, through sharing my own teaching experiences and research, I can highlight the possibilities for expressing meaning through images. Annie's example of a body biography (in the next section) shows how students use visual metaphors to construct and convey meaning about texts, a rigorous and complex achievement.

Body Biography

A body biography is a drawing of a person using symbols, phrases, and quotes to represent the person's physical characteristics as well as his or her personality, journey, and growth (Morawski, 2010; O'Donnell-Allen & Smagorinsky, 1999; Smagorinsky & O'Donnell-Allen, 1998). As a response to literature, the body biography provides a means for students to demonstrate understanding of a character and their experiences. Body biography is a method of literary analysis because "the placement and arrangement of visuals on a body biography indicate how carefully the readers interpreted, analyzed, and evaluated their responses to literary work" (Latrobe & Drury, 2009, p. 61.) When I view students' body biographies, I look for the symbols they draw to represent the character's experiences and inner lives and how they represent abstract ideas such as inner conflict, desires, and personal growth. Annie's body biography (Figure 7.3) illustrates the depth of understanding possible with arts-based strategies.

Annie drew a body biography of Piddy Sanchez, the main character in Meg Medina's (2014) *Yaqui Delgado Wants to Kick Your Ass*. In the novel, Piddy struggles to deal with a bully at school, which leads to feelings of anxiety and depression, as well as conflicts with her mother and friends. The drawing depicts Piddy as a girl with brown hair wearing a blue shirt, black pants, and black shoes. She

FIGURE 7.3. Annie's body biography of Piddy Sanchez.

wears a backpack with a train pass hanging on it and holds a sign with the word "Bullying" inside a red circle with a red slash through it. Annie wrote labels that point to the meanings she made from reading the text. To explain how Piddy's physical features connect to her experiences, Annie wrote: "Eyebrows: Piddy's eyebrows remain as a token from her decision" and "Hairstyle: Piddy no longer wears her hair up to look more intimidating." These statements allude to the ways Piddy altered her appearance to change the way others perceived her, with the intent of appearing menacing to drive away her bully. The items Piddy holds and carries represent her experiences, relationships, and personal characteristics. The label for the sign she holds reads "Antibullying sign: From now on, Piddy will stand up to bullying," which represents both the issue of bullying in schools and that Piddy found strength to stand up to her bully. Piddy's backpack "represents Piddy's intelligence and her final decision to transfer schools." Here, Annie demonstrated her interpretation of the character as smart and ambitious when she decided to attend a science magnet school to achieve her goal of becoming a veterinarian. Lastly, the train pass hanging from the backpack "represents Piddy's friendship with Mitzi, it remains strong." Annie uses the train pass to represent a friendship that endures despite the friend moving to another town that will require taking the train to visit her, but also the conflicts between the friends as they both grow and change. The choices Annie made in designing the body biography show elements of the plot and conflict in the novel, as well as the strategies Piddy used to deal with her conflicts. By representing both surface-level elements of the story, such as plot, and abstract elements, such as the theme of overcoming adversity, Annie's body biography demonstrates the level of literary interpretation expected in a rigorous curriculum.

Creating a body biography of a character requires students to analyze the text to determine which aspects are salient and choose objects and symbols to represent those elements. This process allows students to articulate how they interpreted the text and show connections with it. While I emphasize that drawing symbols does not require background or ability in art, some students still hesitate to take risks, feeling intimidated by any image-making experience. The next section explores how I address this tension.

"What if I can't draw?" Meeting Resistance with Flexibility

Another tension in using arts-based strategies arises when students refuse to participate, saying they are not creative or have no skill. I assure my students frequently that I focus on their expression of ideas and connections to the text. I stress that I *do* expect them to explore new media and take risks, to try new ways of articulating literary interpretations. Most students, even if uncomfortable with drawing, will at least draw stick figures or geometric shapes. On the rare occasion when students refuse to make even a stick figure drawing, I aim for flexibility in offering other, hopefully less intimidating forms of creating images, such as finding public domain images and Creative Commons images and photographs to represent their ideas. Students who are resistant to creating images by hand often describe having been teased and feeling embarrassed about their perceived lack of artistic skill early in life. For these students, I stress that a simply drawn object or symbol can express a complex idea and have multiple meanings (Smagorinsky, 2001). I use examples of how combinations of simple geometric shapes can represent quite complex ideas, such as drawing a square with a triangle on top to represent a house, which can mean both my literal living space and an abstract concept of *home*. I talk about how symbols are socially constructed, in that the meaning we make of a text is situated within our personal, cultural, and historical contexts (Smagorinsky, 2001), and how students' experimentation in symbolizing their understandings in drawings and sharing their insights could help classmates deepen their comprehension of course material (Whitin, 1996). I also explain my teaching philosophy of providing multiple modes of expression and varieties of opportunities to express understanding as a form of differentiation and accommodating student needs (CAST, 2011; Groenke & Scherff, 2010). My hope is that, by creating low-risk opportunities to experiment with formulating and expressing meaning through images, students who feel resistant will find success and increase their self-efficacy in this mode of learning. Collage is one option that exemplifies the possibilities available for image-making on the computer. In the example shown in the next section, Alexis used a collage to highlight how Malala Yousafzai used her strength to overcome a traumatic experience.

Collage

Collage is an assemblage combining multiple images or objects often overlapping one another, and can be paired with creative writing (Olshansky, 1994) and used to increase reading comprehension (Wilhelm, 2004). Collages can be constructed from paper, fabric, or other materials and can also be digital, compiled using images such as artwork, photographs, or clip art. When I introduce the collage prompt, I bring in picture books that use collage in a variety of ways to show the versatility of this medium (Myers & Myers, 1997; Novesky & Brantley-Newton, 2013). For this assignment, students compose a scene from the book or represent characters or themes found in it. The following example shows how students can capitalize on technology skills and social media for creating visual responses to nonfiction.

I chose to do a collage of quotes by Malala Yousafzai for my book response of "I Am Malala." My reasoning behind the collage is because I felt that every single one of these quotes captures Malala's message that she is trying to get across throughout her book. Essentially she is saying that, just because we are woman, we should not let that stop us from getting an education. Malala is a brave, courageous, outstanding woman who was shot by the Taliban for standing up for education. Instead of letting that tragic, horrific event silence her, Malala took that as an opportunity to speak even louder and teach others. This young woman is an amazing and inspiring woman, and I feel that her quotes are perfect ways to get her message out.

FIGURE 7.4. Alexis's collage reflection for *I Am Malala*.

Alexis read Nobel Peace Prize-winner Malala Yousafzai's memoir about her fight for women's right to education (Yousafzai & Lamb, 2015). She composed a digital collage of memes about Malala found online. Her collage has two columns with four rows of memes. Each meme has a photograph of Malala and a quote from her. Examples of the quotes are "I believe in the power of the voice of women," and "I tell my story, not because it is unique, but because it is not. It is the story of many girls." Alexis wrote about why she chose to compose a collage and why she was impressed with Malala's story (see Figure 7.4). She recognized memes as an important vehicle for spreading Malala's message. By composing a digital text, Alexis took advantage of being adept at using social media. She found the memes through search engines and her own social media accounts. She downloaded the images, inserted them, and then arranged them on a page within a word-processing document. Alexis made a collage of quotes and memes, showing that one doesn't need to have a background in art to create a visual response that represents the meaning found in a text. Collage provides an alternative for students who are hesitant to compose their own images. Another tension to consider is the relationship between image and language.

"What is the meaning of this?" Can an Image Stand Alone?

The next tension lies between my view that images can stand alone in representing meaning without the need for language, and my simultaneous need to assess how students represent the meanings they make. Critics have questioned my use of images in assessment with the argument that an image requires language to mitigate its meaning, therefore requiring a verbal explanation from its creator. Publications require captions with figures and museums post titles and descriptions with each piece in art exhibits, thus using language to point to the intended meaning. This expectation assumes that meaning is inherent in the object being observed and that, to understand the object, the viewer must know the intended meaning of its creator. In this view, students analyzing a novel are searching for the author's intended meaning, while teachers evaluating students' responses are searching for the students' intended meanings. However, in a transactional view of meaning construction, meaning is created through interactions between the reader and the text as a set of signs and is dependent on the context of the reader and the interaction (Smagorinsky, 2001). That does not assume that all meaning is relative, but that all meaning is socially constructed in a context whether the text is verbal, visual, aural, gestural, and so on. Students formulate meaning of a novel through interactions with it and associations with their culture and prior experiences, just as a teacher's interpretation of students' visual responses are formulated within the context of the teacher's culture, past experiences, and meanings she formulated for the novel (Zoss & White, 2011). That being said, the purpose of my assignment is to assess students' meaning, and there are times when I am unsure how a student's response connects to the text we read or what the student's intended meaning was. There are also times when a student creates a technically amazing image that doesn't necessarily represent the level of critical thinking I expect in an upper-level literature course, based on my viewing of the image. For these reasons, the visual prompts require students to include labels and annotations with their images to clarify their intended meaning. To illustrate this tension, I discuss Annie's illustration (Figure 7.5).

In looking at Annie's illustration of two wolves (Figure 7.5), I might associate prior knowledge of wolves or remember photographs and nature shows about wolves. I might note the drawing techniques used, such as line, shape, and proportion. However, in the context of the novel *Fighting Ruben Wolfe* (Zusak, 2000), I see much more. I consider it in light of Zusak's use of the wolf metaphor to represent the characters in the Wolfe family. So, not only do I see two wolves nuzzling, I see a representation of two brothers who care deeply for each other. However, to understand the meaning Annie made from the novel, I want to know what *she* thought about when she drew the illustration. Her written reflection of the piece states:

> I chose to draw the metaphor of the wolf pack. I drew two wolves. One wolf on the ground, and the other coming over to check on him. I drew this moment to represent the final fight scene between the two brothers. The love shared between them is clear. Even though they have been forced to fight, the older wolf refuses to "finish" the younger pup.

FIGURE 7.5. Annie's sketch for *Fighting Ruben Wolfe*.

There is one aspect of Annie's interpretation I would not have gotten with-out her written reflection, and that is the allusion to the final fight scene. In the scene, Ruben comes out with only one glove, a signal to Cameron that they will not take the fight seriously and acknowledges that winning isn't everything. When the promotor of the fight yells at Ruben to "finish him," Ruben refuses and catches Cameron as he goes down. Annie's drawing represents not only the wolf metaphor and the love between the brothers, but also the conflicts they overcame to keep their relationship. It alludes to the tension between the boys leading up to the fight and differences in how they reacted to success, failure, and ambition. With that one line, Annie has added depth to her response that I would not have known she intended without her written reflection. For this reason, even though I wish student images could stand alone, for the sake of assessing their meaning making, I ask for index labels and annotations. This tension of whether images can stand alone and how teachers interpret the meaning intended in student responses is directly related to issues of assessing students' visual responses, which I discuss next.

"How do you grade someone's artwork?" Assessing Creative Responses

Both as a high school teacher and as a university professor, I have been questioned about the subjective nature of assessing students' creative responses, in terms of both creative writing and visual compositions. There is an assumption that meaning is inherent in the text and what is important is only the intention of the piece's creator, thus the argument that it is unfair to grade works that are composed in artistic media, whether that means a poem, a drawing, or a musical composition. My reply to these queries is that I use rubrics because they both tell students what I am looking for before they begin work and help me stay focused on how well the composition represents students' understandings and ideas about the text, aligns with the assignment prompt, and demonstrates quality work. I explore these elements below, but first I share a thought on rubrics.

Gates (2017) describes the tensions between objective and subjective assessments in art education. While she writes for art educators, I believe her argument also applies to the context of ELA teachers assessing students' visual responses. Objective rubrics attempt to quantify use of vocabulary, tools, and techniques and delineate right and wrong ways of using them, which Gates critiques, saying "not all learning in the arts can be captured within such a structure" (p. 23). While there is a perception that subjective rubrics are mysterious and ambiguous, Gates argues that descriptive qualitative rubrics "provide opportunities for an educator to be transparent about her expectations, and encourage student self-reflection" (p. 26). She argues that teachers must

(1) engage in the difficult task of creating assessment instruments that assess some of the less tidy aspects of student artmaking that are nevertheless central

to learning in our discipline and (2) consider the ways in which our experience and knowledge both inform and complicate the making of subjective judgements, which are necessary and valuable in assessing art (p. 23)

as well as recognize that "knowing students is an essential aspect of assessing their work" (p. 24). The first point shows it is important not to overlook the messiness of learning, even if it is not easily listed, checked off, and numbered. In ELA classrooms, judging students' comprehension of readings and how they express their analysis and interpretation is rarely cut and dried, which leads to the second point, that assessing students' representations of analysis and interpretations of texts does require expertise in the specific text and a nuanced understanding of how adolescents make meaning of texts. This professional background, together with knowledge of and relationships with students, all goes into assessing their compositions, no matter what form they may take. While not all ELA teachers have the background to evaluate the artistic techniques used to create students' visual responses, there are some areas where quality in artistic compositions and literature response compositions overlap. In defining quality work for myself and my students, I draw on Eisner's (2002) suggestion to look at three features when assessing student artwork: "the technical quality of the work produced, the extent to which it displays an inventive use of an idea or process, and the expressive power or aesthetic quality it displays" (p. 183). I next explain the criteria in my rubric for assessing students' creative responses.

Using Rubrics to Evaluate Responses

In formulating a rubric to assess my students' book projects, I wanted to focus on both how students represent the meanings they made from the text and how they apply literary perspectives to analyze the texts (see Appendix 7B). The four criteria I look at are as follows: (1) conveys a concept of the novel, (2) shows depth of understanding, (3) follows directions, and (4) is on time/edited. The criterion for conveying a concept of the novel evaluates whether students clearly represented aspects of the text such as character, theme, setting, conflict, and plot. Aligning with Eisner's (2002) first two suggestions, I also look at technical characteristics of the response, such as how the concept is articulated with inventiveness, abstract thinking, and use of color or other principles of art and design. I emphasize to students that, while I do not expect their responses to demonstrate the expertise of someone with experience in visual art, I *do* expect them to show that time and thought were put into their construction.

The criterion for showing depth of understanding looks at how students represented their understandings of the text, illustrating expressive power in how they incorporated literary elements such as theme and conflict, represented questions of critical literacy (Lewison et al., 2002), and showed their connections and inferences. Throughout the semester, I engage students in activities to support their growth in these first two categories. For example, in discussing the novels in class, we use a three-column note format for recording what the students notice, where in the text cues are located, and what meanings students attribute to the text and their notes. They can then use these notes when composing their interpretations. The criterion for following directions looks at whether students created a response that is in line with the chosen prompt and includes required elements. While I ask students to follow the expectations expressed in the directions, there is also room for flexibility. For instance, one student took the idea of making a memory box for a character and adjusted it to her idea of painting an object the character would have put in her memory box. Allowing for flexibility within the prompts gives students opportunities to find inspiration for representations outside of the parameters I set for the assignment, frequently with surprising results. The on time/edited category awards or takes off points if the project was turned in late or was not proofread. This category reinforces the idea that the written responses in my courses require attention to detail, just like the images.

A Way Forward with Creative Responses

Eisner (2002) posits that the "arts provide a way of knowing" and "a means for exploring new possibilities" (p. 10). The purpose of the creative response assignment is not for everyone to share the same interpretation of a novel, but for students to consider the meanings they make of the text and to express their interpretations in a variety of modes. The beauty of providing choices in *how* they express literary interpretations is that I get a wider range of interpretations. Sometimes, students' responses repeat what we talked about in class or sit just at the surface of their thinking, but oftentimes students find nuances of meaning or shifts in focus that would have never occurred to me. When students come in excited about an idea of how to design their creative responses, I get excited along with them.

The creative response assignment, the visual prompts discussed in this chapter, as well as the verbal/written and performative prompts (see Appendix 7A) all offer students opportunities to explore the meaning they make from texts through media and genres beyond a traditional book report summary. The students' work samples presented here illustrate the affordances of visual art for expressing ideas and representing interpretations of a text (Eisner, 2002).

Another benefit of this flexible assignment is that it offers students choice and autonomy, building in a structure for differentiating for students' learning preferences and personal interests (CAST, 2011; Groenke & Scherff, 2010). Adding prompts that ask students to express what they visualize as they read by composing images, whether they compose the images themselves or find clip art and photographs that represent their mental images, adds opportunities to explore ideas through visual media in ways that are often missing from our schools (Eisner, 2002). However, integrating the arts is not a plug-and-play instructional model: it does require preparation and forethought to integrate image-making in a meaningful way without undercutting art as the handmaiden to English content (Eisner, 2002).

In my own work, as I continue to revamp my young adult literature course, I wanted to add creative response prompts that were specific to the books we would read. As I reread the books I had picked, I kept getting ideas for responses that I thought would be interesting and fun to create. For instance, as I read *Polly and the Pirates* by Ted Naifeh (2006), which is about a girl who finds out her mother was a famous pirate captain, I kept wondering if there were ever any female pirate captains. And, as I read *Yaqui Delgado Wants to Kick Your Ass* (Medina, 2014), I kept picturing a Latin dance club, as the narrator describes her mother's friends dancing in their living room. I added new suggestions to my prompts list that were tailored to the themes and characters in each text. I wanted projects to push students' thinking about the author's decision making, language use, and character development. What I found in doing this reflection and revision of the assignment was that students had even more enjoyment developing intriguing ideas for representing the novels. Playing on their interest in social media, students designed Twitter and Facebook profiles for characters, or they wrote "what happened next" chapters and alternate endings that were immensely creative and thought-provoking. While I have included my assignment designs with this chapter, my hope is that readers will take these ideas and expand them, considering their own students' interests and strengths, even asking students for ideas on how they would approach the task.

The tensions I shared in this chapter were based on my own experiences, and I continue to struggle with how my work answers these complex and intangible questions of the appropriateness of visual composing in secondary and college classrooms, how teachers make meaning of students' representations, encouraging resistant students to take risks, and fairly assessing how students represent their meanings in visual responses. In any educational quest such as this, there are no easy answers. No instructional method will work in every context, so each of us must mold what we learn to our individual contexts and students. However, my hope is that, by sharing how I have navigated these tensions, I can pave the way for others to feel more confident in taking on this exciting opportunity to open possibilities for students to formulate and represent the mental pictures they use to interpret texts.

Appendix 7A: Young Adult Literature Creative Response Prompts

Over the course of the semester, you will create a book response for each young adult novel we read. There are a variety of prompts listed below as options, but I would like you to explore responses from each category. Some novels will have additional options specific to the themes we discuss. No matter the type of prompt, I will be looking for how well you demonstrate your understanding of the book through *analysis* and *interpretation* with literary theory and literary elements. Each response should include your name, the title and author of the book, and the class.

Performance Responses

Choose at least two musical, film, or performance prompts. (Each should be three to four minutes of audio or video recording.)

- *Prepare a television commercial about a book.* Imagine a book is the basis for a miniseries on television. Prepare and record the television commercials that would make people want to watch it.
- *Convert the events of a story into a ballad or song.* Write the lyrics and music, or adapt words to a melody by someone else.
- *Prepare a book talk about a book.* Script and record yourself giving a book talk describing the novel in a creative way. Be sure to use aspects of storytelling to make it interesting.
- *Poetry in two voices.* Write poems in two voices for two characters in the novel, illustrating opposing viewpoints or conflicting motives.

Visual Responses

Choose at least two image-based prompts. (Each should be on quality drawing paper, at least 5" × 7" or 8" × 10", and include an annotation or index of images.)

- *Make a body biography of a character.* Create a visual interpretation of a character, including symbols to represent the character's personality, identity, life, and conflicts represented in the novel. Include an index of symbols with a short annotation of how each relates to the character.
- *Make a literary map of the author's works and life.* Use references and biographical and autobiographical materials (articles, books, interviews) to

create an informative and colorful map. Label the places and/or time-
line.

- *Be a modern artist.* Using various mediums, create a collage that comments on a particular theme or issue in the book. Write a short annotation explaining the collage or include an index of images connecting
them to the novel.

- *Compile a scrapbook or a memory box.* Choose one of the major characters in
your book, and, as that person, put together a scrapbook or memory box
of special memories and mementos. Include an index of objects with a
short description of each.

- *Sketch-to-stretch.* Create a sketch-to-stretch that includes both visual and
written compositions demonstrating your understanding of elements of
the book (character, plot, setting, conflict, themes).

Verbal Written Responses

Choose at least two written prompts. (Each should be one to two pages.)

- *Write a short playlet based on some character or event in the story.* Be sure to
provide accurate and interesting stage directions.

- *Write an editorial on some controversial issue raised by the book.*

- *Create a playlist for the novel.* List fifteen to twenty songs that you associate with the characters, plot, or themes of the novel. Annotate each song
with a short explanation of why you chose it and how it relates to the
book.

- *Quick analysis.* Using literary theory, write a two-page analysis of the
novel making claims and citing evidence from the novel to support your
interpretation.

- *Produce a wiki or website dedicated to the novel.* Include both images and
written text; maybe try music and video as well.

Adapted from "91 Ways to Respond to Literature" (Glee, n.d.) (see also Latrobe
& Drury, 2009).

Appendix 7B: Young Adult Literature Creative Response Rubric

Criteria	Level 3 (5 points)	Level 2 (3 points)	Level 1 (1 point)
Conveys a concept of the novel	A concept from the novel is clearly conveyed using the response prompt directions.	A concept from the novel is only vaguely conveyed.	The novel is not represented.
Shows depth of understanding	Goes beyond surface interpretation using literary theory and shows depth of understanding of the text.	Presents surface-level interpretation without showing depth of understanding or use of literary theory.	Presents only summary without either surface-level interpretation or in-depth interpretation using literary theory.
On time	Turned in on time in accessible format.	Turned in late or in format that is not accessible.	Not turned in at all.
Follows directions	Follows directions of the chosen prompt and includes required elements.	Follows only some of the directions of the chosen prompt or includes only some of the required elements.	Does not conform to directions of an optional prompt or include required elements of an optional prompt.

References

Atwell, N. (2014). *In the middle: New understandings about writing, reading, and learning* (3rd ed.). Portsmouth, NH: Heinemann.

Bang, M. (2000). *Picture this: How pictures work*. New York, NY: SeaStar Books.

Bradbury, R. (1990). All summer in a day. In *Classic stories 2: From "A medicine for melancholy" and "S is for space"* (pp. 97–103). New York, NY: Bantam. (Original work published 1960)

CAST. (2011). *Universal design for learning guidelines version 2.0*. Wakefield, MA: Author.

Eisner, E. W. (2002). *The arts and the creation of mind*. New Haven, CT: Yale University Press.

Gallagher, K. (2009). *Readicide: How schools are killing reading and what you can do about it*. Portland, ME: Stenhouse.

Gates, L. (2017). Embracing subjective assessment practices: Recommendations for art educators. *Art Education, 70*(1), 23–28. https://doi.org/10.1080/00043125.2017.1247565

Glee, K. (n.d.) 91 ways to respond to literature. Retrieved from http://www.angelfire.com/ok/freshenglish/bookreportideas.html

Groenke, S. L., & Scherff, L. (2010). *Teaching YA lit through differentiated instruction*. Urbana, IL: National Council of Teachers of English.

John-Steiner, V. (1997). *Notebooks of the mind: Explorations of thinking* (Rev. ed.). Oxford, UK: Oxford University Press.

Latrobe, K. H., & Drury, J. (2009). *Critical approaches to young adult literature*. New York, NY: Neal-Schuman Publishers.

Lewison, M., Flint, A. S., & Van Sluys, K. (2002). Taking on critical literacy: The journey of newcomers and novices. *Language Arts*, *79*(5), 382–92.

Marjanovic-Shane, A. (2010). From yes and no to me and you: A playful change in relationships and meanings. In M. C. Connery, V. P. John-Steiner, & A. Marjanovic-Shane (Eds.), *Vygotsky and creativity: A cultural–historical approach to play, meaning making, and the arts* (pp. 41–59). New York, NY: Peter Lang.

Medina, M. (2014). *Yaqui Delgado wants to kick your ass*. Somerville, MA: Candlewick.

Morawski, C. M. (2010). Transacting the arts of adolescent novel study: Teacher candidates embody Charlotte Doyle. *International Journal of Education & the Arts*, *11*(3), 1–19. Retrieved from http://www.ijea.org/v11n3/

Myers, W. D., & Myers, C. (1997). *Harlem*. New York, NY: Scholastic.

Naifeh, T. (2006). *Polly and the pirates* (Vol. 1). Portland, OR: Oni Press.

Novesky, A., & Brantley-Newton, V. (2013). *Mister and Lady Day: Billie Holiday and the dog who loved her*. New York, NY: Harcourt Children's Books.

O'Donnell-Allen, C., & Smagorinsky, P. (1999). Revising Ophelia: Rethinking questions of gender and power in school. *English Journal*, *88*(3), 35–42. https://doi.org/10.2307/821577

Olshansky, B. (1994). Making writing a work of art: Image-making within the writing process. *Language Arts*, *71*(5), 350–56.

Sadoski, M., & Paivio, A. (2004). A dual coding theoretical model of reading. In R. B. Ruddell & N. J. Unrau (Eds.), *Theoretical models and processes of reading* (5th ed., pp. 1329–62). Newark, DE: International Reading Association.

Smagorinsky, P. (2001). If meaning is constructed, what is it made from? Toward a cultural theory of reading. *Review of Educational Research*, *71*(1), 133–69. https://doi.org/10.3102/00346543071001133

Smagorinsky, P., & O'Donnell-Allen, C. (1998). Reading as mediated and mediating action: Composing meaning for literature through multimedia interpretive texts. *Reading Research Quarterly*, *33*(2), 198–226. https://doi.org/10.1598/RRQ.33.2.3

Steinbeck, J. (1947). *The pearl*. New York, NY: Viking Press.

Suhor, C. (1984). Towards a semiotics-based curriculum. *Journal of Curriculum Studies*, *16*(3), 247–57.

White, A. M. (2012). *Artistic frames: An arts-based study of teachers' experiences with arts-integrated English language arts for students with dis/abilities* (Doctoral dissertation). Retrieved from https://scholarworks.gsu.edu/cgi/viewcontent.cgi?article=1104&context=msit_diss

White, A. M., & Zoss, M. (2015). "It's a sad, sad story": Teaching emotional connections and tone in literature. *The Educational Forum, 79*(3), 213–29. https://doi.org/10.108 0/00131725.2015.1037513

Whitin, P. (1996). *Sketching stories, stretching minds: Responding visually to literature.* Portsmouth, NH: Heinemann.

Wilhelm, J. D. (2004). *Reading is seeing: Learning to visualize scenes, characters, ideas, and text worlds to improve comprehension and reflective reading.* New York, NY: Scholastic.

Wilhelm, J. D., Smith, M. W., & Fransen, S. (2014). *Reading unbound: Why kids need to read what they want—and why we should let them.* New York, NY: Scholastic.

Yolen, J. (1997). Brandon and the aliens. In *Twelve impossible things before breakfast* (pp. 109–23). New York, NY: Magic Carpet Books.

Yousafzai, M., & Lamb, C. (Contributor). (2015). *I am Malala: The girl who stood up for education and was shot by the Taliban.* New York, NY: Back Bay Books.

Zoss, M. (2009). Visual arts and literacy. In L. Christenbury, R. Bomer, & P. Smagorinsky (Eds.), *Handbook of adolescent literacy research* (pp. 183–96). New York, NY: Guilford Press.

Zoss, M., & Jones, S. (2007). Enhancing literary reading through visual and language arts practices. In A. O. Soter, M. Faust, & T. Rogers (Eds.), *Interpretive play: Using critical perspectives to teach young adult literature* (pp. 191–209). Norwood, MA: Christopher-Gordon.

Zoss, M., Siegesmund, R., & Jones Patisaul, S. (2010). Seeing, writing, and drawing the intangible: Teaching with multiple literacies. In P. Albers & J. Sanders (Eds.), *Literacies, the arts, and multimodality* (pp. 136–56). Urbana, IL: National Council of Teachers of English.

Zoss, M., & White, A. M. (2011). Finding "my kind of teaching": How a drama project became a teacher's expressive teaching moment. *English in Education, 45*(2), 161–75. https://doi.org/10.1111/j.1754-8845.2011.01

Zusak, M. (2000). *Fighting Ruben Wolfe.* New York, NY: Scholastic.

Using Artistic Response Strategies Meaningfully in the English Language Arts Classroom

8

PAMELA M. HARTMAN, *Ball State University*

JESSICA BERG, *Franklin Central High School*

BRANDON SCHULER, *R. J. Baskett Middle School*

ERIN KNAUER, *Whiteland Community High School*

While using artistic response in the English language arts (ELA) classroom has been shown to increase students' comprehension and engagement (Bustle, 2004; Chicola & Smith, 2005; Grant, Hutchinson, Hornsby, & Brooke, 2008; Holdren, 2012; Marshall, 2008; Miller & Hopper, 2010), many teachers struggle to create meaningful activities and projects that utilize artistic response effectively. By *artistic response,* we mean the process by which readers create concrete representations of their transactions with a text through artistic means, including visual arts (e.g., drawing, sculpture, and painting), drama, and music. In this chapter, we provide several examples of workable and meaningful artistic response activities, along with discussions about the factors that teachers need to take into account when designing or adapting activities for their own classrooms.

Perhaps the most important elements to consider when discussing the use of artistic response are why it works and how it works. Literacy researcher and theorist Louise Rosenblatt (1978) argues that "the benefits of literature can emerge only from creative activity on the part of the reader himself" in what she describes as a *transaction* (p. 276). This "creative activity" requires the reader to control the reading and to activate ideas, emotions, and images to perform this transaction with the text. Thus, both the reader and the text play a vital role in the meaning-making process. We know that this engagement must happen in a relevant, personal manner in order for students to make meaning from these texts. In other words, as readers interact and construct meaning with the text, they must draw from their own pool of knowledge and experiences while taking cues from the text.

According to Rosenblatt (1978), the reader's engagement with the text should be regarded as an event or experience that becomes a part of the reader's overall life experience. Unless the reader can "crystallize" the experience of the story—that is, make it real, substantial, and lasting—using a combination of their own background knowledge, present personality, and the guidance of the text, their transaction with the text will not be meaningful or impact their lives in any significant way. Without a meaningful transaction with the text, the reader will likely forget the reading without learning or growing as a person or reader. Our position is that the artistic responses described in this chapter provide concrete opportunities to help students transact with texts and make their reading experiences real and tangible.

In *"You Gotta BE the Book,"* Jeffrey Wilhelm (2008) supports and applies Rosenblatt's transactional theory in his list of *dimensions of response*. These ten dimensions fall into three categories: (1) evocative, (2) connective, and (3) reflective. The evocative dimension, as the name implies, involves the reader's ability to evoke the story world—to enter and explore it, to relate to the characters, and to enjoy the story. Wilhelm asserts that the evocative dimension is often overlooked or even devalued by classroom teachers in favor of the two other categories of response. These connective and reflective responses include the kind of response activities teachers ask students to do on a daily basis, such as answering comprehension questions, picking apart literary conventions, and writing essays about such traditional literary elements as theme and plot. Without doing evocative work, connective and reflective response are compromised. If we would like students to do the connective and reflective work we want to see in summative assessments, we must remember to help them do evocative work first. Artistic responses are just the sort of work that encourages students to enter, explore, and enjoy stories and characters.

We should also keep in mind artistic response's intrinsic value as a tool to help students enjoy literature and the language arts. The standardization and current testing culture of education can sometimes persuade us to hurry through artistic response activities, to implement them as a filler, or to neglect them completely. We must resist these urges, not only because artistic response is crucial for students' engagement with text, but also because we risk distancing students from the very field we are trying to help them to understand. Rosenblatt (2005) argues that, in many cases, students learn not to embrace literature from their ELA education, but instead to avoid it. They learn that "literature" or the texts that they read in the ELA classroom are only appropriate in school contexts and for certain purposes. The result, unfortunately, is that students are not so much invited into the world of literature as much as they are held captive at the door, answering an endless stream of questions to pass tests they don't care about. Rather than becoming enablers or patrons of their literary journeys, we unintentionally become gatekeepers.

To prepare our students for life beyond tests and to become lifelong readers and learners, it is important that we teach them how to establish effective and powerful transactions with texts. Artistic response is one way to assist them in achieving this goal. Knowing how and why artistic response works can help us design and implement strategies thoughtfully and responsibly. With those goals in mind, we have concluded the following about designing and implementing artistic response strategies: (a) effective artistic response activities, like all classroom activities, should be designed specifically to activate higher-order thinking skills and to support, strengthen, and deepen students' exploration of enduring understandings; (b) ownership and choice are important elements of artistic response because they allow students to explore concepts and solidify their vision of story worlds in a personal way; and (c) teachers should provide multiple models so that students don't think that there is one correct way to produce a final product. If students are communicating their transaction with the text through their response and demonstrating their mastery of relevant concepts, they should be allowed to explore the text through a method that fits them best. Understanding how to adapt and imagine new, high-quality artistic response strategies can help us meet the needs of students and objectives as they change or evolve.

In the sections that follow, we provide examples of strategies that we believe demonstrate careful and strategic use of artistic response: *character portraits, character mirrors*, and *character soles*. By explaining the strategies' potential uses and discussing the logic guiding their design, we hope to clarify what we mean by responses that activate higher-order thinking skills and allow students to evoke, visualize, and crystallize a story. We also hope that teachers will feel empowered to adapt these examples for their own classrooms, or to simply use them as inspiration to design their own artistic response activities that fit their needs and the needs of their students. Our examples are by no means exhaustive with respect to the forms artistic response might take. Instead, we hope that they help further the understanding of artistic responses and that they prove useful to educators who want to incorporate artistic response into their classrooms.

Character Portrait

Inspired by the infamous portrait described in the nineteenth-century work *The Picture of Dorian Gray* (Wilde, 1890/2003), this activity—character portrait—involves recording the internal change of a character over the course of a novel. Starting with an initial representation of a character, students create a series of images to represent that character at critical points in a work. These images can demonstrate a character's change or development through a variety of means, and they can help the student reflect on the character and the author's choices in creating the character. The process of creating the images can help students personalize the character's journey, a necessary step in creating the transaction Rosenblatt (1978) discusses, and one that can also help support students in evoking and exploring the story world by providing them with visuals (Wilhelm, 2008).

In our specific example (see Figures 8.1–8.3), we, as a group of educators, explored the development of the main character Melinda from the novel *Speak* by Laurie Halse Anderson (1999). Instead of illustrating the character's physical appearance literally, we used a more figurative means to show her character growth by representing her as a tree, an important recurring symbol in the book. For the initial image (Figure 8.1), we focused on Melinda at the beginning of the book and drew the image on a sketchpad with a marker and colored pencils. The first image of the tree is dark, gray, and dormant. This image is meant to show Melinda, at the onset of the novel, as deeply depressed, isolated, and passive.

The next images symbolize several critical moments (or turning points) throughout the novel that best represent Melinda's development. To create these images, we layered translucent tracing paper over the original image

and used its shape and outline as a base to add new details to represent the character's development. This layering shows the character's continuous development as a coherent whole. For example, when Melinda's only friend gave her a note ending their friendship, Melinda goes through a period of distress and desperation. We represented this development by incorporating red into the image on that layer and using rougher and harsher shapes than those used for the previous image (Figure 8.2).

Throughout this process, the first image of the tree that represented Melinda remained the base of these drawings, emphasizing the connection between the character at the start and end of the book. For a character like Melinda, whose growth is difficult and painful, this layering can help students better visualize and empathize with the fact that recovery is possible even after devastating

FIGURE 8.1. Character portrait of Melinda at the beginning of *Speak*.

FIGURE 8.2. Character portrait of Melinda's continuing development in *Speak*.

FIGURE 8.3. Final character portrait of Melinda in *Speak*.

traumas. The artistic representation also makes it clear that past hardships do not disappear; they become part of who the character is—a lesson that students can relate to their own lives and struggles.

In making this drawing, we found that thinking of the character and creating visuals that were grounded firmly in specific events that happened in the novel was an excellent way of making the character's journey concrete and memorable. In terms of Rosenblatt's (1978) emphasis on fixing the work as an experience in the mind of the reader, this exercise was successful in connecting important events of the novel and highlighting their effects, both short and long term, on the character. This strategy is especially effective since it requires students to deliberate on and decide which of the events in the book affect the character the most. It requires the reader to step back from the story, process everything that happened, and make judgment calls, which compels them to use the higher-order thinking skills of analysis and evaluation. The character's journey and growth is also emphasized through the creation of images that represent it, which can help students gain greater empathy for characters and their hardships—an important step in helping them evoke the story world and proceed to other connective and reflective tasks (Wilhelm, 2008).

In terms of the challenges and difficulties in using this strategy in the classroom, teachers should keep in mind that this type of task likely would not work well with shorter texts or with characters who do not experience significant, long-term growth. For instance, the main character, Louise Mallard, in "The Story of an Hour" by Kate Chopin (1894/2001) may initially seem like an ideal candidate for this kind of activity, but, upon closer inspection, this short text might not prove to be the best fit for this strategy. In the story, Mrs. Mallard is informed of her husband's death and, after her initial grief, slowly reveals her secret desire for freedom from social and marital obligations, which could now actually be available to her through the death of her husband. When her husband then walks through the door, alive and well, the shock and implied anguish from losing this new freedom literally kills her. This kind of change in character may seem to provide a basis for the character portrait artistic response we described. However, we argue that, because the story is so short and the change so obvious and radical, constructing several images to show the changes would not encourage higher-order thinking skills in the same way that a different and more appropriate response activity could. If the teacher is the one choosing the text for a unit, they should be sure that the characters exhibit the kind of significant, long-term, and gradual growth that would require students to do the meaningful cognitive work of choosing important events that impact the character and deciding how to best represent the character's growth or changes in their images. Likewise, if the students are the ones choosing their texts or characters, some guidance should be offered about what kind of character to choose, and why they should select one that can be successfully represented as changing throughout the novel.

Another point of concern in regard to this strategy relates to choosing artistic materials. For us, using tracing paper worked well, but, if features of the character do not expand upon previous features—that is, if some element of the previous image must be removed in the next image—tracing paper would not be ideal. All aspects of the previous images are visible in future images when using a material like tracing paper. Perhaps the easiest way to adapt or modify this activity to accommodate different contexts and student responses would be to make a series of images that are drawn separately. We suggest that teachers experiment with the ways they might adapt this aspect of the project. They could encourage students to strategically use construction paper to build upon, alter, or reimagine the previous image, making it into more of a multilayered paper-craft piece of art, or they could allow students to use digital media to layer images. The material element of this project may be one of the most challenging for teachers, but multiple possibilities exist that would be just as successful as our own response proved to be.

This artistic response strategy can be adapted in a variety of other ways, especially if students are given a level of choice in forming their response. For instance, based on the story they read and how they read it, students could be invited to decide whether a figurative or symbolic representation of the character would be more appropriate than a literal rendering of their character's physical appearance. Allowing students to choose how best to represent their chosen character would most likely create an adaptation appropriate for the needs of that student and the text they are exploring. For instance, our students have chosen to create their representation through a collage, storyboard format, and diorama where each image represents a different stage in a character's life.

No matter what form the students' artistic responses take, teachers can assess their students' mastery of relevant concepts and skills being taught. For instance, when using this activity, teachers could assess students' abilities to form a cohesive and well-supported argument, to analyze a character's development, to use both images and text in ways that work together to communicate an idea and persuade their audience, and to engage their audience. It is often helpful for teachers to construct a rubric, in advance, to consider what skills and knowledge they want to focus on and assess (in Appendix 8, we provide a sample rubric that could be modified in accordance to the needs of the teacher). In addition, when provided with a rubric, students will better understand the purpose of the activity.

Students could begin this project after they have read the entire novel, which may help them recall important events, make connections, and solidify the work in their minds. They could also make sketches as they read as visual checkpoints representing their thinking at key points in their reading, and the students could reflect, either in groups or in writing, on the reasoning behind the choices they make. Even if the images do not directly build on each other in this adaptation, they can provide a visual for students to examine how they saw the character differently at various points in the novel as well as analyze if and how the character developed. At the end of the novel, the students could then analyze all the images they have made over the course of the novel and attempt to create a representation that synthesizes their interpretations into a single, unified image. This image could be used to initiate discussions about authorial intent as well as to crystallize the student's transaction with the text and characters. In fact, this adaptation of the character portrait artistic response strategy helped us to envision our next strategy, the character mirror.

Character Mirror

The idea of the character mirror strategy was first conceived as an adaptation of the character portrait response. We decided to separate them into two sections in order to emphasize how altering a response task can dramatically change the way we interact with texts. Unlike the character portrait response, which looks at a character over the course of an entire text and seeks to explore their development, the character mirror response focuses more on a character's nature—personality, desires, and fears. The character mirror strategy was inspired by the "Mirror of Erised," the magical mirror from J. K. Rowling's (1997) *Harry Potter and the Philosopher's Stone* that reflects a person's innermost desire to them. The goal of this strategy is for each student to understand the characters, their motivations, vital traits, treasured possessions or relationships, and strengths or weaknesses. It works best when the reader focuses on the character's point of view rather than the point of view of an objective observer.

The character mirror strategy requires students to draw a "reflection" of the character standing in front of a mirror. The drawing can contain only the mirror and the reflection, or, as with the Mirror of Erised (Rowling, 1997), it can also include the character standing in front of the mirror. The teacher can provide a specific question for the students to respond to, such as "What does this character desire most?" or "What would be the character's ideal future?" The students can also choose to come up with their own question or concept, such as the character's worst fears, the character's greatest hopes, or the character's best qualities. To complete the task, the students must turn to the text and put themselves in the mind of the character to better understand the character's intentions, motivations, personality, and relationships with other characters. Through this process, students both gain empathy for the character and learn to discover textual clues to help them infer subtle or unstated aspects of the character. Doing this creative work helps students to crystallize the character in their own minds, and it prepares them to do other complex thinking, such as examining authorial intent and how the author's choices in craft bring the character together and pace their characterization.

To further emphasize how the character mirror strategy can create a different kind of response from those of the character portrait, the character mirror can also feature treasured possessions, important relationships, or idealized scenes that may not exist in the actual text. This is different from the character portrait, which is focused on the character at specific points in time within the actual text. In contrast, the character mirror strategy encourages students to take more creative liberties with the text, providing room for inference or speculation. Thus, this activity supports not only the transaction between reader and text, but also higher-order thinking.

Another way that the character mirror strategy inspires different interactions with the text and with the characters can be illustrated through our application of it to Chopin's (1894/2001) "The Story of an Hour." While earlier we argued that the character portrait strategy would not work well for this story or other similar short stories, the character mirror strategy would be effective in scaffolding a lesson on characterization using abbreviated texts.

For example, in one eighth-grade English classroom, we implemented this strategy after the students had read "The Story of an Hour" (Chopin, 1894/2001). Students were asked to examine Mrs. Mallard and her internal conflicts throughout the story. We asked the question, "If Mrs. Mallard had looked into this magic mirror, what would her reflection have shown?" We then instructed students to draw a representation of this reflection. The final products were quite different from one another. For instance, even though two students chose to draw Louise in the moments after she learned of her husband's supposed death, they chose completely different symbols, and those symbols uncovered how their thinking varied and even, perhaps, how they contradicted each other. The first student chose to represent Louise's emotional journey through masks (see Figure 8.4).

She explained in a written reflection that "Louise is holding a mask of herself crying, while she is smiling behind it. I drew this because I thought that Louise was confused about how to feel during her husband's death. She's happy because she's free, but she's sad because her husband died." This student's drawing focused on her belief that Louise held conflicted feelings about her situation and her husband's death.

The second student drew a bird to represent Louise, a chain to represent Louise's emotional attachment, and two versions of a birdcage to represent the marriage (Figure 8.5). She explained, "I drew the cage's door open, the chains broken, and a reflection of the cage broken in half that represented Louise's new-found freedom within her husband's death. She no longer had to have her husband controlling her and how she lived, she had 'broken free' into a new

FIGURE 8.4. Character mirror of Louise with a mask from "The Story of an Hour."

FIGURE 8.5. Character mirror of Louise as a bird from "The Story of an Hour."

life." She indicated in class that the two cages represented different realities about the marriage. The first cage shows how Louise sees her marriage—as a cage, but one that is necessary. However, she said the cage is not necessarily the problem in this case; the problem may be the husband, which she represented through chains. These chains were holding her in the cage and had to be broken in order for the character to be free. The second image shows a cage that is less visible and already broken in half. This broken cage representing marriage shows that it is a broken institution—one that Louise should have been able to recognize and maybe had support to escape from. Interestingly, these ideas on marriage align with Chopin's (1894/2001) themes, both in this story and other writings. This drawing, and the student's thinking, could be used as a catalyst for discussing these themes.

Both the character portrait and character mirror strategies could be used separately to help students develop the skills, tools, strategies, and procedures involved when analyzing texts and characters. These strategies also could be combined to scaffold students' ability to apply that knowledge to a new kind of task and to build on it. For example, the character mirror could be used at an early point in a text to facilitate students' understandings of a character or character's perspective. This could be followed by the character portrait strategy, which could be used to explore a character's changes throughout the text, and it still could be used at the end of a text to synthesize all of the individual impressions of the character into one unified vision that represents the reader's overall impression of the author's intent. Through the combination of the two strategies, students would learn how to (a) pay attention to important aspects of characterization, (b) analyze and evaluate these aspects, (c) follow the character's development throughout the text, and (d) come to their own conclusion about both the character's actions and the author's narrative choices. The focus, through the whole process, is the development of important reading skills and the thinking that allows students to use these skills productively. As we discussed earlier, teachers should be clear about the intentions of their teaching and the knowledge and skills that they wish students to develop.

In this way, they will be better able to develop and implement artistic response strategies and to assess students' learning.

When teaching the character mirror strategy, particularly when used without something like the character portrait strategy, it is important to remember that students may take too much creative liberty with their interpretation of the character and forget to return to the text for evidence to support their interpretation. Students may overemphasize a character trait or conflict that they find particularly relatable, or they may distance themselves from a trait or conflict they find distasteful or troubling. This can especially be true if students have forged personal connections with the characters. Although this difficulty may seem problematic from a teaching standpoint, it may actually create the exigency for a number of productive conversations about both academic and humanistic topics, such as the importance of close reading or the power of fiction to help us to better "read" ourselves and the world (Applebee, 1996; Freire & Macedo, 1987; Rosenblatt, 1978). We suggest that, should a teacher choose to use this or other artistic strategies that encourage empathy with a particular character, the teacher can be ready and willing to interact with the more personal elements in the response as well as the academic elements in order to meet the emotional needs of the students alongside their cognitive or academic needs.

Another issue that might affect teachers' use of this strategy as well as the character portrait strategy might be student anxiety relating to their artistic ability. Some students may shy away from this kind of response if they feel they are expected to draw everything entirely by hand. This might be particularly true if they are attempting to portray the complex nature of the scene as they envision it. Teachers may alleviate some of the students' anxiety by providing a variety of materials for the students to manipulate into a collage or other multimedia form of response. Such materials could include magazines, newspapers, and found objects like scraps of cloth and beads. Students can also benefit from access to digital tools and the internet. By giving students choice in how they create their image, they will think more creatively, feel more ownership in their product, and, hopefully, feel less anxiety in using the strategy.

Character Soles

The last artistic response strategy we developed is character soles. This strategy was inspired by the trend of drawing on white canvas tennis shoes, and involves students illustrating their thinking about a story directly onto a single shoe or pair of shoes. These illustrations may include visual representations of rhetorical devices used by the author, such as symbolism and theme; important story elements and scenes; and portraits of characters. Students are also encouraged to integrate key phrases and short quotations as part of the illustration.

One of our first considerations when developing and implementing this strategy was the fact that not every student enters the classroom with funds to buy an additional pair of tennis shoes. When we used this strategy, we encouraged students to share the expense with a friend so that each had one shoe. We found that the one shoe allowance made more students keen on the idea. For those students who did work on two shoes, we asked that they brainstorm ways of connecting the two. For instance, one shoe might represent the author while the other focuses on a main character, which can help students think about authorial intent. One shoe might represent the beginning of the story or the main character at the onset of the novel, while the other shoe represents either the resolution or the character's changed state at the end of the novel, in a way similar to the character portrait strategy. Because of the multitude of possibilities, this strategy is easy to adapt to different needs and contexts or to combine with other strategy ideas to introduce a new kind of thinking.

The character soles strategy is effective in helping students understand the importance of theme, plot structure, and use of rhetorical devices and literary terms as they relate to a work, in part because the shoes are designed for a peer audience. Unlike the other response strategies we've discussed, the character soles activity produces a wearable product that students can incorporate into their daily lives. Knowing this, we pitched the idea of the shoes as an advertisement for the novel they depict, and we encouraged students to consider their audience when choosing their designs. At the same time, we reinforced their knowledge about theme, plot structure, and literary devices as a means of thinking about their novels and making artistic choices with their shoes. Because one of the goals of the finished products was to interest others in the novel, the students were encouraged to choose images, quotations, and scenes that were both interesting to the audience and significant in terms of plot, themes, or literary merit. We also felt that the shoes provided a unique means for students to reflect on and share their experience of the novel with others. We stressed that whatever a student enjoyed in their reading of the novel (i.e., whatever grabbed them and caused them to begin a transaction, as described by Rosenblatt, 1978) should be something they should highlight in their creative response, so that peers would be similarly drawn to the novel. As mentioned in our introduction to this chapter, accomplishing any of these tasks successfully requires students to use their knowledge to evaluate the novel, and the strategy served as a scaffold to lead them from the evocative into the connective and reflective dimensions of reading (Wilhelm, 2008).

Another way the character soles strategy can be implemented is through the empathy-building symbolism inherent in the phrase "to walk in someone else's shoes." In this version of the strategy, students may focus on the motivations or internal life of a character, and their designs on the shoes figuratively represent their attempt to walk in the character's shoes. This take on the strategy can create a response and inspire thinking in a way similar to the character mirror strategy, but with a stronger emphasis on the student's connection with and reading of the character.

The character soles strategy is useful because it can be implemented in many different ways while still inspiring higher-order thinking skills, and we found that students can make the choice regarding how they want to use the strategy. For instance, with this response, the students can make any of the following decisions to fit their own needs: "Will you complete a pair, or just one shoe?" "Will the shoes be themed?" "Will they fit together in some way, like friendship necklaces?" "Is one focusing on the author while the other covers a main character?" "Is one shoe inspired by the film version of the novel, so the pair analyzes their differences somehow?" When we implemented the strategy, we began by providing students books to choose from and allowing them to pick any science fiction novel they wanted to read. We also offered a variety of choice in what and how they represented their novel on the shoe. We found that this method worked well and gave students ownership over their shoes, which is an important consideration since they would be the ones wearing them.

Because of the amount of choice we offered to students, we had them write a rationale to explain why they chose their particular response to best represent or advertise their novel and to defend the artistic choices they made in creating the product. This additional component solidified much of the thought process for students and incorporated a level of metacognition into the task. We knew this expectation required models as well, so a fellow teacher, Jordan Kubaszyk, created a model for our lesson (see Figures 8.6 and 8.7), focusing on *The Silence of the Lambs* (Harris, 1998). Discussing the model, using it as a springboard for a whole class discussion, and dissecting the elements of the shoe designs helped encourage students who were at first daunted. Through these discussions, we modeled the thought process we hoped students would have, including the higher-order thinking skills they would use while working. We wanted to be sure that their drawings, quotes, themes, and so on were purposeful and carefully selected. Along with models, teachers can provide students with a rubric, which might further clarify what is being learned through the activity and the level of mastery they should achieve.

FIGURE 8.6. Character sole for Hannibal Lecter from *Silence of the Lambs.*

FIGURE 8.7. Character sole for Catherine Martin from *Silence of the Lambs.*

A gallery walk after students completed the task made the audience real and relevant for the students, which further helped them to think critically about the presentation of their ideas. Student work benefited from the knowledge that peers would also be providing feedback and seeing their final products. We believe that this gallery walk also cemented the connection between the character soles response and the idea of a book talk. Most students agreed that they enjoyed being able to see the shoes and the rationales and walked away with a couple of books they wanted to read next. Students also agreed that it was obvious when someone had not read their entire book, saying that "there wasn't much detail in their reason." For some students, this realization may help them understand why the work of reading and the effort of completing their responses thoroughly are important to performing well academically.

An important point to keep in mind when implementing this strategy or others like it, particularly strategies that create an object that the students might use or incorporate into their lives, is that ownership is important for student engagement. A student may be more invested in an object that they might want to wear or display. For this reason, choice is especially important for this kind of strategy. Whether the students are making shoes, T-shirts, or other usable objects, the teacher should allow them to personalize their response when creating their product so that they feel ownership and pride in their work. The authenticity of the task is, in part, connected to the use of the product; if the students think that they will not use the item, the audience for the task will be lost and so too the exigency of creating the product for that audience. At the same time, the thinking processes that are at the center of this artistic response should remain the core focus of the strategy. A careful balance between the teacher's goals and the students' must be struck for this strategy to meet its optimal potential.

Conclusion

The strategies we've described are only an introduction to artistic response. Understanding how and why a strategy works is key to its success. All artistic response activities should support classroom goals and objectives, scaffold student thinking, and foster the development of creative attitudes and skills that successful readers use, and not just appear to be fun and engaging at a surface level. All our artistic responses include rationales and reflections that express skills and strategies we meant to scaffold. We feel that these discussions are the most critical part of this chapter, because, when we create artistic response strategies, we strive to understand the theories and goals behind the response well enough that we can articulate them to students, parents, administrators, and other teachers. This measure pushes us to ensure that we have accomplished the kind of thinking necessary to create an appropriately rigorous artistic response strategy. In addition, teachers must reflect on the strategies after they implement them in the classroom to check that the goals of the strategy have been met. This reflective activity is critical to the long-term success of teaching these strategies. Teachers should not be afraid to adjust any strategies to fit the changing needs of their own classrooms and student populations.

Teachers interested in developing and implementing their own artistic response strategies should also keep in mind the following:

- Students should not feel that their artistic or creative ability is the focus of evaluation, and teachers should not evaluate based only on criteria such as artistic talent or completion. Asking students to accompany the artistic response strategy with an artist rationale or reflection is a good way to ensure that teachers are evaluating student thinking as much as possible and that students know they are not being graded solely on their artistic ability. Student–teacher conferences, gallery walks, and peer or self-evaluations are also possible means of assessment that allow students to discuss their thinking and defend their choices effectively.

- Providing choice is often key to success. Students who can choose the best way to interact with the text are more likely to create an authentic response that helps to make their reading a meaningful experience. Since our goal in creating artistic response strategies involves helping students to complete a transaction and to crystallize their reading, we should not underestimate the value of allowing them choice and ownership whenever possible.

- For each strategy, both models and modeling are necessary to solidify students' understanding of the task and the kind of thinking necessary to create a successful transaction with the text. Modeling the thinking process behind the creation of an example in particular can help students with their focus on the process as much as their final product. Showing students some possible forms their response might take is also much more helpful than trying to describe the task on a handout, and students can use the models to get different ideas for how they may approach their response.

- Planning and implementing effective artistic response activities is a time commitment for teachers both before and during implementation in the classroom. Although this commitment might be a concern for teachers who are worried about working through a curriculum or overwhelmed by high-stakes testing, the outcome of using artistic response strategies is worth the time and effort. We encourage teachers not to give up if students initially need a little extra time and instruction in order to adopt the kind of rigorous thinking needed for the strategies, especially if they have not had much classroom experience with artistic response in the past. Over time, we hope students will use artistic response strategies with more confidence and more independence.

We have only scratched the surface of potential response strategies. We have demonstrated how inspiration can be found in many places; our strategies were inspired by literature and popular culture, and these are only some of the many places teachers can find ideas. We encourage teachers to examine their lives and the lives of their students for ideas when thinking of new strategies to create. Teachers might conceptualize new response strategies by considering how common objects can be manipulated in interesting ways or how the environment of the classroom can be utilized. In addition, while most of our example strategies largely focus on character, similar strategies can focus on other literary elements depending on the teacher's goals. As long as teachers are seeking to help students transact with texts, experimenting with ideas can prove productive. Our imagination is our ally. Just as our response strategies aim to help students apply new ways of thinking to their reading, we can test the limits of our own creativity in constructing response strategies for our classrooms.

Appendix 8: Character Portrait Rubric

	Excellent	Good	Fair	Unsatisfactory
Focus of design and argument	Images and text effectively unify the project around a central idea; uses convincing evidence to support a coherent and persuasive analysis of a character.	Images and text organize examples around a central idea; uses relevant evidence to support a coherent analysis of a character.	Has a central controlling idea; uses some relevant evidence in the analysis of a character.	Lacks controlling idea and/or contains little or no evidence presented to support the analysis of a character.
Validity of interpretation	Shows insight about the character and makes strong connections. May present original ideas and a new understanding.	Shows a reasonable understanding of the character and makes appropriate connections, recognizing patterns of characterization.	Makes some attempt to show an understanding of the character, but shows few connections or a recognition of patterns of characterization.	Provides little or no interpretation of the character or uses faulty analysis.
Integration of textual and visual features	Both textual and visual elements are present and work together to contribute to strong communication and persuasion.	Both textual and visual elements are present and work together to contribute to communication and persuasion.	Both textual and visual elements are present and somewhat work together to contribute to communication and persuasion.	Visual or textual elements may not be present and/or do not work together to communicate or persuade.
Visual impact/ appeal	Dynamic images and text. Use of color and symbols shows conscious effort to engage the audience through clever and thoughtful design.	Appealing images and text. Some consideration for color and design is present but is secondary to message or not cohesive.	Somewhat appealing images and text. Little consideration for design, space, or color is given, even after allowing for artistic ability.	Student did not complete image, or image is inappropriate for the assignment.

References

Anderson, L. H. (1999). *Speak*. New York, NY: Farrar, Straus and Giroux.

Applebee, A. N. (1996). *Curriculum as conversation: Transforming traditions of teaching and learning*. Chicago, IL: University of Chicago Press.

Bustle, L. S. (2004). The role of visual representation in the assessment of learning. *Journal of Adolescent & Adult Literacy*, 47(5), 416–23. https://doi.org/10.1598/JAAL.47.5.6

Chicola, N., & Smith, B. (2005). Integrating visual arts into instruction. *International Journal of Learning, 12*(5), 167–75.

Chopin, K. (2001). The story of an hour. In B. Lawn (Ed.), *40 short stories: A portable anthology* (pp. 73–75). Boston, MA: Bedford/St. Martin's. (Original work published 1894)

Freire, P., & Macedo, D. (1987). *Literacy: Reading the word and the world*. London, UK: Routledge & Kegan Paul.

Grant, A., Hutchinson, K., Hornsby, D., & Brooke, S. (2008). Creative pedagogies: "Art-full" reading and writing. *English Teaching: Practice and Critique, 7*(1), 57–72.

Harris, T. (1998). *The silence of the lambs*. New York, NY: St. Martin's Press.

Holdren, T. S. (2012). Using art to assess reading comprehension and critical thinking in adolescents. *Journal of Adolescent & Adult Literacy, 55*(8), 692–703.

Marshall, J. (2008). Visible thinking: Using contemporary art to teach conceptual skills. *Art Education, 61*(2), 38–45.

Miller, S., & Hopper, P. (2010). Supporting reading goals through the visual arts. *Reading Improvement, 47*(1), 3–6.

Rosenblatt, L. M. (1978). *The reader, the text, the poem: The transactional theory of the literary work*. Carbondale: Southern Illinois University Press.

Rosenblatt, L. M. (2005). *Literature as exploration*. New York, NY: Modern Language Association of America.

Rowling, J. K. (1997). *Harry Potter and the philosopher's stone*. London, UK: Bloomsbury.

Wilde, O. (2003). *The picture of Dorian Gray*. New York, NY: Penguin. (Original work published 1890)

Wilhelm, J. D. (2008). *"You gotta BE the book": Teaching engaged and reflective reading with adolescents* (2nd ed.). New York, NY: Teachers College Press.

Teaching High School English with Drawings and Large-Scale Visual Projects

9

Michelle Zoss, *Georgia State University*

In Las Vegas, Nevada, the older high schools have rooms with either no windows or very small windows located near the ceiling of the room. The room where I taught English was large, windowless, and located on the other side of the building from all the other English teachers. There were bricks on one wall, cinder blocks on all the rest. There were no bulletin boards, and getting anything to stick to the walls was a challenge. So I devised my own version of bulletin boards by hanging long, vertical lengths of craft paper from the ceiling. Each thirty-six-inch-wide section of paper served as a gallery space to display student work, posters, and other visual information.

During one project, students used the entirety of several vertical lengths of paper to draw line art based on Mayan, Incan, and Aztec designs. They worked on these large-scale drawings in between sessions of reading creation stories from all three civilizations. They also created comic strips retelling these stories, so I used more long sheets of craft paper to hang this work alongside the ten-foot murals. By the end of the year, the walls were festooned with work by students that included comics, drawings, essays, and poems. The room was a gallery of the work they completed. And then, each spring, we "buffed" the walls, as graffiti artists put it, so that they could create a space for the annual Literary Faire. One spring term, my room became the Greek Underworld and, the next spring, it became the landscape of the United States. In these large-as-life installations, students composed new gallery spaces to highlight their work both individually and in collaboration with one another. My big room and the hall outside of it became the canvas on which student work shined. In this chapter, I discuss how I arrived in this teaching and learning space, the difficulties and the delights that I encountered, and the crucial conversations I had to have with colleagues, parents, and administrators about how honoring image and language in my classes supported students in high school English.

Entering the Profession with Art and English Hand in Hand

I went into teaching because I was fascinated by the prospect of talking with people about their thinking. As an English teacher, I could talk with students about what they thought about their own writing, about their lives, and about the literature we read. I went into my English job in Las Vegas as both a language and an image person. I was certified to teach both English and art, and, the year before, I worked as an art teacher at three elementary schools. Bringing language and image together was something I was accustomed to doing. During my undergraduate career, I completed degrees in studio art and in English and did additional honors theses for each major. I illustrated a novel for my English honors thesis, a move that perplexed some of the committee members in the English department. Alongside the nearly 100 images I composed, I also developed a complete written thesis about the ideas that my images brought to life. In that project, image and language had to function as equal partners to meet the requirements of the honors thesis committee in the English department. Years later, I started teaching with the knowledge and the courage to see and use images and language as two distinct yet, in my mind, inseparable ways of knowing in an English classroom setting.

When I set up my room to teach English at Clark High School in Las Vegas, there were a lot of images involved. I had posters from a teacher store, paintings from calendars that I had collected over the years, and posters of artists and art that I bought while in college. I hung this collection of visual material on the long sheets of craft paper in yellow, orange, green, and blue. These ceiling-to-floor banners had room for student work as well as bulletins from the school administration. No windows? No problem. The artwork and the images on these panels served as views beyond the confines of the four bricked-up walls.

The students at Clark were an eclectic bunch, typical of the populations found in urban schools. There was a diversity of race, ethnicity, religion, and language. The students in my classes came from working-class and middle-class families. In a city like Las Vegas, parents and youth work around the clock because the city is always open. Some of my students had large families with multiple siblings, and some had three generations living together in the same home. Some students had smaller families with one parent and no siblings. My students identified as African American, European American, and Latinx, as well as newcomers from China, Honduras, Mexico, and Peru. Within their families, they practiced a wide range of religions and identified themselves as agnostics, Catholics, Christians, Hindus, Mormons, and Muslims. They also liked music of all sorts, as well as sports, drawing, skateboarding, reading, and watching movies. My classes were tracked into two groups by the school administrators: Ninth Grade English and Ninth Grade Read–Write English. The assumption was that the students in the unmarked English classes would not need extensive help in completing the course; the students in the marked classes required more support than a typical student to complete the requirements for English in the first year of high school. What I found was that students in both classes struggled for different reasons, and the struggle often depended on the text—a finding that Beers (2003) confirms.

While teaching, I noticed that many of the students doodled in their notebooks. Two students, P. J. and Mauro, spent a lot of time drawing intricate designs on their folders. Another student, Jose Angel, used a needle-sharp pencil to draw roses and names in a gothic alphabet style. These preferences for making images during class intrigued me as a teacher because I remember doing similar practices myself. I drew people and eyes in the margins of my notes in all my classes throughout high school. During English, math, and history classes, I drew in the margins when I needed to listen carefully and there were no other images or words to focus on. I doodled when there were lulls in the conversation, when I was waiting for the next activity to begin. As a teacher seeing students doing similar drawings in their notebooks, I watched to see how they responded during discussions. The students with doodles participated as regularly as students who did not doodle. I did notice that when Mauro, in particular, brought out his colored pencils or markers, his attention seemed to divert toward the drawing more than the action in class. So I set up a ground rule that drawing was acceptable, but, when students began to focus on changing colors or markers, they needed to pause and regroup to refocus their attention on the topic at hand.

Encouraged by the possibility of what drawings could do for students to help them learn in my classes, I began teaching a modified version of *two-column notes*. Walter Pauk introduced the notion of two-column notes in the 1960s, emphasizing that students divide their notepaper into two columns, with important information listed on the right and questions, topics, and potential headings on the left (Pauk & Owens, 2014). This method of note-taking is also called the Cornell method, because Pauk was a professor at Cornell University. The modification I used for these notes focused on adding small drawings on the left side to supplement the topics and headings. I learned this method from my friend and department chair, Joanne Ho, who also used it with students in grades 9 through 12. We used this method because it fitted a need we identified in our student population. Other researchers have also employed drawings to support students. For example, Fu (1995) shows that students who struggle with language can open up and develop their English language communication when given the opportunity to include drawing in their repertoires for expression. Likewise, Smagorinsky and his colleagues studied several students who used drawings not only in English class (Smagorinsky & Coppock, 1994; Smagorinsky & O'Donnell-Allen, 1998), but also in classes for interior design, ranch design, and architecture (Smagorinsky, Cook, & Reed, 2005; Smagorinsky, Pettis, & Reed, 2004; Smagorinsky, Zoss, & Reed, 2006). Since both Joanne and I saw that our students sometimes struggled with the language of school and literature, depending on the texts we were using, we opted to use the modified, visual Cornell method to draw on the strengths our students already had and further develop their linguistic understandings of the literature.

The Delights of Teaching with Drawing

When my classes moved on to reading Homer's *The Odyssey*, I showed them how we could use small drawings and minimal words to learn the background story of Homer's prequel story, *The Iliad*. In this instance, we used what I called *visual notes*. I began by drawing two circles to represent the islands of Sparta and Troy. I gave a brief retelling of the story and continued to add to the

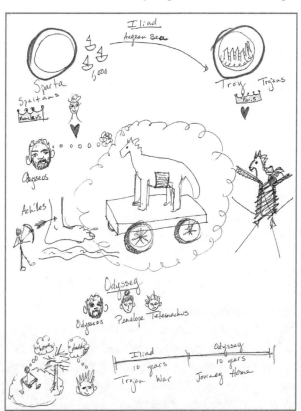

drawing. I asked students to draw the shapes on their papers as well, so that they could retell *The Iliad* for themselves and also refer to it while reading *The Odyssey* (see Figure 9.1). By the time we reached the bottom of the page, we had set the stage to begin the story of Odysseus making his way home. We continued to use drawings like this to summarize the action within *The Odyssey*, using quick sketches that I made to encourage students to remember details (see Figure 9.2). Figures 9.1 and 9.2 illustrate how I created these drawings and used them with students.

The modified Cornell notes and the visual notes were useful components to support students' understandings and responses to characters, plot lines, and literary details. Whitin (1996, 2005) argues that, with writing, students can simply fall back on

FIGURE 9.1. Visual notes for *The Iliad*.

retelling and summarizing a story; with drawing, however, they interpret, transmediate (Suhor, 1984, 1992), and carefully consider how to show their understanding in a different way. By *transmediate*, I mean that the students had to take the ideas located in the language of the literary text and then shape their thinking into a visual text. Suhor (1984) shows that people make these kinds of moves from one sign system to another all the time. When I tell someone about my favorite meal, I can use words, I can find images or make

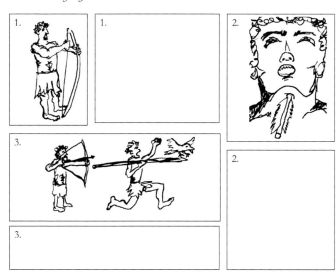

The Odyssey: "The Great Bow" & "Death at the Palace"

FIGURE 9.2. Visual notes for *The Odyssey*.

drawings, and I can gesture with my hands to convey my thoughts. In using words, images, and gestures, I employ at least three different sign systems: linguistic, visual, and gestural, respectively. I can use these sign systems simultaneously and successively and do so often without fanfare. In schools, teachers tend to use multiple sign systems to explain and introduce concepts and texts, but the real action for students comes in the construction of linguistic texts. There is more cachet in many schools for what students read and write strictly with language than there is for making images, films, and other nonlinguistic forms that also show thinking, imagination, and understanding. Making drawings an important part of learning is a move that Suhor argues is key to tapping into the ways that humans already communicate. He contends that the limitations of the school curriculum in focusing almost entirely on language and, at times, numbers unnecessarily reduce the varieties that exist in human expression. In my classes, I made a concerted effort to bring images and image-making into the curriculum, because I saw that students used images in their own practices and I, too, used them in mine.

Using drawings paired with language while reading texts helped students to think about the literary texts, respond to those texts in more than one sign system, and think in multifaceted ways about both what they were reading and what they were composing. To be sure, making a drawing as a response to literature is neither a simple task nor a duplicative task to writing about literature; instead, drawing is a complementary activity that gives students alternative and different means for thinking through the meaning and significance of a text (Eisner, 2002; Smagorinsky & O'Donnell-Allen, 1998; White & Zoss, 2015). The argument supporting the complexity of thinking involved in making images contrasted with thinking in language and numbers goes all the way back to Dewey (1934/1980): "To think effectively in terms of relations of qualities is as severe a demand upon thought as to think in terms of symbols, verbal and mathematical" (p. 46). The "qualities" that Dewey refers to are the perceived elements of art—essentially, the stuff that the senses take in when a viewer comes upon a work of art. His argument is that to take line, shape, pattern, and color and then compose those qualities into drawings, sculptures, paintings, and other artwork is an act of extraordinary thinking no less demanding than what it takes to express ideas using words and numbers.

When I taught high school students to consider literary texts like *The Odyssey* as sources for thinking and composing, I did so knowing that they could express themselves with drawings and words. I made this move because I knew that words are sometimes not enough to encompass the whole of what can be articulated. Eisner (2002) makes it clear that, when students work on a drawing paired with a written response, they are not simply doing the same work twice. Rather, they are thinking differently when developing the image than when they are developing the words. In these cases, students are thinking about the literary texts from multiple angles and for more than one purpose, so they have to consider the text from nuanced positions. Such thinking and expression from informed perspectives seems to be the essence of critical thinking and higher-order thinking, as those concepts are laid out in national curriculum documents (National Governors Association Center for Best Practices & Council of Chief State School Officers, 2010). Indeed, in order to make a credible image and essay, students have to take the original literary text into account to show how their thinking links up with and/or resists the ideas they encountered.

When students in my classes worked on line art based on images from ancient Central and South American communities, they had opportunities to think about and see those communities in different ways than the origin stories alone could have provided. With those large-scale drawings that were reproductions of carvings, pottery, and tapestries, they could trace the curves and lines that artists centuries before them had engraved, painted, and sewn into rock, clay, and fabric. Our process was this: We read the stories in English (a necessary translation for a US public school focused on teaching with the English language), and then students traced the designs using line drawing reproductions (also a necessary translation because we needed a means of enlarging the images and did not have access to the original works). The translation of language is something that reflected an issue that I could not provide access for—I did not read or write in the original languages of these stories. The images, though, were perhaps a closer link to the cultures that we explored. That is, students could move their hands along the lines that the artists had made, could see the intricacies of pattern and the interplay of positive and negative spaces, and could begin to feel the magnitude of scale that some of these artworks had in their original locations on walls and monuments. Figure 9.3 shows three students at work on one of the drawings.

FIGURE 9.3. Students working on large-scale drawings.

When working on nearly ten feet of craft paper, an image begins to feel different to the person working on it than an image that is contained within a ten-inch square of paper. Large-scale images have room for details and nuances that might not be possible in smaller-scale pieces. But the importance here is not in the image alone.

The tall, mural-length images were coupled with reading origin stories, taking notes using the modified two-column system, and an assignment to choose one of the stories to retell using sequential art, or comic strip–style, drawings. Students worked collaboratively on the mural drawings, with the line art projected onto the paper from the light of an overhead projector. They next outlined their pencil drawings with permanent markers and then colored in the shapes with pastels. They took notes after reading passages within the textbook as part of large group instruction that I led and participated in by drawing the images they suggested on a projected image of the notes. They worked on the sequential art after the reading and note-taking was complete and the murals were in the coloring stage. The resulting sequential art that students developed reflected the notes, the stories, and the murals. Characters in their comic strips had qualities that we had discussed as a group, and the settings and details of the objects in the art included patterns of lines like those found in the murals.

To assess the work that students produced, I sought methods that were as varied as the ways we explored the creation stories. In keeping with the practices of the English department, I tested students on their knowledge of the creation stories using quizzes with short answers and multiple-choice responses. I also asked students to self-evaluate their contributions within their small groups: "What was your role?" "What did you contribute to the drawings?" "How well did you work with your group members?" For the sequential art projects, I used a rubric that looked at how the students incorporated story details from the textbook and qualities of the designs used on the murals. I also looked at how they showed their own perspectives of the stories in the ways that the students organized an entire origin story in six to eight panels. For the qualities of design in the sequential art, I looked at their use of speech bubbles and narration, color and line to see how they used these elements to convey their understandings of the stories. By using a variety of assessment options, I gauged students' recall of details, as well as the completeness and overall quality of the work they produced in class. Approaching my English classes from the perspective that learning required a variety of teaching methods and assessments helped me to support students in the school's annual exhibition of English language arts learning.

The Possibilities of Teaching with Large-Scale Visual Projects

One of the highlights of working at Clark High School was that the English department had a long-standing tradition of holding an annual Literary Faire. Intended to showcase the practices within the discipline that science and STEM fairs display, the Literary Faire was a celebration of learning about reading literature and composing new texts related to a shared theme. Students across the school transformed every English teacher's classroom space to visually connect with a body of literature. The culmination of the festival was an evening celebration in which students invited their friends and family to see, hear, and feel the work in person. There were four alternating themes—Shakespeare, American literature, poetry, and world literature.

During my first year, the theme was world literature and my classes had already read creation stories from the Greeks, Aztecs, Incas, and Mayans. I polled my four classes and they opted to focus on stories from Dante's *Inferno*, focusing in particular on the geography of the journey of the dead as they moved from Hades, Tartarus, and Elysium and across the Rivers Styx, Lethe, Acheron, Cocytus, and Phlegethon. The culminating experience required students to do both an independent project and contribute to the classroom experience that involved creating three levels of the Underworld, replete with various rivers, creatures, and characters. Together, we explored the role of the Fates, Cerberus, and other gods and goddesses who played roles within Greek stories. We created a passageway of spaces within my room by using the same craft paper that I had used to display student work earlier in the year. However, instead of hanging the paper from the ceiling in a vertical orientation, we instead created paper walls by taping together twelve- to fifteen-foot long strips of the paper and then attaching those long pieces to the drop ceiling tiles using yarn. These panels of paper were massive, so we had to keep them rolled up and stored in a corner of the room until the day of the Faire. The school custodial staff was tremendous that week, removing our desks and chairs to a temporary storage location so that all the English rooms could transform into new literary spaces.

Because my classroom was on the far side of the school, away from all the other English teachers' spaces, the students developed a plan to get visitors to come to our installation. Students dressed as Hermes and Iris served as messengers to go to the other end of the school and read out welcome messages on scrolls of paper. They also brought with them a jar of pennies to distribute, thus providing the required passage fee for each person wanting to enter our Underworld. When arriving in the hall near my room, guests found two more students who alternated playing Charon, the boat pilot who delivered the dead along the River Styx. Charon's job during the Faire was to carry the visitors from one end of the hallway to the entrance of Hades. Charon accepted the pennies as passage fares from five to six passengers at a time. The boat was made of long pieces of cardboard, folded in half and made to look like a large rowboat, open at one end, that moved through pretend water by the feet of the passengers (much like the cars in *The Flintstones*). Just inside the entrance of Tartarus, guests encountered three students playing the Fates. They used yarn, scissors, and prewritten fate messages to give guests their destinies. Further into the room, a three-headed Cerberus made of paper and standing more than four feet tall guarded the entrance to Hades. Even deeper into the room, in the space of the Elysian Fields, students displayed their individual projects. The Elysian Fields functioned like a gallery space and a hallway of honor to highlight the work students had done outside of class. In the individual projects, students created drawings, paintings, dioramas, essays, and poems that expressed what they had learned about characters they studied in Greek mythology. The overall effect was remarkable— the room transformed into another world. Students smiled as they guided and explained to their family members what they had learned and how they showed that learning in the three-dimensional experience they had created.

The assessments I used for these large-group and individual projects were again varied like those I used in the creation stories projects. During and following our reading and exploration of Dante's work, I gave students quizzes to see what they recalled from our readings, discussions, and activities. I also asked them to do self-reflections and evaluations related to transforming the room into the Underworld and their individual studies of characters. I asked them to write about what was important to them in these projects: "What did you learn about working with both small and large groups to create a project that required the thinking and talents of everyone in four English classes?" "What was challenging about completing the projects both as a group member and as an individual?" "What did you learn by doing the individual project that you had not learned in class?" "What piqued your interests when you saw what other classes had created throughout the school?" "What made the Underworld experience successful for you as a learner and for visitors?" "What made this project memorable and what might you take away from this project that you could use in the future?" These assessments required students to use language to express their thoughts. With the individual projects in hand, and the entire room renovated into a literary representation, I could see what the students learned from these projects. I could discern from group interactions how they got along with their classmates and came together, or not, to create the vision of the Underworld that they imagined. I was pleased that, at the end of doing several weeks of work that used images, language, literary texts, and group work, the students could spend some time in class writing about their experiences.

It was necessary in assessing student work to use some language to convey both my expectations and the evaluation that I gave them. This was an English class after all, and I was comfortable with doing this work using language. The notion of critiquing student work using language was a familiar practice for me: when completing my studio art degree at the University of Iowa, we regularly paused our painting or drawing once every two weeks, or even during each studio session, to conduct a critique discussion. During *critique*, as we called it, we brought all our work to a central location within the studio so that everyone could see all the work at once. We sat on stools, chairs, the floor, or stood as needed, and the professor began the session with time to look at the work. Then we began a discussion about what we could see and not see in the images before us; we discussed questions we had about the images our classmates had made; and we pondered the possibilities of what other moves might be made in the images to change them. These exchanges often worked on the model that is used by English teachers called "Save the Last Word for Me" (Beers, 2003, pp. 172–73), in which one student's artwork is the focus of discussion, and the artist is the last person to comment. In this scenario, the discussion focuses on what the class perceives without having knowledge of what the artist intended. Then the artist can comment or follow up after the discussion reaches a point of conclusion—a moment often identified by the teacher.

There are several parallels here to reading a literary text. Students and teacher read a shared piece of literature, they discuss it as a class based on what they've read, and then they may or may not consider biographical or critical sources to learn more about the author's intent. I used my knowledge of both literary discussions and visual arts studio critiques to inform my assessment of student work. I asked students to talk with me or write about what they were doing in their literary responses. I also evaluated the sequential art, the individual projects, and the large-group projects based on the ways that those projects could display details and ideas about the texts to which they were connected. As an educated artist, I made judgments about the quality of the designs. I looked for a sense of composition: Does the image cohere as a unified composition? Can I see a sense of balance or proportion in ways that are consistent with the design that the student chose? Can I see evidence that the student invested thinking, time, and connections to the goals of the project? What can I identify as strengths within the piece? What can I identify that could use further attention to clarify the meaning and/or the composition? This last question is important because the meaning of a thing is part of the form (Eisner, 2002). If a drawing composition does not have a sense of connection within itself or toward a specified goal, then the drawing falls flat.

As a teacher who strives to integrate the arts, I am never disappointed when the focus turns to writing. The key for me is that writing is not the only driving force for expression in my classes. In the Literary Faire experience, students showed that they could collaborate to build an entirely new space, and that they understood the geography, characters, and stories that drove their decisions for designing and building that space. Students used a full range of sign systems to express their ideas and they delighted in the results. On the night of the Literary Faire, students were excited to share their knowledge and their accomplishments both as members of a group and as individual composers. In written reflections and conversations in class on the day following the Faire, students said they enjoyed having something that their families could not only see, but also walk into and experience. They were proud of what they had accomplished both as a group and as individuals. The success of that Literary Faire, however, was something I had to defend to administrators in subsequent years.

Conversations with Critics

For me, the many projects that required writing and drawing in my English classes were a success. These projects required a full representation of how students could encounter, perceive, and respond to literary texts in ways that were collaborative and individual, as well as linguistic and visual. Students had to show what they were learning during and after reading, a responsibility that Wilhelm (2008) and Smagorinsky and his colleagues (O'Donnell-Allen & Smagorinsky, 1999; Smagorinsky, Daigle, O'Donnell-Allen, & Bynum, 2010) have shown is vital to the development of students' literacy practices. In the years since teaching at Clark, I have continued to explore these ideas with a teacher who also used drawings to teach literature with middle school students (Zoss, 2010; Zoss & Jones, 2008; Zoss & White, 2011). From a student perspective, they found the project to be challenging but not impossible, and many appreciated learning about cultures and stories that required them to do something more than just write about the text. The Literary Faire was a project well received by my colleagues and department chair. Because I was teaching in a room on the opposite side of a large campus from all the other English teachers, I had a sense of autonomy that further reinforced my decisions for visual art integration. Joanne, my department chair, was fully supportive and did much of the creation stories project with her students as well. My overall sense was that the drawing and writing in English classes was not only well received throughout the school, because all the English teachers supported this pedagogical choice, but that it was also an important component of student learning.

It was not until after the school year ended that I learned what the school administrators had to say about all the visual and linguistic work that Joanne and I had been doing. They were displeased with the idea of spending school budget money on markers, scissors, and craft paper. The rolls of craft paper were expensive and they did not see why anyone in the school needed to have such luxuries. Joanne told me this story:

> The new assistant principal won't allow us to have any art in our lessons this year. She said that, because our students' test scores are so low, we have to concentrate on the basics, and "there is no room in an English classroom for art."

The leadership was unconvinced that the good work we had been doing was worth the time and expense. Perhaps the pushback came because this administrator was new and had not yet seen the potential and promise of our arts-integrated curriculum. Perhaps this administrator did not have the imagination to see what was possible when students have opportunities to express themselves beyond words alone, a possibility that had already found success in this school and elsewhere (Zoss, 2009). Perhaps this administrator and others had not considered the complexity of thinking required to make images alongside essays to respond to literary and informational texts (Eisner, 2002). The work that I have since done with teachers, teacher education students, and my own students at Clark High School has been to examine just these possibilities and develop rationales and scholarship to investigate and better understand what it means to integrate drawing and visual art in English curriculum (White & Zoss, 2015; Zoss, Siegesmund, & Jones Patisaul, 2010; Zoss, Smagorinsky, & O'Donnell-Allen, 2007; Zoss & White, 2011).

If I had the chance to talk with that administrator today, my conversation would begin with the work that I describe and show in this chapter. In the hands of students, visual arts–integrated English classes are exciting places to be. The room buzzes with energy and conversation both about and surrounding the texts as students work. This work requires a teacher who has the wherewithal and artisanry (Huberman, 1993) to address many different student questions, often at a rapid pace. Students working in small groups encounter challenges to getting the work done, but they also learn in that milieu how to work with others, to problem-solve, and to develop ideas that are workable beyond simply their own desires—they come to a sense of what the group needs or wants and find ways to get to shared goals. In these groups that work on visual and verbal texts, students learn about the strengths they possess and the strengths their classmates possess. They learn who is good at locating the big picture, at homing in on the details, at finding the best words to describe an idea, and at contouring a line to capture an image or pattern. When working with both images and language, students learn that they can use more of the sign systems available to them to express themselves (Zoss, 2009).

Eisner (2002) has argued for decades that there is more to human expression than what words alone can contain. Schools typically acknowledge the importance of mathematics alongside language as paramount to student success, whatever that success might look like. The indicator that mathematics and language are valuable to schools can be found in the testing and accountability practices that schools and local governments choose to use for determining school quality: schools test mathematics and English language arts consistently from elementary through high school (Nichols & Berliner, 2007). Schools do not consistently test for artistic, gestural, theatrical, physical, or social knowledge. So, indeed, language is important. But it is not the only means necessary within an English curriculum to develop student thinking and expression. Why limit the tools that students might use to articulate their understandings when they live in a world that is saturated with both moving and still images, with digital tools of computing power that can bring images and language together within seconds only to be shared across the globe in just a few seconds more? With the advent of the printing press, books and literature became more widely available. With the onset of social media platforms and unprecedented access to information via the internet, literature, images, and films are nearly always available and located as close as one's pocket or handbag. To limit students to language-only responses and tools within an English class designed to expose students to literature from within the United States and across the world seems short-sighted at best and punitive at worst.

I share my experiences in this chapter so that readers can see what is possible in classes with students who struggle for a variety of reasons. My students struggled with the origin stories because the mythology textbook was designed for twelfth-grade readers and the class was filled with ninth graders. They struggled because of language differences and social obligations at home that superseded their responsibilities at school. They struggled because the standardized tests assumed they shared all the same cultural mores the test designers imagined they should have. These students may have had low test scores according to the administrator, but that did not mean that they could not think in complex and nuanced ways about the literature curriculum. How do I know what they were thinking? I looked to their drawings and writing for indications. I looked to see if the sequential art could convey the nuances of the origin stories with a fidelity to the details: Did they name the characters and show their physical qualities according to the descriptions in the original text? Could they show key details within a limited number of panels and still get a sense of the complete story? Could they use color and speech bubbles or other details to convey a sense of what the characters were like—tricksters or supplicants, gods or mortals? These evaluations of quality could be performed by three groups: me as the teacher, the students themselves in self-evaluation, and other students in peer evaluation.

Bringing drawings and large-scale visual projects into English classes like those described here requires thoughtful planning, execution, and assessment. Like all good teaching, these practices take time to develop and they require thoughtful teachers to make the experiences meaningful for students. Teachers have to know the content well and they need patience to help students learn to express themselves in a variety of ways. It is no accident that students in my classes had more than one opportunity to draw and write in class. They had opportunities to practice expressing ideas using both images and words throughout the year. Teachers who use these activities teach students how to determine quality in the projects so that both teacher and students can share understandings about what is produced. Doing this work requires time to think and plan. In my own work, I find that having another teacher to work with and reflect with is an invaluable resource to help me work through ideas (Zoss et al., 2010). While I was in Las Vegas, my friend and department chair, Joanne, was a key reason that I found my way as a new teacher. She was highly supportive of the arts-integrated work I did and she employed similar methods in her own classes. While we had some support from the changing administration in the school, we also found resistance there. But we approached those administrators as a team with shared goals.

From a day-to-day perspective, integrating drawing into an English curriculum can be tiring. It takes a lot of energy to talk with kids about their work multiple times during a given class period. When students constructed the walls and geography of the Underworld, I moved from group to group, answering both individual and group questions. I monitored the action happening both within the confines of my room and in the hallway just outside where students built the boat and attached blue paper to walls to transform them into a river. At the end of each class period, students and I gathered to give the next class a set of directions for where to take the projects to the next goal. First period left instructions for second period, and so on. During fourth period, the students set tasks for the first period to tackle the next morning. Students left notes for one another and they initiated conversations about the project in the corridors. Keeping track of all these details was something that we all had to share. I could not do it myself, so students shared the responsibility. I went home tired on those days, yet I returned the next day with plans to help the students continue to move toward the goals they set for themselves.

The results were projects that I could not have imagined. I was surprised by what students produced because I did not have a fixed answer for what the project should become. Valuing this sense of surprise and having questions that do not lead to fixed answers are qualities that the arts bring to education (Eisner, 1992). As a high school teacher and now as a college professor, I still value this sense of surprise that is possible in teaching. I love finding out how students think about ideas from my classes. I frequently offer at least one project per course that requires students to produce a project that is driven by their imaginations and desires. Having projects that are open ended can make both teaching and assessing student work an enjoyable experience. Smagorinsky (2019) explains this phenomenon in his English methods book when he illustrates how teachers who ask for a singular essay with limited response possibilities end up becoming bored with marking student papers. If the questions and the means for responding to literature can be open-ended and include language and image, the possibilities become magnificent.

Conclusion

The value of teaching English with drawings is in the opportunities: Students can look, feel, and talk about literature in ways that move beyond recitation and multiple-choice assessments. In the moments of working with students as they grappled to find the right images and words to explicate their thoughts, my goal was to both honor the tools of expression they already had and broaden the range of tools available to them. If one word could not convey what a sketch could, then they had a choice to find or create an image. Likewise, if a sketch was insufficient to say what a phrase could, then they had a choice to write something new. I also emphasized that learning need not be solitary. We worked together to develop the modified two-column notes, and the students worked across classes to create the large-scale installation for the Literary Faire. Students had choices here as well—they chose the parts they wanted to work on, and they made decisions daily about what needed to be done in subsequent classes to make their vision of the Underworld fit the visions they shared.

My teaching choices were thus informed by an ethic of care (Noddings, 1992), of striving to be open in my thinking and in my teaching practices to see what excited students. Noddings (1992) argues that one important quality of teaching is making sure that students feel cared for; in my teaching, having options for visual and linguistic expression was a way that I attended to students' needs. They showed me that drawing was important to them, and I gave them space to explore multiple ways of making meaning about the English curriculum that included both drawing and language. Similar to Noddings, Eisner (2002) invites educators to seek out ways to value students as whole, expressive beings who need a multiplicity of ways to be, hear, feel, see, and experience the world. He further argues that students also need ways to show their thinking about those experiences. In my teaching at Clark and in my classes today, I continue to create learning experiences for students that showcase their strengths and challenge them to think expansively. By integrating drawing and visual art in high school English, I reinforced for students the vitality and importance of practices that honor the variety of ways students can and should express themselves in school.

References

Beers, G. K. (2003). *When kids can't read, what teachers can do: A guide for teachers, 6–12.* Portsmouth, NH: Heinemann.

Dewey, J. (1980). *Art as experience.* New York, NY: Perigree Books. (Original work published 1934)

Eisner, E. W. (1992). The misunderstood role of the arts in human development. *Phi Delta Kappan, 73*(8), 591–95.

Eisner, E. W. (2002). *The arts and the creation of mind.* New Haven, CT: Yale University Press.

Fu, D. (1995). *My trouble is my English: Asian students and the American dream.* Portsmouth, NH: Heinemann.

Huberman, M. (1993). Teachers' work: Individuals, colleagues, and contexts. In J. W. Little & M. W. McLaughlin (Eds.), *Professional development and practice series* (pp. 11–50). New York, NY: Teachers College Press.

National Governors Association Center for Best Practices & Council of Chief State School Officers. (2010). *English language arts standards*. Washington, DC: Author. Retrieved from http://www.corestandards.org/ELA-Literacy/

Nichols, S. L., & Berliner, D. C. (2007). *Collateral damage: How high-stakes testing corrupts America's schools*. Cambridge, MA: Harvard Education Press.

Noddings, N. (1992). *The challenge to care in schools: An alternative approach to education.* New York, NY: Teachers College Press.

O'Donnell-Allen, C., & Smagorinsky, P. (1999). Revising Ophelia: Rethinking questions of gender and power in school. *English Journal, 88*(3), 35–42.

Pauk, W., & Owens, R. J. Q. (2014). *How to study in college* (11th ed.). Boston, MA: Wadsworth Cengage Learning.

Smagorinsky, P. (2019). *Teaching English by design: How to create and carry out instructional units* (2nd ed.). Portsmouth, NH: Heinemann.

Smagorinsky, P., Cook, L. S., & Reed, P. M. (2005). The construction of meaning and identity in the composition and reading of an architectural text. *Reading Research Quarterly, 40*(1), 70–88.

Smagorinsky, P., & Coppock, J. (1994). Cultural tools and the classroom context: An exploration of an artistic response to literature. *Written Communication, 11*(3), 283–310.

Smagorinsky, P., Daigle, E. A., O'Donnell-Allen, C., & Bynum, S. (2010). Bullshit in academic writing: A protocol analysis of a high school senior's process of interpreting *Much Ado About Nothing. Research in the Teaching of English, 44*(4), 368–405.

Smagorinsky, P., & O'Donnell-Allen, C. (1998). Reading as mediated and mediating action: Composing meaning for literature through multimedia interpretive texts. *Reading Research Quarterly, 33*(2), 198–226.

Smagorinsky, P., Pettis, V., & Reed, P. M. (2004). High school students' compositions of ranch designs: Implications for academic and personal achievement. *Written Communication, 21*(4), 386–418.

Smagorinsky, P., Zoss, M., & Reed, P. M. (2006). Residential interior design as complex composition: A case study of a high school senior's composing process. *Written Communication, 23*(3), 295–330.

Suhor, C. (1984). Towards a semiotics-based curriculum. *Journal of Curriculum Studies, 16*(3), 247–57.

Suhor, C. (1992). Semiotics and the English language arts. *Language Arts, 69*(3), 228–30.

White, A. M., & Zoss, M. (2015). "It's a sad, sad story": Teaching emotional connections and tone in literature. *The Educational Forum, 79*(3), 213–29. https://doi.org/10.1080/00131725.2015.1037513

Whitin, P. (1996). *Sketching stories, stretching minds: Responding visually to literature*. Portsmouth, NH: Heinemann.

Whitin, P. (2005). The interplay of text, talk, and visual representation in expanding literary interpretation. *Research in the Teaching of English, 39*(4), 365–97.

Wilhelm, J. D. (2008). *"You gotta BE the book": Teaching engaged and reflective reading with adolescents* (2nd ed.). New York, NY: Teachers College Press.

Zoss, M. (2009). Visual arts and literacy. In L. Christenbury, R. Bomer, & P. Smagorinsky (Eds.), *Handbook of adolescent literacy research* (pp. 183–96). New York, NY: Guilford Press.

Zoss, M. (2010). Keeping ideas and language in play: Teaching drawing, writing, and aesthetics in a secondary literacy class. In C. M. Connery, V. P. John-Steiner, & A. Marjanovic-Shane (Eds.), *Vygotsky and creativity: A cultural–historical approach to play, meaning making, and the arts* (pp. 181–97). New York, NY: Peter Lang.

Zoss, M., & Jones, S. (2008). Enhancing literary reading through visual and language arts practices. In A. O. Soter, M. Faust, & T. Rogers (Eds.), *Interpretive play: Using critical perspectives to teach young adult literature* (pp. 191–209). Norwood, MA: Christopher-Gordon.

Zoss, M., Siegesmund, R., & Jones Patisaul, S. (2010). Seeing, writing, and drawing the intangible: Teaching with multiple literacies. In P. Albers & J. Sanders (Eds.), *Literacies, the arts, and multimodality* (pp. 136–56). Urbana, IL: National Council of Teachers of English.

Zoss, M., Smagorinsky, P., & O'Donnell-Allen, C. (2007). Mask-making as representational process: The situated composition of an identity project in a senior English class. *International Journal of Education & the Arts, 8*(10), 1–41.

Zoss, M., & White, A. M. (2011). Finding "my kind of teaching": How a drama project became a teacher's expressive teaching moment. *English in Education, 45*(2), 161–75.

Putting the Public in Publication: Guerilla Art in English Language Arts

10

Stephen Goss, *Kennesaw State University*

A new student entered my classroom a few days into the second quarter of the school year. His name was Fernando and he had just moved to the state of New York from Puerto Rico. On his first day, I asked the class about internal and external expectations in their lives, as part of a district- and school-mandated lesson aligned with the Common Core State Standards. Fernando wrote that one of his internal expectations was "to be known." He said that he didn't want to be "famous," only "known" to others; the extent of that knowing didn't matter.

I asked Fernando to turn his thought into a mini-poster, to write the statement on a piece of construction paper. When he was finished, I gave him a roll of tape and he hung the paper at the front of the classroom. In the days, weeks, and months that followed, other students asked about Fernando's poster. Later, it became an important part of ongoing discussions around dystopian literature and what it means to lead a meaningful life. In the process, Fernando's desire to be known was achieved, even if it was on a relatively small scale. Fernando's poster was a catalyst for other students and further conversation in the classroom. These ongoing conversations became existential discussions about the nature of schoolwork and its value outside of the classroom. I shared Fernando's statement with all of my classes, which in turn stimulated similar conversations throughout the school year. One conclusion reached by all of my classes was that much of the previous work students had done in English language arts (ELA) seemed to be busywork, having little or no value, purpose, or meaning outside of school. Students were extrinsically motivated to complete the work solely to obtain a grade. I also believe that this simple activity of posting a statement, and the fact that Fernando's words were published, sent an important message to him on his first day in my class. What we did in our ELA class was important and valuable beyond a grade, and different from what he had experienced in the past.

I think that many students want to be known, to be seen, by their peers and teachers and the larger community. They want to be recognized for who they see themselves becoming and as important members of their school spaces. However, too often test-centric curricula do not give enough space for students to be themselves, find themselves, express themselves, and then share that expression in real ways. To have a real experience and not just a simulated one. To have a real audience and not an imagined one. To have the space and support to ask real questions that can be answered through research and inquiry. To work on assignments and projects with meaning and value beyond a grade, a smiley-face sticker, or a high five from the teacher. These things are what's important and relevant in ELA.

Context

This chapter discusses experiences from classrooms in two different schools. The first was a tenth-grade classroom in a large northeastern urban district that comprised students who were lifelong residents of the city. Horizons High School (all names have been changed) was funded in part by the Bill and Melinda Gates Foundation and offered a five-year program during which students took traditional high school classes as well as classes at a local community college, beginning in their junior year, with the opportunity to graduate with a diploma and an associate's degree.

The second classroom was at City Prep, where I taught ninth- and tenth-grade ELA. City Prep was a comprehensive public school for grades 5 to 12 that drew heavily on the growing immigrant population of the city. More than forty languages were spoken by the students who commuted to City Prep from neighborhoods spread throughout the city, and the school did not receive outside funding.

Origin Story

When I tell teachers and preservice teachers about the various projects that my students have created (including the ones discussed in this chapter), they most often react by saying these projects would never work in their classrooms, citing various constraints, including no space in the Common Core curriculum, a need to focus on preparing students for state testing, low-performing students, lack of funding, and little support coupled with high expectations from the school administration and other English teachers on the staff. These concerns are indeed valid; however, they are not insurmountable and, as I argue in this chapter, based on my experiences, the constraints often provide structure from which creative and effective lesson designs can develop. My history as a teacher is largely a history of overcoming or working with constraints, changes, and roadblocks. Indeed, I have learned throughout my career that overcoming obstacles is part of what it means to be a teacher.

I taught at two other schools in the district before teaching at City Prep. It was during these placements that my students started publishing ELA products/content via public art installations, mini-posters, QR codes, and conceptual art pieces, all of which we later started calling *Guerilla English*.

At the time of my return to the high school classroom, I applied for an ELA position within the district, which I assumed was for the following school year. However, the very next day, the district coordinator offered me a temporary, full-time substitute position at one of the largest high schools in the district, to replace a teacher whose teaching certificate had expired. That position led to other temporary full-time positions. I soon began to see myself as a hired gun brought in to teach in difficult situations and broken, forgotten classrooms, abandoned by their teachers, with little to no guidance from school administrators. All of these placements started with less than a week's notice, during which I met with the various principals who went over job requirements and expectations. Each principal provided me with a detailed curriculum and then asked me to follow it closely.

For example, on my first day at City Prep, the principal leaned over her desk, held out a sheet of paper, and said, "Today is the last day of the third quarter. The teacher you are replacing will not be back for the rest of the school year. Here is the required tenth-grade curriculum for the fourth quarter." I took the paper in my hands and quickly looked it over. There were three columns; the first was a poetry-heavy list of required texts and authors—William Shakespeare, Edna St. Vincent Millay, D. H. Laurence, Alice Walker, Robert Hayden. . . and the list went on. There were also several essential questions, such as "What tools do authors use to craft engaging, vivid texts?" and "How does a poet use form to evoke meaning?" The second column listed suggested texts and authors: Walt Whitman, Carl Sandburg, and Robert Frost. "You are expected to cover all of the first column and most of the second," the principal said, handing me the grade book for the classes I would be teaching. I flipped through the pages. The majority of the students had failing or near-failing grades for the first three quarters. In each class, there was a handful of students whose grades were so low they mathematically could not pass the year, as well as a handful who had consistently achieved high grades throughout.

The principal then took me to my classroom, which I shared with the ninth-grade English teacher. When we entered the room, the ninth-grade teacher was standing behind a podium reading from a textbook. The desks were arranged in rows. Some students in the front rows seemed to be following along as she read, others had their heads down; a group of young men in the corner kept reaching over and hitting each other, and another student loudly and randomly repeated words that the teacher had read. The room vibrated with disinterest. The principal disrupted the class and introduced me to the teacher and the students. One student leaned in my direction and whispered, "Yo mister, can you teach our class? This teacher boring as hell." The teacher stopped reading, and asked: "Can anyone tell me why Romeo wears a mask to the party?" The class was silent. After a moment, the teacher answered her own question. The principal showed me my desk, handed me my schedule, and said, "Your first class starts in ten minutes," and then left the room.

The challenge I faced in each school was to design lesson plans in a short period of time that would be highly engaging, highly effective, and aligned with the curriculum—or, at least, I needed to be able to argue that they were aligned. I knew that I wanted to create space for the students to explore their worlds in order to build toward curricular concepts (Sheehy, 2004). I also needed to accelerate the development of a classroom culture that supported the kinds of small- and large-scale creative projects that I imagined. Finally, in addition to managing all of this, I also had to satisfy my administrators and the district that I was following the district-mandated curriculum and that my lessons where driven by data per district requirements. In each class, I was successful in these endeavors, based on my own observations and data that I collected. Similarly, the schools also found my work to be "highly effective" on principal observations and data collected from my students through mandatory standardized tests given every five weeks. Yet there was always a moment at the beginning of each of these placements when I thought the task before me seemed impossible. So I fell back on the various educational theories that I believe in, my core: namely, that literacy—and, by extension, learning—are social activities.

"No one knows we exist": Moving from "Social" to "Super Social"

The idea that literacy is socially situated (Gee, 2004) fundamentally changed how I thought about teaching English and what I thought was possible in my teaching. But, as I returned to the classroom, I needed to figure out what that would actually look like when put into action. How would I change my pedagogy to accommodate my new understanding of sociocultural theory (Smagorinsky & O'Donnell-Allen, 2000; Vygotsky, 1978; Wertsch, 1991)? On my first day at Horizons High School, I broke the ice by having my students design sneaker colorways (i.e., the color styling of a sneaker) that reflected their life experiences

(Moll, Amanti, Neff, & Gonzalez, 1992). We talked about several popular sneaker designs and their celebrity endorsers, and how the sneaker product often personifies the athlete. Then we watched several Nike commercials that feature athlete endorsers, including "I Am Not a Role Model," a Nike commercial with Charles Barkley (Nike, 1993/2013). The students explained that, like the sneaker designs, the commercials further reflected and reinforced the persona and image of the athletes. Using these examples as entry points, students wrote poems to accompany the shoes that they designed (Klingel & Jarosch, 2010). I encouraged students to write poems that gave some insight into their lives and experiences. I asked them to think as if they were creating a commercial for their sneaker design and to imagine that their poem was the script to that commercial. Once most of the class was writing, I taught a short mini-lesson about "I Am" poems (Fink, n.d.) to those students who were struggling with writing. Students then shared what they had been working on with a partner and gave feedback to each other. Once they had a final draft of their poem, they wrote the poems on and/or around the sneaker. During the next class, the students shared their poems in small groups, then to the whole class. Finally, we hung all of the sneakers in the hallway outside our classroom (see Figures 10.1 and 10.2). The sneakers immediately caught the attention of passersby and it was quickly apparent that the project was not only engaging for my students, but it also captured the attention of kids who happened to be walking by as we posted the work. For the next several weeks, small crowds of students often gathered in between classes to read and explore the sneakers. Some discussed which sneaker design they actually wanted to wear. They talked about which poems and designs best represented their authors, and which ones seemed inauthentic.

After we hung the project, we had a class discussion. I asked, "How do you think the Sneaker Project went?" The class came to a quick consensus that the project went "extremely well." Then multiple conversations broke out about whose piece was the best or worst, and which ones would be on discount at the store. As these arguments wound down, I gave my comments about the project. I shared that I was shocked by how many students were stopping to read their work. That I had never seen such rigorous arguing about poetry before. Then I told them about all the teachers who had commented on, and praised, the project. Finally, I asked my students how we could get even more people to see their work. Malcolm, a tenth-grade student, started talking first. He said it was not possible to get a larger audience because, as he put it, "No one knows we exist." No one in the classroom argued against this statement. One of the issues was that Horizons High School was located on the first and fourth floors of a downtown office building. There were no signs or markers of any kind indicating the existence of the school aside from a small brass placard inside the building next

FIGURE 10.1. "Be Cool Blue" sneaker poem.

FIGURE 10.2. "I Am Bubble Love" sneaker poem.

to the elevators. Indeed, no one knew we existed, let alone that we were doing exciting things.

In the weeks that followed, Malcolm's statement became a class mantra. "No one knows we exist" was enshrined on a mini-poster hanging in the front of the room above the entryway. Several times, I began class by quoting Malcolm, using his statement as a challenge to the class. I asked, "How can we let the outside world know that we exist, that we do great things? How can we show others that the work we do in school is important, meaningful, and deserves to be seen outside of the realm of school?" All the while, the idea that literacy is a social activity was on my mind. If literacy is a social activity, what if my classes worked to make it more social—super social—which to me meant that my students' writing and thinking needed be to be shared with an audience beyond the classroom.

Jenny Holzer and Jay-Z's Boom Box

I started researching artists who use text in their artwork, searching for an idea or method that my students could borrow to help them publish their work. One of the first artists that came to mind was Jenny Holzer. Holzer is recognized for publishing provocative statements in public spaces (Smith, 2009). During this same time, a student was reading Jay-Z's (2011) autobiography. One day, the student showed me a picture from the book of Jay-Z's first boom box, and asked if we could somehow use the image in one of our projects. I later showed the boom box as well as some of Jenny Holzer's work to the class. After some discussion, the class decided to publish their own provocative or important statements using the boom box as a method of delivery.

The next day, I supplied the class with a large stack of photocopies of the boom box. I asked the class to read through their daily journal entries. These included responses to various anticipatory writing prompts, short personal narratives, and poetry modeled after works by Gwendolyn Brooks, Langston Hughes, and other authors we had read as part of the district curriculum. I asked the students to highlight the most important and meaningful statements from their entries, and then to find a partner and share these statements. After getting feedback from their partners, the students selected one statement they agreed was the most powerful and then they wrote the statements on the photocopied boom boxes. I had previously met with the principal and asked for permission to hang students' work around the school. So, as students left the classroom, I gave them pieces of tape and they "published" their statements by hanging them somewhere inside the school (see Figures 10.3–10.5).

FIGURE 10.3. "Learn or die" boom box statement.

FIGURE 10.4. "Education is for US not just THEM" boom box statement.

FIGURE 10.5. "Kindness is key" boom box statement.

I repeated this activity with all my classes, and, by the end of the day, over one hundred of the boom box statements were on display throughout the school. Soon they became a major topic of discussion among the student body. In between classes, students could be seen up and down the halls reading the various statements. The majority of students had no idea where the statements came from. This mystery spurred interest in the project.

At the end of the day, there was a staff meeting. I arrived early and, as teachers took their seats, a veteran teacher entered the room holding two handfuls of crumpled-up boom boxes over her head. She stood at the front of the room and announced, "Some student is putting these up all over the school. If you see one, please tear it down and throw it out." Just then, the principal entered, interrupted the teacher, and briefly explained the project and that the boom boxes came from my classes. She encouraged the staff to consider displaying more student work. At that moment, the room erupted in conversation around the project and several teachers came and sat next to me, asking for more details.

After the meeting, still more teachers came up to me praising my students' work. The next day, I told the story of the staff meeting to each of my classes. At first, students were outraged that another teacher destroyed their work. Some were mad at me for not protecting their work, for not announcing the project to the school prior to publishing. But, as the conversations continued, most classes came to the conclusion that the destruction of a few projects was actually a good thing. It was evidence that the students had the power to elicit real reactions from a real audience. Instead of discouraging the students, it encouraged them to think about new ways to publish their work. I asked each class a rhetorical question: "When was the last time a teacher felt so emotional about your schoolwork that they wanted to destroy it?" Soon they came to see that the teacher's bombastic action and announcement to the staff worked to spread the word about what we were doing in our classes. They agreed that the principal's defense of our work gave it additional weight and importance on a schoolwide level.

Word Walls and Word Birds

The district required all teachers to have a *word wall*. While I knew this requirement was interpreted in different ways across the district, at my school, it meant every teacher had to do the same thing. Each teacher had to post two vocabulary words in the cafeteria every five-week marking period, accompanied by an image, definition, and sentence for each word. I didn't want to do it. I didn't, and still don't, see the value in it. In talking with the other teachers, I learned that most of them begrudgingly put up their walls, and that they never even discussed the words with their students. This lack of purpose and interest for teachers and students alike resulted in ignored, heartless word walls filled with decontextualized vocabulary and generic clip art.

I decided that, instead of *me* completing this required assignment, I would open the wall space to my students. I wanted them to display something that was theirs and not mine. I took inspiration from an idea my wife had come up with. Around the same time, my wife and I were painting and redecorating our bedroom. She had found and purchased a small flock of ceramic swallows to hang on the wall and she arranged them so that they appeared to be flying through our bedroom and out of a window. Inspired by her idea, I traced one of the birds and photocopied it onto bright pieces of paper, two birds per sheet. I also printed a list of the 1,000 most common SAT words. I set up a small station in the back of my room with the bird photocopies, the SAT words, and several pairs of scissors and tape. In the upcoming class periods, I directed students who were finished with their work to go to the word bird station and read through the SAT words until they found one that they wanted to learn, that appealed to them, or that they found interesting or useful. Then students wrote the word, the definition, and a sentence using their chosen word on a bird. They cut out the bird, shared it with a classmate, and then hung the bird in our allotted space in the cafeteria (see Figure 10.6).

Within a week, most students in my classes had created and hung a bird. It became apparent that there was not enough space on the word wall for the birds they created. Also evident was that students generally enjoyed making the birds and most wanted to make more than one. The bird station continued to be open to any student who had extra time. Students began making the birds without me asking them to do so. Other students in the school who were not in my classes became curious about the project and asked questions about the birds. Many asked if they too could make a bird. So I started bringing the necessary supplies to the cafeteria during my daily lunch duty. Students from every grade ended up participating. Soon the birds filled the official word wall space, and then spilled out into the hallways; bright flocks of them covered the walls and windows of my classroom. About a month after I started teaching at the school, a ninth-grade student whom I had never met before stopped me in the hall and said that my classes had "transformed the school."

Since this first time experimenting with the birds, I have reused and reconfigured their purpose for different schools and classrooms. In one iteration, students wrote personal narratives describing a defining moment in their life. We published final draft versions of their narratives using large, three-foot-by-three-foot birds (see Figure 10.7).

FIGURE 10.6. The word bird wall.

FIGURE 10.7. Personal narrative word birds.

In my most recent classroom, students wrote on small birds as part of a writing project at the beginning of the year. I had my students write about their expectations and goals for the school year and their futures in general. Students first wrote and shared journal entries, brainstorming ideas and setting goals as well as plans to achieve those goals. The students wrote a final draft version of what they had written in their journals on a bird, shared with the class, and placed the bird somewhere outside or inside my classroom. I left these vision birds up, and kept them up until the end of the year, when students took theirs down, re-read it, and wrote a final journal reflection about their goals and what they had or had not achieved and why.

I have found that starting the school year off with a project like the one I just described eases students into the idea of publishing their work. In the beginning, many students are apprehensive about sharing their writing with a partner, so the idea of sharing with a large audience can be daunting. So I start small with projects like the word birds and boom box statements and move somewhat slowly, building gradually to larger and more public projects.

Letter from Birmingham Jail Stairway

At City Prep, English teachers were required to follow modules developed by New York State (EngageNY, 2014). According to the module, "In 10.2.1, students read Martin Luther King Jr.'s [1963/2018] *Letter from Birmingham Jail*, focusing on how King develops his argument for universal acceptance of equal human rights. Students also analyze how King uses rhetoric to advance his purpose" (EngageNY, 2014, p. 2).

My classes spent several weeks conducting a close reading of the text as outlined in the module. As such, during class discussions and activities, students often explored how Martin Luther King Jr. (1963/2018) developed an effective argument through rhetoric and word choice. But I believed my students should have the opportunity to explore the text in personally meaningful ways, and to connect what they were reading to issues that they've encountered in their own lives.

I dealt with many issues and challenges while teaching this text the way it is outlined in the 577 pages of the New York State Learning Module for the second quarter of tenth grade. My international students had little to no context in which to place the text. Most were unaware of the Civil Rights Movement in the United States and many did not know who Martin Luther King Jr. was or why he is important. As a result, my classes spent a lot of time building up background knowledge around the text. We talked about the Civil Rights Movement, and then students made connections to their own experiences and histories. This helped them contextualize *Letter from Birmingham Jail* (King, 1963/2018). We watched excerpts from the videos *African Americans: Many Rivers to Cross* (Gates, 2014) and *Black America since MLK: And Still I Rise* (Gates, 2017), and then we discussed what we had seen. In another activity, we listened to, analyzed, discussed, and wrote about Nina Simone's (1964) song "Mississippi Goddam." The song and videos proved to be a powerful entry text that further helped students contextualize *Letter from Birmingham Jail* and opened up important discussions about the Civil Rights Movement and the Jim Crow South. Since the song is short and easily digestible in comparison to *Letter from Birmingham Jail*, students found it immediately accessible and were able to analyze the lyrics for word choice and rhetoric, as required in the district-mandated curriculum. My classes were quickly able to confidently respond to the mid-unit assessment of the module, which required students to "[d]etermine a purpose in *Letter from Birmingham Jail* and analyze how King uses rhetoric and specific word choices to advance that purpose" (EngageNY, 2014, p. 1).

Soon after we started reading *Letter from Birmingham Jail* (King, 1963/2018), it became apparent through discussions that the students believed Martin Luther King Jr.'s argument for protest in Birmingham was potentially applicable to many political and civil struggles in the world today. International students in my classes discussed and wrote about issues in our school building, neighborhoods, and their home countries. For example, a group of Bengali students connected the US Civil Rights Movement to the mistreatment of women in Bangladesh. Students wrote their various ideas and responses on brightly colored paper and taped them to a wall in the classroom, which eventually formed a quilted mosaic of issues from around the globe. They highlighted the various ways people have fought and argued for change, issues still prevalent today, as well as what action students could take to advance change.

At the end of the unit, students selected one sentence or statement from *Letter from Birmingham Jail* (King, 1963/2018) that they believed to be most meaningful in their world. They typed each line into a Word document on our classroom computer and, using the same large font, printed the line onto bright paper. Then they cut the paper into strips and adhered them to each riser of an often-used stairway that led from the first to the third floor of the school building. The final product was bright and visually appealing, with vertical neon bars, framed by high-gloss black-painted woodwork (see Figure 10.8). Students also published essays that they had written connecting their selected line to a present-day issue. The essays were displayed on the walls going up the stairs, so that viewers could stand on a stair and read a student's perspective about the selected line and its relevance in the world today.

FIGURE 10.8. *Letter from Birmingham Jail* stairway.

Counternarrative Interactive Maps

The *Letter from Birmingham Jail* stairway in Figure 10.8 highlights the need to give students space in the curriculum to personally reflect and react to course content, as well as provides opportunities to apply the ideas gleaned from that content to present-day events and their own lived experiences. In October 2016, at City Prep, I started class by stating, "Donald Trump said that where we live is an urban hell," and then the class watched a video clip of a Trump campaign speech (ABC News, 2016). I asked the ninth-grade students if they thought it was true. "Do you live in an urban hell?"

Some agreed and some disagreed, but most were somewhere in the middle. One student, Bishop, called out, "Mister, you wear those shoes in my neighborhood, you gonna lose 'em," pointing to the Nike sneakers on my feet. "You better wear sandals." However, Ashley disagreed and said that most neighborhoods aren't that bad, just "full of regular people, doing regular things."

After more discussion, I had the students think back to a few weeks earlier when they watched the TED Talk "The Danger of a Single Story" by Chimamanda Adichie (2013), and asked, "Is Donald Trump telling a single story? And, if so, is it dangerous?" The students answered both questions with a resounding "yes." I handed out blank sheets of fluorescent paper and announced, "Let's write stories that complicate Trump's single story." I asked the students to write and then audio-record counternarratives about places in their neighborhoods that contradicted Trump's single story of the city where they lived and attended school. *Counternarrative* is used by critical scholars to complicate and contradict dominant narratives, or single stories, about people and places (Solórzano & Yosso, 2002). In particular, counternarratives expose the problematic assumptions made by the dominant narrative that presents one group of people as the default (e.g., white students living in suburbs) and marginalizes anyone who is different as the other (e.g., students of color living in urban centers). These dominant narratives are particularly dangerous when they essentialize and marginalize people based on race, class, immigration status, gender, sexuality, religion, and additional intersections of difference. Counternarratives have the potential not only to expose systems of oppression, such as racism (Solórzano & Yosso, 2002), but also to humanize people who have been erased or maligned by the dominant narrative (Souto-Manning, 2013).

Once these stories were written and their audio recorded, the class held a listening party and voted to select which stories to publish. Our publication was an interactive digital map of our city. These counternarrative pieces were digitally pinned to the map, enabling the viewer to touch a pin and listen to a student's story. The map was created using ArcGIS (Esri, 2018), an online mapping tool with which users can create detailed, data-rich maps.

We unveiled the final map at the school's Cultural Night. At this event, parents were invited to meet with teachers and enjoy food from the many cultures of the school. Inside my classroom, students projected the map that they created onto an interactive smart board. A group of student volunteers presented the map as parents entered the room and showed them how to use it. Parents walked up to the map and were able to touch any pin on the screen. Each pin was linked to an audio story voiced by the student who wrote it. Their narratives talked about an important moment in their life and the place where it happened.

Toward the end of the night, a parent walked into my room looking dejected. Her child, Angeliz, was struggling with academic and behavioral issues in all of her classes, including mine. The parent explained that Angeliz was failing and was refusing to do work in every subject. While she was also failing my class, I told her mother that there was still hope. I pointed to one of the pins on the map and Angeliz's mother walked up to it and touched it. Angeliz's voice began to tell a story about a family party. Her mother couldn't believe that the person speaking was her daughter and commented that her voice sounded so confident. At the end of the recording, Angeliz's mom was crying. I asked her if she was OK, and she said that the recording was the only positive thing she had heard that night. Although Angeliz was struggling in school and refusing to participate, she had participated in the mapping project and she recorded something meaningful and relevant. In my class, she had worked hard with her classmates to create something that she found to be important. In talking with Angeliz and many other students who struggle in school, I have found that many, including myself as a student, resist school when assignments appear to be meaningless and intangible. The interactive maps, and projects like it, disrupt the traditional nature of schoolwork. The meaningfulness of these projects is evident throughout the learning experience. When students see that what they are doing in my classroom will eventually be displayed in public and/or be a part of a large public art project, they engage with the content in new ways, with new purposes, and do so not merely to earn a grade, but, rather, to be a part of something that they know to be important.

Discussion

When teachers design lessons that give students opportunities to publish their work for an audience outside the classroom, they give them power. Designing lessons with sociocultural and social aspects of learning presents an avenue for teachers and students to truly collaborate and to combine ideas. The classroom becomes a space of social possibility, a space that students can feel comfortable and inspired in to work and create.

Classrooms are fundamentally changed when students come to understand that there is a potential audience out in the world that may actually care about the work they are creating inside school. Local media has taken notice of my students' work several different times. Each time a news story has been printed or aired on public radio, my students came to realize that the work they do in my classroom is important and represents more than just a grade. Students approach schoolwork differently when they know that their work might be, or eventually will be, published in a public space (physical and/or digital) and viewed by hundreds or thousands of people. Daily writing assignments and journal entries take on new import and purpose when students start to see them as part of a process that will eventually lead to something bigger.

Rethink What Is Possible

I am constantly inspired by my students, school spaces, buildings, surrounding areas, and my own current and past life experiences. It should go without saying that teaching should be exciting for students—learning should be inspired. Teachers should be excited by lesson designs that they unfurl every day. Energy needs to come from both parties; the classroom space needs to be a team space. A classroom should be a place where everyone involved participates and makes something meaningful. When students start to talk to each other and the teacher through authentic conversations, new ideas and possibilities pop up.

Final products, like the public art projects discussed in this chapter, have the potential to affect schools and communities in positive ways, including encouraging teachers, professors, and students to share their ideas, to speak, and to be heard. Public art has the potential to transform the inside and outside of schools to actually look like places of learning, covered by important ideas developed, articulated, and presented by the learners in that space. These projects can raise awareness of the school within communities.

Conclusion

The examples in this chapter represent a few of the projects students have completed. These assignments have transformed the way I teach, how I think about my classroom, and what is possible within it. The lesson and project designs that I have developed are a product of what my students needed, combined with what has been required by administrators and the district.

Creative, outside-the-box projects that include art integration give students voice and agency by repositioning them as producers of content, not passive consumers. In publishing their work, students in my classrooms took up positions of guerilla street artists by creating both written pieces and audio pieces, and by directing and taking part in the creation of their own writing and learning. Giving students a role in their own education is essential if we want engaged, imaginative, well-rounded pupils who are invested in their own learning. Following along with a scripted curriculum is not working for a vast majority of students; it was not working for mine. I needed my classroom to represent who my students were and could become, and not what the educational system in which they were entrenched thought they should be.

References

ABC News (Producer). (2016, October 26). *Trump warns of inner city "hell" for blacks where Trayvon Martin was shot* [Video file]. Retrieved from http://abcnews.go.com/Politics/video/trump-warns-city-hell-blacks-trayvon-martin-shot-43066713

Adichie, C. N. (2013). *The danger of a single story* [Video file]. Retrieved from https://www.ted.com/talks/chimamanda_adichie_the_danger_of_a_single_story

EngageNY. (2014). *NYS common core ELA & literacy curriculum: Grade 10, module 2 overview.* Retrieved from https://www.engageny.org/sites/default/files/downloadable-resources/2014/Jun/ela-10.2.pdf

Esri. (2018). ArcGIS [Computer software]. Retrieved from https://www.arcgis.com/features/index.html

Fink, L. S. (n.d.). Creating classroom community by crafting themed poetry collections: ReadWriteThink. Retrieved from http://www.readwritethink.org/classroom-resources/lesson-plans/creating-classroom-community-crafting-391.html?tab=4#tabs

Gates, H. L. (2014). *The African Americans: Many rivers to cross* [Video file]. Arlington, VA: Public Broadcasting Service.

Gates, H. L. (2017). *Black America since MLK: And still I rise* [Video file]. Arlington, VA: Public Broadcasting Service.

Gee, J. P. (2004). *Situated language and learning: A critique of traditional schooling.* New York, NY: Routledge.

Jay-Z. (2011). *Decoded.* New York, NY: Spiegel & Grau.

King, M. L., Jr. (2018). *Letter from Birmingham jail.* London, UK: Penguin Books. (Original work published 1963)

Klingel, H., & Jarosch, D. (2010). *The sneaker coloring book.* London, UK: Laurence King.

Moll, L. C., Amanti, C., Neff, D., & Gonzalez, N. (1992). Funds of knowledge for teaching: Using a qualitative approach to connect homes and classrooms. *Theory into Practice, 31*(2), 132–41.

Nike. [GloopTrekker]. (2013, April 13). *I am not a role model* [Video file]. Retrieved from https://www.youtube.com/watch?v=4gqk4WPnrpM (Original work published 1993)

Sheehy, M. (2004). Between a thick and thin place: Changing literacy practices. In K. M. Leander & M. Sheehy (Eds.), *Spatializing literacy research and practice* (pp. 91–114). New York, NY: Peter Lang.

Simone, N. (1964). Mississippi Goddam. On *Nina Simone in concert* [Record]. New York, NY: Philips Records.

Smagorinsky, P., & O'Donnell-Allen, C. (2000). Idiocultural diversity in small groups: The role of the relational framework in collaborative learning. In C. D. Lee & P. Smagorinsky (Eds.), *Vygotskian perspectives on literacy research: Constructing meaning through collaborative inquiry* (pp. 165–90). New York, NY: Cambridge University Press.

Smith, R. (2009, March 12). Sounding the alarm, in words and light. *The New York Times.* Retrieved from http://www.nytimes.com/2009/03/13/arts/design/13holz.html

Solórzano, D. G., & Yosso, T. J. (2002). Critical race methodology: Counter-storytelling as an analytical framework for education research. *Qualitative Inquiry, 8*(1), 23–44.

Souto-Manning, M. (2013). Critical for whom? Theoretical and methodological dilemmas in critical approaches to language research. In D. Paris & M. T. Winn (Eds.), *Humanizing research: Decolonizing qualitative inquiry with youth and communities* (pp. 201–22). Los Angeles, CA: SAGE.

Vygotsky, L. S. (1978). *Mind in society: The development of higher psychological processes* (M. Cole, V. John-Steiner, S. Scribner, & E. Souberman, Eds.). Cambridge, MA: Harvard University Press.

Wertsch, J. (1991). *Voices of the mind: A sociocultural approach to mediated action.* Cambridge, MA: Harvard University Press.

11

Radical Visions for the Future

Michelle Zoss, *Georgia State University*

Katherine J. Macro, *SUNY Buffalo State College*

Several years ago, Michelle's friend and department chair, Joanne Ho, asked her a pointed question: "When are you going to write something that we can use to show administrators that art really can be an effective part of the English curriculum?" In many ways, this book is a response to Joanne's question. She and Michelle both struggled and triumphed to teach with the arts at the center of their practice. They also encountered administrators who were skeptical and nonplussed by the expense of having markers and large paper available for students. But they never backed down from the argument; teaching through arts integration made sense to both of them and they carried on accordingly.

Kathie faced a similar question about the arts being part of the curriculum when she attempted to conduct research for her dissertation. After submitting a detailed and lengthy proposal to study the way that drama functioned and affected both students and teachers in an English language arts classroom, Kathie's request was denied due to the "amount of instructional time spent on drama activities for those students." The implication of that refusal was clear: drama was not a necessary part of the instructional time and therefore would have taken time away from the kind of teaching that really mattered. The district seemed to miss the point that drama *was* the method of instruction rather than additional exercises that would take extra time. But why is it that administrators seem so adamant about questioning the value of the funding and time required to make the arts in language arts a priority? Part of the issue is perception: people think that making drawings and acting out scenes are better left to younger students, the children in elementary schools, because there might be play and imagination involved. These same people might also pay handsomely to see live music, plays, and film productions, and to own images that delight them. The baffling part is that they do not see the value of doing this work that focuses on creating, thinking, and feeling during school hours. Instead, they want to make sure that the students can perform on the standardized exams, many of which are high-stakes requirements for graduation. They want to measure and count all the things that students can do, because, while measurement and counting can be complex operations, the reporting of those numbers can be done in efficient and seemingly precise ways. Reporting on test scores can be done in sound-bite-length statements that can also be enhanced with graphs and tables. Watching and listening to a student perform a song, or poem, or scene takes time; seeing student artwork in a gallery walk takes time and space. None of these activities is easily quantified or distributed through headline-length statements. Instead, these activities require investment by the school, teachers, and students in order to produce high-quality results. And, yes, there are results. But these results need not be used to stratify and rank one school or student against another; rather, the results are creations that show what and how students have been thinking and feeling, and what they are capable of becoming.

Radical Vision to Focus on Creating

In our radical vision, we focus on what it would mean if English classes focused on what students create. When the aim of a class lesson is creating something, students produce knowledge, embody their ideas, and examine their thinking. The logic seems simple. Teach students to think so they can participate in democracy and contribute to the community. The problem is that the current culture of accountability (Sowerbrower, 2014) shifts the aim from creating knowledge to testing knowledge. This testing and accountability culture forges students into test takers (Freire, 2000). The result is people who perform well on tests. But can they create knowledge and think for themselves when situations arise that they have not encountered before? Can they think for themselves when not taking a test? Can they create for themselves and others when not prompted by an exam?

Extending the questions further, we wonder about the ways in which testing requires students to react. Testing does not necessarily require students to create. It is creation that is at work in all the arts-based pedagogies in this book. Arts integration requires students and teachers to create, not simply to react. To be sure, student reactions and reflections are key components to each of the arts examined here, but the work does not stop there. Whether it is through composing a song, a poem, a scene, or a drawing, all the work that happened in the classrooms described in this book showed students creating something with their ideas. The teachers and writers in this book collectively ask students to grapple with ideas and texts to produce something that was not there before. These strategies and activities show the trajectories of student learning, but they do so in a wide variety of ways that are not standardized. This book represents and illustrates ways of grappling with the curriculum in English language arts that result in surprising creations. We gathered educators together so that this book could be used as a set of tools for doing that grappling. There is not one answer here, just as there is not one answer for the best way to teach English in secondary classes. Teachers can use this book to help them find the tools they need to meet the needs of their students, class by class, student by student. Our hope is that they might take the visions here to help students create their way through secondary school, rather than just react to it.

Radical Vision for Complexity

In this radical vision, we refuse to minimize the complexity of feedback and determinations of quality in student work with a single letter grade or set of points. When giving students feedback on their written and oral expression in English classes, teachers already use a wide range of words. Conscientious teachers who want to sustain the cultural plurality of their students give feedback that affirms student identities while also challenging students to think, read, write, and express their ideas (Paris, 2012). Teaching students to revise, re-think, re-see, and re-hear their ideas is hard to do, and yet teachers do it all the time. And they accomplish this hard work using many tools available to them, including language, gestures, and numbers. A problem arises when the feedback is limited to a letter grade or a number evaluation. What could have been a discussion about what excites, puzzles, and informs the teacher about a student's project instead becomes a sanitized and detached grade. We know that grades are deeply embedded in the mindset of everyone involved in the education enterprise in the United States, but that does not mean that grades and rankings should be the driving force for teaching literature and writing in secondary English. What would it look like if, in this radical vision, teachers focused on substantive, complex forms of expression and feedback?

Teachers in this vision ask students to reflect on what they see, hear, feel, and think when they are working through the arts in English classes. It is virtually impossible to avoid language in English, but it is possible to design a curriculum that puts at the core the thinking and sign systems used for the creation of music, drama, poetry, and art. Suhor (1984) argues that, when teachers put sign systems like gestures, images, constructions, and music on more equal terms with language, then students have opportunities to express themselves in ways that are more in line with what they do outside of school. To ask students to write music, speak through poetry, draw about their reading, and embody literature through gesture and talk is to challenge those students to see and feel the world differently than what is possible simply through oral discussion or written essays. Language will not cease in schools, but it does not have to dominate the ways of thinking and expressing ideas about language, literature, and composition. Instead, language can be a partner that supports thinking in the full range of arts available to English classes.

When music teachers evaluate the quality of songs their students write, they use language to help them articulate both what they expect students to do and the degree to which students meet those expectations. When drama teachers evaluate the quality of student performances, they use language to help students explore how different moves and choices about voice, gesture, costumes, and movement inform the ways that characters can be portrayed. When art teachers evaluate the quality of student images, they use language to help students see elements and principles of design within the images and consider how viewers perceive the work. When poetry teachers evaluate the quality of student poems, they use language to help students convey emotions and details through word choice, cadence, and the juxtaposition of words in surprising ways.

For teachers to focus on the nuances of arts-based approaches to teaching, they do need to have or foster a sense of openness, a willingness to be surprised. Teachers need time to slow down, to consciously pause in order to get beyond recognition and into perception (Dewey, 1934/1980). When teachers and students have an opportunity to linger, even if only briefly, they can think, see, hear, and feel, rather than just recognize what is at hand and move on to whatever comes next. These are the moments when time seems to stretch, and everyone in the room seems to come together in that moment. These are the moments when there is potential for the lesson to become a meaningful part of who students become as they see and feel and react to the world around them. These are the moments that the arts offer.

So, what's next? How do teachers ensure that students have more of these moments? The future of arts integration needs to be one that embraces embodied, multimodal learning, with opportunities for expression and exploration for growth and development rather than for the sake of a grade or a test. It is made of hands-on, meaningful, and applicable professional development that places the arts at the center of instruction rather than at the fringes in extra credit projects. The future of arts integration is made by teachers sharing their successes, like the ones found in this book. The future for English language arts is created every time teachers and students come together to share what they learn, express what they feel, and imagine what might be possible.

References

Dewey, J. (1980). *Art as experience*. New York, NY: Perigree Books. (Original work published 1934)

Freire, P. (2000). *Pedagogy of the oppressed* (30th anniversary ed.). New York, NY: Continuum.

Paris, D. (2012). Culturally sustaining pedagogy: A needed change in stance, terminology, and practice. *Educational Researcher, 41*(3), 93–97.

Sowerbrower, K. (2014). *Opening the classroom doors: Stories of English teachers' experiences with three eras of educational reform* (Doctoral dissertation). Retrieved from https://scholarworks.gsu.edu/cgi/viewcontent.cgi?article=1010&context=mse_diss

Suhor, C. (1984). Towards a semiotics-based curriculum. *Journal of Curriculum Studies, 16*, 247–57.

Resources

Resources for Drama

Videos/Films/Websites

- American Shakespeare Center—see https://americanshakespearecenter .com/

- The ArtsLiteracy Project at Brown University—see http://www.artslit.org/

- Chicago Shakespeare Theater—see https://www.chicagoshakes.com/

- Folger Shakespeare Library's Education Program—see https://www.folger .edu/teach-learn

- Globe Education at Shakespeare's Globe—see http://www.shakespeares globe.com/learn/teaching-resources

- myShakespeare—see https://myshakespeare.com/

- Royal Shakespeare Company—see https://www.rsc.org.uk/education/ teacher-resources

- Tate Britain—see http://www.tate.org.uk/visit/tate-britain

Books

Banks, F. (2016). *Creative Shakespeare: The Globe education guide to practical Shakespeare*. London, UK: Bloomsbury.

Gibson, R. (2016). *Teaching Shakespeare: A handbook for teachers* (2nd ed.). Cambridge, UK: Cambridge University Press.

Royal Shakespeare Company. (2013). *The RSC Shakespeare toolkit for teachers: An active approach to bringing Shakespeare's plays alive in the classroom* (Rev. ed.). London, UK: Methuen Drama.

Resources for Music

Videos/Films/Websites

- *American Songwriter* magazine—see http://americansongwriter.com/
- Broadcast Music Incorporated—see https://www.bmi.com/
- RhymeZone rhyming dictionary—see https://www.rhymezone.com/

Books and Articles

Cornett, C. E. (1999). *The arts as meaning makers: Integrating literature and the arts throughout the curriculum.* Upper Saddle River, NJ: Merrill.

Dethier, B. (2003). *From Dylan to Donne: Bridging English and music.* Portsmouth, NH: Heinemann.

Duggan, T. J. (2003). *Uses of music in the high school English/language arts classroom in South Dakota: Teacher perceptions and practices* (Unpublished doctoral dissertation). University of South Dakota, Vermillion, SD.

Duggan, T. J. (2007). Ways of knowing: Exploring artistic representation of concepts. *Gifted Child Today, 30*(4), 56–63.

Johnson, L. L., & Goering, C. Z. (Eds.) (2016). *Recontextualized: A framework for teaching English with music.* Rotterdam, Netherlands: Sense Publishers.

Resources for Poetry

Videos/Films/Websites

- "25+ Slam Poems Appropriate for Middle School (and Others)"—see http://teacheroffduty.com/20-slam-poems-you-can-use-in-your-classroom-tomorrow/
- Brave New Voices—see http://youthspeaks.org/bravenewvoices/watch/
- "Can We Auto-Correct Humanity?"—see http://www.youtube.com/watch?v=dRl8EIhrQjQ
- Eyes on the Prize: America's Civil Rights Years 1954–1965 (series)—see http://www.pbs.org/wgbh/amex/eyesontheprize/
- "Hugo Ball's Dada Manifesto, July 1916"—see https://www.wired.com/beyond-the-beyond/2016/07/hugo-balls-dada-manifesto-july-2016/

- *King: A Filmed Record . . . From Montgomery to Memphis*—see https://www.kinolorber.com/film/view/id/1288

- *Louder Than a Bomb*—see http://www.louderthanabombfilm.com

- "Performance and Discussion of *Nappy Hair* by Carolivia Herron: Performance with Dr. Neal A. Lester'"—see https://vimeo.com/59694234

- "Slam Nation: The Sport of Spoken Word"—see http://devlinpix.com/slamnation/

- "Taylor Mali on 'What Teachers Make'"—see http://www.youtube.com/watch?v=RxsOVK4syxU

- "Ten Spoken Word Performances, Folded like Lyrical Origami"—see http://blog.ted.com/2012/12/07/10-spoken-word-performances-folded-like-lyrical-origami/

- *The Unspoken Word*—see http://topdocumentaryfilms.com/unspoken-word/

Books

Fisher, M. T. (2007). *Writing in rhythm: Spoken word poetry in urban classrooms*. New York, NY: Teachers College Press.

Jocson, K. M. (2008). *Youth poets: Empowering literacies in and out of schools*. New York, NY: Peter Lang.

Weiss, J., & Herndon, S. (2001). *Brave new voices: The Youth Speaks guide to teaching spoken word poetry*. Portsmouth, NH: Heinemann.

Resources for Visual Arts

Videos/Films/Websites

- "Americans for the Arts: Public Art"—see https://www.americansforthearts.org/by-topic/public-art

- Free Art Friday—see https://www.facebook.com/FreeArtFriday/

- Metropolitan Museum of Art—see https://www.metmuseum.org/

- National Gallery of Art—see https://www.nga.gov/

- San Francisco Museum of Modern Art—see https://www.sfmoma.org/

- Smithsonian American Art Museum—see https://americanart.si.edu/

Books and Articles

Albers, P., & Sanders, J. (Eds.). (2010). *Literacies, the arts, and multimodality*. Urbana, IL: National Council of Teachers of English.

Blake, J. (2006). *The full English: An A–Z handbook of English teaching activities*. Sheffield, UK: National Association for the Teaching of English.

Burnaford, G., Aprill, A., & Weiss, C. (Eds.). (2001). *Renaissance in the classroom: Arts integration and meaningful learning*. Mahwah, NJ: Lawrence Erlbaum.

Carter, J. B. (2007). *Building literacy connections with graphic novels: Page by page, panel by panel*. Urbana, IL: National Council of Teachers of English.

Connery, M. C., John-Steiner, V. P., & Marjanovic-Shane, A. (Eds.) (2010). *Vygotsky and creativity: A cultural–historical approach to play, meaning making, and the arts*. New York, NY: Peter Lang.

Efland, A. D. (2002). *Art and cognition: Integrating the visual arts in the curriculum*. New York, NY: Teachers College Press.

Eisner, E. W. (2002). *The arts and the creation of mind*. New Haven, CT: Yale University Press.

Essley, R., Rief, L., & Rocci, A. L. (2008). *Visual tools for differentiating reading and writing instruction: Strategies to help students make abstract ideas concrete and accessible*. New York, NY: Scholastic.

Flood, J., Heath, S. B., & Lapp, D. (2008). *Handbook of research on teaching literacy through the communicative and visual arts* (Vol. 2). New York, NY: Lawrence Erlbaum.

McDonald, N., & Fisher, D. (2002). *Developing arts-loving readers: Top 10 questions teachers are asking about integrated arts education*. Lanham, MD: Scarecrow Education.

Olson, J. L. (1992). *Envisioning writing: Toward an integration of drawing and writing*. Portsmouth, NH: Heinemann.

Underwood, W. (1987). The body biography: A framework for student writing. *The English Journal, 76*(8), 44–48.

Walling, D. R. (2005). *Visual knowing: Connecting art and ideas across the curriculum*. Thousand Oaks, CA: Corwin Press.

Whitin, P. (1996). *Sketching stories, stretching minds: Responding visually to literature*. Portsmouth, NH: Heinemann.

Glossary

ARTeacher Fellowship Program A three-year course of professional development for teachers in Arkansas designed to create teacher leadership in arts integration, especially at the secondary levels.

Arts Integration Curriculum and pedagogy that bring together the arts and another content area and in which the arts are an equal partner in the teaching and the learning. *Arts-based curriculum* refers to a course of study designed to blend techniques and concepts used within the arts with English language arts content. *Arts-based pedagogy* refers to methods of instruction that incorporate various art forms and the practices of actors, artists, musicians, and writers.

Avant-garde A general descriptor for any artist, technique, or style that challenges social ideals and inspires controversy because of its innovative vision.

Body Biography A drawing of a person, often a character from a novel or short story, using symbols, phrases, and quotes to represent the person's physical characteristics as well as his or her personality, journey, and growth.

Bridge A structural component of many songs with lyrics that includes a different musical framework than the verses and chorus, and typically occurs in the middle or in the second half of a song. The bridge is sometimes used to reflect a turning point in narrative songs.

Chorus A structural component of a song with lyrics that typically repeats the same lyrics and musical progression. Often, the lyrics in a chorus reflect the theme of the song.

Cognitive Pluralism A sociocultural model of thinking developed by Vera John-Steiner that describes the diversity of modes for representing one's thinking as well as expressing ideas.

Collage Both a technique and an artistic product. It involves fusing or arranging bits of existing materials to create something wholly new by combining multiple images or objects, often overlapping each. Collages can be constructed from paper, fabric, or other materials, and can also be digital compositions created using images such as artwork, photographs, or clip art.

Creative Drama The use of dramatic exercises such as tableau, role-play, and other theatre games to explore and understand a text and its elements.

Creative Response Assignments Assessments of students' understandings of literary texts demonstrated in forms and media other than formal essays, such as creative writing, scripting a performance, or image-making.

Dadaism Also known as Dada, Dadaism refers to a European avant-garde arts movement in the early twentieth century that sought to transcend the constraints of cultural convention. Dadaism was anti-war, anti-bourgeois, anti-capitalist, and anti-art. Collage, photomontage, and **found poetry** originated in the work of the Dadaists.

Differentiation Designing curricula to address the needs of a variety of learners by offering multiple ways to access course content, engage with the content, and demonstrate learning. (See also **Universal Design.**)

Drama Beyond the genre, drama refers to exercises (physical and mental) that an actor uses to prepare for a role or performance, as well as the performance itself.

Dual-Coding Theory A cognitive model of reading developed by Allen Paivio to understand students who have trouble visualizing what they read. It has been used to develop instructional methods for teaching students how to create mental pictures and verbally describe them to improve reading comprehension.

Exquisite Corpse A drawing game developed by a group of surrealists in the 1920s. The figures that resulted from the drawings were absurd composites, metaphors for the disruption of convention and social order.

Found Poetry The literary equivalent of a **collage**. It borrows words, phrases, and passages of language from existing texts and reorders them to create the quasi-metrical lines of a poem. Methods of generating found poems include erasing words from the original text leaving only select words behind, excerpting words and phrases, uniting entire lines from disparate works, and cutting or tearing up a text into words and phrases to be rearranged.

Gallery Walk An activity in which student work is displayed on walls or desks. Students and teachers move through the room, viewing the work. The viewing leads into conversations and continued thinking about student work. Gallery walks can also be used with drama activities like **tableau.**

Instrumental Break A structural component of many songs that features musical sound without lyrics. The breaks are used not only to showcase instrumental prowess of the musicians, but to bring forward the emotional tone of the piece.

Kent State Massacre During a mass protest on the campus of Kent State University, the Ohio National Guard fired on unarmed college students on May 4, 1970, following which four students were killed and nine wounded.

Key Change A structural component of some songs that features a change in the musical key to heighten the emotional intensity of the song. An *ascending* key change is a change that moves the notes higher, such as a change from the key of C to the key of D.

Musical Adaptation The process of retelling a story in a piece of literature (or an entire work of literature) through song.

Musical Exploration/Extension The process of profiling a character in a story and composing a song that reflects that character's inner monologue. Also, the process of taking a key concept in a piece of text and writing a song that explores that concept in some depth.

Musical Theme (Leitmotif) A musical signature for a character or a concept within the instrumental component of a composition. The musical theme or leitmotif typically features more than one note and occurs whenever the composer wishes to focus listener attention on that character or concept.

Poetry Slam An event in which poets perform and are scored by judges.

Pointillism The term was first used by art critics in the late 1800s to describe the style of painting developed by George Seurat and Paul Signac, French impressionists whose paintings employed distinct dots of color, rather than traditional brush strokes. In this technique, the point of the paintbrush dots the canvas to create patterns of color that appear blended.

Sequential Art Images drawn in a series in order to tell a story. Most often seen in comic strips and graphic novels.

Setting (in music) The musical aspect of a song with lyrics. Literally, the progression of chords, notes, key changes, instruments, etc., that form the nonlinguistic aspects of the song.

Signs and Sign Systems Signs are anything that might be used to represent something else. Language and images serve as everyday examples of signs within linguistic and pictorial systems of signs.

Sketch-to-Stretch A method of deepening comprehension through the recursive process of drawing, writing, and talking about the text.

Social Activism A group or an individual taking an action for a cause with the goal of changing something—a policy, practice, or another action.

Social Constructivism A theory that human development is innately social and knowledge is constructed with others.

Spoken Word Poetry Poetry that is performed for an audience.

Surrealism An artistic and literary movement that explored the unbridled imagination of the unconscious mind. Surrealists experimented with new modes of expression, such as "automatism" or automatic writing. Surrealist works often purposefully confused fantasy and reality, drawing on dreams and unexpressed desires as influences. Salvador Dali is perhaps the best-known surrealist painter.

Tableau A posed or frozen scene created by using the bodies of participants. Tableaux are living statues that can be used to recreate scenes, characters, emotions, or concepts within a text.

Think-Aloud An instructional method to demonstrate how to do something by verbalizing thinking.

Transmediation The process of responding to texts using a variety of sign systems that are different from the original text; for instance, translating the meaning found in a piece of artwork through talking or writing about one's impressions, or reading a story and drawing about what the story means.

Verse A structural component of a song with lyrics that typically recurs two or more times with a similar musical progression but different lyrics.

Visualization Creating a mental picture to process information and create meaning; it is an important part of reading comprehension. The metaphor of making a film in one's head is often used to describe visualization for students who are struggling readers.

Index

Note: An *f* following a page number indicates a figure.

classroom examples, 6–11, 14–15
definition, 186
in M.A.S.T.E.R. framework, 2–3
and setting, 14–15
and songwriting process, 5–6, 8–9
Musical explorations/extensions
classroom examples, 11–16
definition, 187
in M.A.S.T.E.R. framework, 3–4
Musical themes, 3, 187
Myers, M., 53, 54, 63
My Shakespeare (film), 96

Newlin, Nick, 88
Noddings, N., 154
Note-taking, 141–42. *See also* Visual notes

The Odyssey (Homer), 142–43, 143f
O'Meara, Mari, 93
Open mic, 44–45
"Ophelia" (Merchant), 82
"Ophelia" (The Lumineers), 82
Opt-out movement, xiv–xv
"Over the Rainbow" (song), 4

Parallel curriculum model, 14
The Pearl (Steinbeck), 100–101
Pence, Mike, 28
Performance
assessments of, 15–16
approaches to teaching Shakespeare, 88–91
audience feedback, 41–42
classroom examples, 26–27
in M.A.S.T.E.R. framework, 5
prompts for, as creative responses, 116
publication of texts as, 57–58
reading circles, 57–58, 62
spoken word poetry, 43, 44–46
and writing choices, 93
Perlowski, Julia, 89
Petit Jean Mountain State Park, 6
Phillips, Sam, 32
Pinar, W. F., 53, 55
Play and playfulness, 79–80, 81

Poetry. *See* Drama; Found poetry; Spoken word poetry
Poetry clubs, 46
Poetry slams, 41–42, 44–45, 187. *See also* Spoken word poetry
Poetry videos, 46
Pointillism, 54, 187
Practice, curriculum of, 14
Problem solving, 8, 53
Protest songs, 19, 21–25, 27–29
Public art/guerilla art
Boom Box project, 163, 164f, 165
interactive digital maps, 171–72
Letter from Birmingham Jail (King), 168–69, 170f
power of, 172–73
Sneaker Design activity, 160–61, 161f
Word Walls, 165–66, 167f, 168
Publication. *See* Performance

Readers, 53, 56. *See also* Learners
Readicide, 92
Reading
dimensions of response to, 122
enhanced by found poetry activity, 63
as pleasurable, 99
prereading activities, 86, 88–89
as transaction, 121–22, 123
Reading circles, 57–58, 62
Reflection. *See* Assessments
Relevancy, of material, to learners, xvi–xvii, 31, 38, 73, 85, 157–58, 165, 168, 170, 172
Rivera, T., 41, 44
Role-playing, 73–74
Romeo and Juliet (Hinds), 91–92
Romeo and Juliet (Shakespeare), 14–15, 91–92
Rosenberg, D., 22
Rosenblatt, L. M., 53, 56, 62, 121–22
Rowling, J. K., 128
Royal Shakespeare Company, 88
Rubrics, 113–14, 118, 127, 137

Safe spaces, 83–85

Editors

Katherine J. Macro is currently a full-time lecturer in English education at SUNY Buffalo State College. For the past seven years, she has taught courses in literacy, and English education at University at Buffalo, Niagara University, and SUNY Buffalo State College. Macro's passion for working in the field of teacher education has always been fueled by her passion for the arts and the way that drama, in particular, can foster literacy, learning, and growth. She was the co-chair of the Com-  mission on Arts and Literacies, a special interest group within NCTE, for six years. Prior to her work in teacher education, Macro taught high school English, theatre, and acting in a suburb of Buffalo for twelve years.

Michelle Zoss is an associate professor of English education at Georgia State University. She frames her research within a sociocultural perspective to study the possibilities of visual arts integration in English language arts classrooms. She examines the meaning making of teachers and students as they compose visual texts within ELA curricula. Her publications include analyses of student-made visual texts, teacher curriculum and pedagogy decisions, preservice teachers'  understandings of aesthetic experiences, and advocacy for integrating drawing and images throughout K–12 literacy curricula. Zoss's interests in the connection between literacy and visual arts stem from her professional experiences while teaching art and English in elementary and high schools in Las Vegas, Nevada. Currently, she serves as co-chair of the Commission on Arts and Literacies, a special interest group in NCTE that brings together English teachers and teacher educators dedicated to supporting the arts.

Contributors

Jessica Berg received both her bachelor's degree in English literature and her license in English education from Ball State University, Indiana. She now works at Franklin Central High School in southern Indianapolis, Indiana, where she teaches eleventh-grade General English. She is teaching her first speech class this year as well as sponsoring the school's first ever Japanese Language Club.

Timothy J. Duggan is an associate professor of English education at Northeastern Illinois University in Chicago. For the past six years, he has coordinated a partnership between Northeastern Illinois University and Amundsen High School in Chicago. Duggan has been an educator for thirty-four years, seventeen of which have been spent in teacher education. He is also a songwriter and performing musician with six recordings, including *Language Arts 101* and *Language Arts 201*, collections of songs from Shakespeare and musical adaptations from numerous authors. He frequently conducts teaching workshops with Team Shakespeare at the Chicago Shakespeare Theater on Navy Pier. Duggan has cultivated a long-held interest in arts integration in English language arts classes, including his doctoral dissertation research on music incorporation.

Toby Emert, a former high school English and drama teacher, is a professor in the Department of Education at Agnes Scott College, Georgia, a small liberal arts college for women. He teaches courses in language and literacy, digital pedagogies, and the arts. He has also been on the faculty at Kennesaw State University, Lesley University, and the University of Kentucky, where he was chair of the English Education program and director of the National Writing Project affiliate, the Bluegrass Writing Project. His research includes studying the integration of arts-based instructional strategies, especially for learners who struggle to demonstrate success in traditional academic settings.

For more than a decade, he has partnered with the Fugees Family nonprofit organization to offer a summer literacy and arts program for children of refugee families on the Agnes Scott campus. He also currently serves as coeditor, alongside Joseph Rodríguez, of NCTE's flagship publication for English language arts teachers, *English Journal*.

Christian Z. Goering is a professor of English education at the University of Arkansas, where he directs the Northwest Arkansas Writing Project and works with the licensure programs in English education and theatre/communications. Goering taught high school English in Topeka, Kansas, and is a National Board–certified teacher. He has published three books to date: *Critical Media Literacy and Fake News in Post-Truth America* (2018), *Recontextualized: A Framework for Teaching English with Music* (2016), and *The Arkansas Delta Oral History Project: Culture, Place, and Authenticity* (2016). He's a singer–songwriter in his spare time and organizes a monthly Songs in Progress event in the community.

Stephen Goss is an assistant professor of English education at Kennesaw State University, Georgia. He has most recently taught seventh- and eighth-grade English language arts in western New York. Over the course of his career, he has taught English language arts in a variety of settings, including rural, urban, and suburban schools. In each context, he has worked hard to help his students publish their writing and ideas digitally and via large public art installations. His research focuses on art integration, teacher stance, culturally relevant teaching, student publication, New Literacies, and meaningful integration of educational technologies into classrooms.

Pamela M. Hartman is an associate professor of English and director of English education at Ball State University, Indiana, where she teaches courses in language arts methods, reading, and contemporary multicultural and young adult literature. She is advisor for the English Education club at Ball State University and treasurer for the Gender and Literacy Assembly (an NCTE affiliate), as well as a former chair of the NCTE Commission on Social Justice in Teacher Education Programs. She has taught English for twenty-five years, at both high school and college levels.

Erin Knauer is a third-year secondary English language arts educator who is always learning and growing from her American literature and creative writing students. She recently participated in the Hoosier Writing Project Summer Institute, and is excited by new opportunities to learn from colleagues too.

She is currently working on building a blog, a stronger professional presence through platforms like Instagram and Twitter, as well as a TeachersPayTeachers presence. In her classroom, she both supports and challenges her students to break through their comfort zones and to take active, routine ownership over their learning.

Amy Matthews is a National Board–certified English teacher with twenty years of experience teaching English in grades 7 to 12. She has a master of arts in teaching and a bachelor of arts in English from the University of Arkansas. Matthews currently teaches Creative Writing and Senior English at Fayetteville High School, Arkansas. She is a member of the ARTeacher Fellowship organized by the University of Arkansas's Center for Children & Youth in collaboration with Crystal Bridges Museum of American Art and the Walton Arts Center. Matthews is also a National Writing Project teacher–consultant, and is on the board of directors for Arts Live Theatre, northwest Arkansas's dedicated nonprofit youth theatre company.

Pauline Skowron Schmidt is an associate professor in English education, a co-advisor for an NCTE student affiliate, and a 2015 Pennsylvania Writing and Literature Project fellow at West Chester University. She teaches undergraduate methods courses, as well as a seminar about teaching Shakespeare at the secondary level, and supervises student teachers. She attends NCTE and Pennsylvania Council of Teachers of English and Language Arts conventions annually and shares her research about infusing the arts into the English language arts curriculum at both conferences. She is currently working on a cowritten manuscript with Matthew Kruger-Ross about reenvisioning teaching philosophies through digital technologies.

Brandon Schuler received his bachelor's degree in digital media production from Ball State University, Indiana, in 2014. As a post-baccalaureate student, he received his teaching license in May of 2016. Brandon currently works as a seventh- and eighth-grade English teacher at R. J. Baskett Middle School in Gas City, Indiana. He also teaches courses in drama, film literature, and creative writing, and cosponsors his school's creative writing club.

Laura B. Turchi is a teacher educator specializing in English language arts and student teacher performance assessment. She coauthored *Teaching Shakespeare with Purpose: A Student-Centred Approach* (2016) with Ayanna Thompson. Before joining the faculty at the University of Houston, Turchi was clinical professor in the English department at Arizona State University and director of the Teaching Foundations Project, creating rigorous, inquiry-based, content-rich lower-division/general studies courses for future teachers. For twelve years, Turchi chaired the Education department at Warren Wilson College, in Asheville, North Carolina. She's been a member of NCTE since forever, when she taught secondary English language arts in Tucson, Arizona, and Naperville, Illinois.

Alisha M. White is an associate professor at Western Illinois University in the Department of English. She teaches courses in young adult literature, English education methods, and college writing, and a seminar on topics in literature. Her research on arts-based pedagogy and young adult literature has been published in *English Journal, The Educational Forum, English in Education, Visual Inquiry: Learning & Teaching Art,* and *First Opinions, Second Reactions,* and images from her arts-based research have been published in the literary journals *Of-With: Journal of Immanent Renditions* and *Oddball Magazine.* White's current research on the college experiences of students with disabilities won Western Illinois University's Best in Track for Research and Creative Activities award in 2017.

Wendy R. Williams is an assistant professor of English education at Arizona State University. She studies creative expression and multimodal writing, including songwriting, spoken word poetry, and visual narratives. Her book *Listen to the Poet: Writing, Performance, and Community in Youth Spoken Word Poetry* (2018) takes readers inside a youth spoken word poetry organization in Arizona. At Arizona State University, Williams directs the Young Authors' Studio, a free writing program for young people that is administered by university students, and she organizes the Sparky Slam, an annual poetry event. She also teaches courses on writing, literature, and film. Before becoming a professor, she taught high school and middle school English for nine years.

This book was typeset in TheMix and Palatino by Barbara Frazier.

The typeface used on the cover is Museo.

The book was printed on 50-lb. White Offset paper by Seaway Printing.